CHURCHGOING AND CHRISTIAN ETHICS

Robin Gill argues that once moral communities take centre stage in ethics – as they do in virtue ethics – then there should be a greater interest in sociological evidence about these communities. This book examines recent evidence, gathered from social attitude surveys, about church communities, in particular their views on faith, moral order and love. It shows that churchgoers are distinctive in their attitudes and behaviour. Some of their attitudes change over time, and there are a number of obvious moral disagreements between different groups of churchgoers. Nonetheless, there are broad patterns of Christian beliefs, teleology and altruism which distinguish churchgoers as a whole from nonchurchgoers. However, the values, virtues, moral attitudes and behaviour of churchgoers are shared by many other people as well. The distinctiveness of church communities in the modern world is thus real but relative, and is crucial for the task of Christian ethics.

ROBIN GILL is Michael Ramsey Professor of Modern Theology, University of Kent at Canterbury. He has written many books on both Christian ethics and the sociology of religion, including *Christian Ethics in Secular Worlds* (1991), *Moral Communities* (1992), *The Myth of the Empty Church* (1993), *A Textbook of Christian Ethics* (revised 1995), *Moral Leadership in a Postmodern Age* (1997), and edited *Euthanasia and the Churches* (1998). In addition, Robin Gill is the series editor for New Studies in Christian Ethics.

NEW STUDIES IN CHRISTIAN ETHICS 15

Christian ethics has increasingly assumed a central place within academic theology. At the same time the growing power and ambiguity of modern science and the rising dissatisfaction within the social sciences about claims to value-neutrality have prompted renewed interest in ethics within the secular academic world. There is, therefore, a need for studies in Christian ethics which, as well as being concerned with the relevance of Christian ethics to the present day secular debate, are well informed about parallel discussions in recent philosophy, science or social science. New Studies in Christian Ethics aims to provide books that do this at the highest intellectual level and demonstrate that Christian ethics can make a distinctive contribution to this debate – either in moral substance or in terms of underlying moral justifications.

Other titles published in the series

1 KIERAN CRONIN
Rights and Christian Ethics

2 IAN MCDONALD
Biblical Interpretation and Christian Ethics

3 JAMES MACKEY
Power and Christian Ethics

4 IAN S. MARKHAM
Plurality and Christian Ethics

5 JEAN PORTER
Moral Action and Christian Ethics

6 WILLIAM SCHWEIKER
Responsibility and Christian Ethics

7 E. CLINTON GARDNER
Justice and Christian Ethics

CHURCHGOING AND CHRISTIAN ETHICS

ROBIN GILL

CAMBRIDGE
UNIVERSITY PRESS

PUBLISHED BY THE PRESS SYNDICATE OF THE UNIVERSITY OF CAMBRIDGE
The Pitt Building, Trumpington Street, Cambridge, United Kingdom

CAMBRIDGE UNIVERSITY PRESS
The Edinburgh Building, Cambridge CB2 2RU, UK http://www.cup.cam.ac.uk
40 West 20th Street, New York NY 10011-4211, USA http://www.cup.org
10 Stamford Road, Oakleigh, Melbourne 3166, Australia

First published 1999

Printed in the United Kingdom at the University Press, Cambridge

Typeset in [CE]

A catalogue record for this book is available from the British Library

Library of Congress cataloguing in publication data

Gill, Robin.
Churchgoing and Christian ethics / Robin Gill.
p. cm. – (New Studies in Christian Ethics)
Includes bibliographical references and index.
ISBN 0-521-57058-1 (hardback)
ISBN 0-521-57828-0 (paperback)
1. Christian ethics – Great Britain – Public opinion.
2. Christians – Great Britain – Attitudes. 3. Church attendance – Great Britain
4. Public opinion – Great Britain. I. Title II. Series.
BJ1275.G55 1999
241'.0941–dc21 98-53583 CIP

ISBN 0 521 57058 1 hardback
ISBN 0 521 57828 0 paperback

To Jenny

Contents

Tables

Preface

This is the fifteenth book in the series *New Studies in Christian Ethics*. Originally its title was to be *Moral Communities and Christian Ethics*, but I worried that the term 'moral communities' was just too vague. For reasons to be explained shortly, I became increasingly critical of this vagueness in others. As *Churchgoing and Christian Ethics* the book is now distinctly more concrete. Whatever the title, it at last brings together my empirical research on churches and my theoretical research on Christian ethics.

For the last ten years I have been engaged in detailed empirical research on churchgoing, while continuing a rather separate interest in the role of Christian ethics in society at large. In *The Myth of the Empty Church* (1993) I mapped out churchgoing patterns in Britain from census data going back to the 1830s and suggested some physical reasons for an initial increase followed by a very lengthy decline in churchgoing. I was aware at the time of a limited amount of data from attitude sample surveys linking churchgoing with distinctive moral and theological beliefs. Yet I could not see how to study such data longitudinally or systematically. In that book attitudinal data formed little more than a partial observation about present day churchgoers. However, a visit by the American sociologists C. Kirk Hadaway and Penny Long Marler, armed with a well marked copy of *The Myth of the Empty Church*, convinced me that I was mistaken. There is a large amount of data from attitude surveys of religious and moral beliefs and behaviour in Britain over the last fifty years which, surprisingly, has never been systematically compared. Together we collected data specifically about religious beliefs from well over one hundred surveys and finally published the results in the article for the *Journal for the Scientific Study of Religion* which is reported in chapter three. I am most grateful to both of them for this stimulation.

As a result of this I then discovered the major new sources of data which I use in chapters four to seven. These new sources of British data form the backbone of this book. However they prompted me to gather large amounts of comparative data while travelling in different parts of the world – especially Australia, North America and elsewhere in Europe – which are also reported here. I had to learn how to process the new data myself as well as how to use the appropriate statistical tests in SPSS. Dr Mohammed Jabir did invaluable initial work processing and testing some of the earliest data and then showing me how to do the same. I am most grateful for his help. Dr Edwina Bell and Professor Leslie Francis both gave me vital help on the statistical tests and Leslie read through the entire empirical part of this book. Professor David Fergusson read chapter one, Bishop Peter Selby chapter nine, Richard Allen chapter eight, and Dr Michael Northcott chapters one to seven. All were immensely helpful. I also gave parts of the book as papers at Free Amsterdam, Edinburgh, Lancaster and Reading Universities, at a meeting of the Sociology of Religion Study Group of the British Sociological Association, and at a variety of Universities and Theological Colleges in Australia. Testing the material in this way, and then modifying and revising it, has been crucial.

Throughout the long process of researching and writing this book, while I have also been acting as general editor of the series, successive religious studies commissioning editors at Cambridge University Press – Alex Wright, Ruth Parr, and now Kevin Taylor – have all become friends and helpers. Academic theology and religious studies are deeply indebted to each of them.

Finally as ever to Jenny my love. Although I love statistics, I love her far more.

Abbreviations

ACC	Anglican Consultative Council
ANSS	Australian National Social Science Survey
BBC	British Broadcasting Corporation
BHPS	British Household Panel Survey
BIPO	British Institute of Public Opinion (now Gallup Poll)
BSA	British Social Attitudes
CRA	Christian Research Association
ESRC	Economic and Social Research Council
EVSSG	European Value Systems Study Group
IBA	Independent Broadcasting Authority
ICM	Inter-church Movement
ITA	Independent Television Authority
ITC	Independent Television Commission
IV	International Version
MORI	Market and Opinion Research Institute
NCLS	National Church Life Survey
NEB	New English Bible
NISA	Northern Ireland Social Attitudes
NIV	New International Version
NOP	National Opinion Polls
RSV	Revised Standard Version
SCPR	Social and Community Planning Research
SPSS	Statistical Package for Social Scientists
STV	Southern Television
URC	United Reformed Church

Introduction

Virtue ethics – whether secular or Christian – raises some curiosities which are only just beginning to emerge. For example, there is much discussion today about the importance of 'communities' as carriers of moral virtues, but an odd vagueness about the actual communities involved. Amongst Christian ethicists there is a renewed emphasis upon churches as moral communities, but little empirical analysis of the moral effects of churchgoing. There is an enthusiasm about 'character' and 'identity', yet little corresponding interest in those sociological methods which have usually been concerned to measure and analyse community, character and identity. In short, too much is too vague and ill grounded in social reality.

Virtue ethics, the very discipline which has challenged moral philosophy to take history, traditions and local communities seriously – the discipline which has argued that there is more to morality than the individualistic, narrowly rational concern about moral decision-making as construed by so many post-Enlightenment moral philosophers – has been curiously bashful about putting forward actual moral communities that can be analysed and measured. If anything, Christian ethicists have recently been even more bashful and reluctant to admit that sociology has any constructive role to play in their discipline. It is rare to find a Christian ethicist prepared to examine data about the moral effects of churchgoing. Instead Christian communities have become far too idealised.

This book sets out to challenge and reverse this situation. It starts with a theoretical issue, namely that posed by virtue ethics. Yet it soon finds that theologians and sociologists alike have tended to assume that Christian communities, at least in their identifiable form as congregations that meet together and worship regularly, have little (beneficial) moral effect upon churchgoers. Sociologists of religion who are satisfied with this assumption can then safely ignore churchgoing as a social phenomenon, regarding it simply as an epiphenomenon. Theologians, in contrast, tend to argue that it is churches as they ought to be, especially churches as depicted in the New Testament, and not churches as they actually are, which are crucial for virtue ethics.

It is at this point that my investigation begins. Is it really the case that churches as they are have little or no moral effect within present-day society? In seeking to answer this question I will show that there is a great deal of evidence, much of it largely ignored, which challenges current biases. As it happens, whether or not someone goes to church regularly is a very good indicator of a whole range of beliefs and moral attitudes and behaviour. Churchgoers are more distinctive than is often imagined. Once these data are properly examined, it will then be important to return to the broader issues raised by virtue ethics. What implications does churchgoing, when studied rigorously, have for ethics in a fragmented and, perhaps, postmodern age? Is it possible that identifiable Christian communities offer more concrete and morally effective 'moral communities' than most other forms of 'community' in such an age?

Many of the monographs already published in this series, *New Studies in Christian Ethics*, have been deeply influenced by the agenda raised by Alasdair MacIntyre's *After Virtue.* Most see weaknesses in the Enlightenment moral tradition as it has come to be interpreted in the late twentieth century. Specifically most share a scepticism about the ability of secular individualism and rationalism to resolve moral issues adequately. They believe that ethics should not be reduced either to a non-principled personalism or even just to the two principles of autonomy and individual non-maleficence. Instead, inter-personal virtues such as responsibility, altruism, moral order and justice are also considered to be essential within ethics. Monographs in the series point in various ways to the importance of various individual and corporate virtues being held in tension and see moral character rather than moral decision-making as the main focus of ethics. As a result of this focus upon virtues and upon moral character, most stress that it is moral communities that carry and sustain these virtues and mould this character. Finally, they argue in various ways that Christian ethics has something relevant and distinctive to say about these themes – virtues, character and community – even within a modernist, and especially within a postmodern, age.

For example, William Schweiker's *Responsibility and Christian Ethics* argues that an approach based upon responsibility has much to contribute to the present-day debate about ethics. He also believes that Christian ethics has a distinctive and valuable contribution to make to this approach. Within the secular world an awkward combination of increasing pluralism and technological power makes a notion of responsibility imperative. As power increases in the modern world – not just in the political and military orders but also in such areas as biotechnology – so ironically does pluralism. The latter ensures that people become increasingly confused about the bases of public morality just at the very moment that they are possessing an unprecedented amount of power. Schweiker, in contrast, argues that an ethical approach based upon responsibility (both individual and corporate), which has moral integrity as its aim, is more apposite.

Following the philosopher Charles Taylor, Schweiker argues that responsibility is linked to our capacity to reflect upon and then revise or transform our lives through criticism of what we care about. He does not follow those Christian ethicists who have tended to regard responsibility in individualistic terms as a personal revelation or intuition. For Schweiker responsibility involves cognition and critical reflection/interpretation and is a requirement both for individuals and for moral communities. It is based upon critical reflection aimed at thc question of what has constituted our lives under the respect for others – and, for theists, our lives under God:

> Personal and social identity is formed and assessed through acts of radical interpretation founded in a commitment to some moral project, some orienting faith. This means that self and community are always measured by a good which transcends immediate existence, the good of the integrity of life . . . Conscience is not a faculty of the soul, a divine spark in the mind; it is the practice of radical interpretation within which personal and social identity is constituted and formed in terms of the imperative of responsibility.[1]

Like other authors in the series, Schweiker seeks to show that Christian faith does have a distinctive contribution to make beyond the confines of Christianity, in this instance to the general discussion about responsibility. For Christians genuine moral integrity is an indirect consequence of seeking to respect and enhance the integrity of all life before God. An approach which is based simply upon personal autonomy and authentic fulfilment always faces the temptation in a troubled world of the will to power. But for Christians ultimate power is God's alone and faith in this God provides a confidence to live and act amid the fragmentations of life in the present-day world and beyond a culture based simplistically upon personal fulfilment and 'authenticity'. Christian faith offers a vision of 'goodness' shining through the fragmentariness and travail of existence. A Christian notion of responsibility is based upon an ultimate power, namely God, who is good and a finite world that is graciously respected by God.

There are obvious points of contact with several other monographs in this series. Kieran Cronin's *Rights and Christian Ethics* repeatedly links secular language about 'rights' to Christian notions of duty and responsibility. He also argues that Christians have deeper 'justifying reasons for acting morally' than secularists precisely because moral behaviour for Christians is a part of their relationship to God. So, having provided a very thorough critical account of different philosophical notions of 'justice', the final theological chapter of his book argues as follows:

> In this chapter my main intention is to take the major models of rights

[1] William Schweiker, *Responsibility and Christian Ethics*, Cambridge University Press, Cambridge and New York, 1995, p. 185.

I have been using: freedom, power and covenant, and to relate them in turn to a further model which may be thought of as the ultimate foundation of rights. This model has been mentioned in passing throughout this work. It is the notion that humanity's dignity comes from being created in the image of God. I want to argue here that having and exercising rights are a vital aspect of that dignity, and that being made in God's image gives a specifically religious justifying reason for acting morally.[2]

James Mackey's *Power and Christian Ethics* offers a notion of power as moral authority located finally in God which is also very close to William Schweiker's thesis. For Mackey Christian communities at their best offer a 'radical and encompassing sense of life as grace' which 'enlightens and empowers people to imagine and create an ever better life, and also to overcome the forces of destruction which one could otherwise only join and increase, but never beat'.[3]

Ian Markham's *Plurality and Christian Ethics* makes a number of similar points. Whilst he takes the claims of modern pluralism seriously, Markham finally believes that theism offers 'a more coherent description of life than any alternative world perspective' – it 'makes sense of the objectivity of value and the intelligibility of the universe'.[4] Similarly for Schweiker the very discipline of Christian ethics is finally 'faith seeking moral understanding'. The central problem that concerns Markham is how Christianity should relate distinctively (but without being exclusive) to a pluralistic political and economic order. In what appears to be an increasingly fragmented world – intellectually, culturally, and morally – how is Christian ethics to be done today? He argues for a position between secular relativism and religious exclusivism. In identifying a tradition of 'plurality', which he finds to be more apparent in America than in Britain, he believes that there is such a mid-path. In the final section of *Plurality and Christian Ethics* Markham proposes his bold claim

[2] Kieran Cronin, *Rights and Christian Ethics*, Cambridge University Press, Cambridge and New York, 1992, p. 233.

[3] James P. Mackey, *Power and Christian Ethics*, Cambridge University Press, Cambridge and New York, 1994, p. 203.

[4] Ian S. Markham, *Plurality and Christian Ethics*, Cambridge University Press, Cambridge and New York, 1994, p. 171.

that it is theism which makes most coherent sense of this mid-path.

Very similar themes can also be found in Jean Porter's *Moral Action and Christian Ethics*, Clinton Gardner's *Justice and Christian Ethics*, and Peter Sedgwick's *The Market Economy and Christian Ethics*.[5] For all of these writers moral action is a product of a subtle and complex juxtaposition of interdependent moral virtues – including, crucially, notions of responsibility and justice. However much one stresses such virtues as autonomy, authentic fulfilment, and individual non-maleficence, a strong notion of moral order, altruism, responsibility – both individual and corporate – and of social justice do seem to be required by Christian ethics. Porter's analysis returns specifically to Aquinas. Arguing against an understanding of ethics based simplistically upon moral rules, she seeks to re-interpret Aquinas' understanding of moral actions. For her the moral life consists of a subtle interplay between human dignity grounded in restraint and forthrightness, kindliness and decency built up out of caring, and fairness and responsibility forming a basis for justice. These virtues are interdependent and become seriously distorted if adopted in isolation, as they frequently are in secular forms of ethics. They combine both self-regarding and other-regarding aspects: they are at once both individualistic and social. In arguing for this understanding Porter shows the influence of other Catholic philosophers, notably Alasdair MacIntyre and Elizabeth Anscombe.

However, the contribution to the series which provides the most substantial theological and philosophical appraisal of Alasdair MacIntyre's *After Virtue*, as well as of the more specifically theological contributions of Stanley Hauerwas and George Lindbeck, is David Fergusson's *Community, Liberalism and Christian Ethics*.[6] What Fergusson offers is an appreciative, but finally critical, account of this debate, which takes communitarianism

[5] Jean Porter, *Moral Action and Christian Ethics* (1995), E.Clinton Gardner, *Justice and Christian Ethics* (1995) and Peter H.Sedgwick, *The Market Economy and Christian Ethics* (1999), all Cambridge University Press, Cambridge and New York.

[6] David A. S. Fergusson, *Community, Liberalism and Christian Ethics*, Cambridge University Press, Cambridge and New York, 1998.

seriously without abandoning all of the achievements of realism and liberalism. Unlike theologians such as Stanley Hauerwas and John Milbank, he offers an account of theology which is radical but not radically postmodern. In doing this he sees himself more as a neo-Barthian than as a post-liberal.

What is at stake here? Within modern theology there is an increasing division between those who see themselves as a part of the liberal arts, engaging with secular disciplines and seeking to influence the wider political order from within, and those, in contrast, who argue that theology must abandon liberalism in any form, looking instead to the unique resources of the Christian community, and building up a radical theological critique of post-Enlightenment thought. Within secular social and political thought there is also an increasing division between libertarians who emphasise the autonomy of the individual and the centrality of individual choice, and communitarians, on the other hand, who stress the need for community, tradition and interdependency. David Fergusson seeks to offer a bridge between what he regards as unnecessarily polarised positions. For him it is essential that Christian ethics *is* distinctively Christian, albeit focused less upon the church than upon God made known in Jesus Christ. He is suspicious of those who exaggerate the distinctiveness of actual Christian communities and believes, instead, that Christians must still engage centrally with secular society. Liberalism has made real gains both within society and within Christian communities which he believes do need to be recognised. For David Fergusson an appreciation of their distinctive contribution can be combined with a positive account of some of the central features of liberalism.

For all of these writers Christian virtues held together in creative tension, and in the process moulding Christian character, do need to be carried in and sustained by moral communities. All of them admit that the actual communities that exist, in the form of church congregations, are fallible and flawed. Nonetheless, Christian ethics is essentially done within these communities and is shaped by the traditions and virtues that they carry but do not always exemplify. Actual Christian communities are bearers and harbingers of the Christian virtues of altruism, responsibility, moral order and justice, amongst other virtues, which shape and mould the lives and characters of individual Christians. Inherent within this understanding of Christian ethics is a stress upon community, character and virtues held in tension. Christian ethics is no longer regarded as a discipline concerned with individualistic problem solving. All of the writers in the series have also been concerned in one way or another with the two key aims of *New Studies in Christian Ethics* – namely to promote monographs in Christian ethics which engage centrally with the present secular moral debate at the highest possible intellectual level and, secondly, to encourage contributors to demonstrate that Christian ethics can make a distinctive contribution to this debate.

The aim of my study is to build critically upon these conclusions. Whilst I am convinced by the general thrust of post-MacIntyre Christian ethics, I also believe that it often underestimates some of the theological and especially sociological problems involved. It tends to produce a theological understanding of churches as moral communities which underestimates the synchronic and diachronic plurality of Christian resources. In addition it tends to produce a picture of churches as moral communities which fits ill their social reality. It can also treat the 'secular' world as being distinctly more secular than it actually is. *The challenge I believe is to find ways of expressing Christian distinctiveness which do not exaggerate the theological and sociological distinctiveness of churches as moral communities.* As yet this a challenge which has occupied the attention of too few Christian ethicists. Making grand claims is just too easy. Making claims which actually fit the ambiguities of churches and society is much more difficult.

This study will seek to clarify and reinforce some of the philosophical and theological grounds upon which the conclusions presented in the previous studies in the series have been made. However, above all else, it will seek to clarify the specifically sociological factors involved in them. It is the latter which have yet to be faced adequately in most of the other monographs. James Mackey's *Power and Christian Ethics* comes nearest to facing them. He acknowledges more frankly than others the weaknesses of existing Christian institutions if they are to be regarded as responsible moral communities in the modern or postmodern world. He challenges existing Christian communities with the paradigm of community presupposed in the New Testament. Specifically he argues that power as coercion soon becomes the dominant mode both in society at large and in the churches in particular, whereas in the message of Jesus of Nazareth power is commended only in the mode of moral authority. Yet, having made this challenging analysis, Mackey remains vague about its actual implementation. In short, he is clear about the ambiguities and paradoxes of power in relation to existing 'moral' communities, but he is less than explicit about the specific social structures and institutions that might carry and contain power responsibly.

What is needed, I believe is a clearer philosophical, theological and especially sociological understanding of moral communities in relation to the current debate about values in a fast-changing world. The term 'moral communities' was used in a philosophical and eminently sociological sense by Durkheim, intimately linked with his understanding of the function of religion in society. Few of the other writers in the series have engaged at length with the functionalist literature which depends so heavily upon Durkheim despite its obvious relevance. I have argued elsewhere[7] that this literature suggests three levels at which the links between Christian ethics and moral communities can be explored critically. In sociological language these are the levels of legitimation, socialisation and institutionalisation. In more theological terms they concern the issues of justification and apologetics, Christian nurture and formation, and ecclesiology. The bulk of this book will be concerned with the middle level, since it is this which is treated too summarily in much of the virtue ethics literature. However the final chapter will return to the first and third levels.

If a more sociological approach is taken, then it becomes important to examine closely the empirical evidence about Christian communities. Particularly important are the attitudes

[7] See my *Moral Leadership in a Postmodern Age*, T. & T. Clark, Edinburgh, 1997.

and behaviour of those who participate regularly in these communities. Do they show signs of being shaped and moulded by specifically Christian virtues? To focus this question more sharply, do regular churchgoers show distinctive evidence of altruism and moral order? Do churchgoers differ in their moral behaviour and attitudes from nonchurchgoers? It is, I believe, important to ground this theoretical discussion of Christian ethics in the evidence that these questions might help to uncover. MacIntyre himself has always moved between the two worlds of sociology and moral philosophy. Unfortunately his critics and followers alike have tended to ignore the sociological.

Of course a sociological description of the characteristics of churchgoers can never provide a sufficient basis for Christian ethics. Those of us who are churchgoers will be only too aware of our frailties and ethical shortcomings. Nevertheless, an account of Christian ethics which so emphasises character and community would be very unwise to ignore evidence of actual Christian communities. Yet this is the very serious weakness of theologians such as Hauerwas and Milbank that they move too quickly from actual to idealised Christian communities. It is to them I must turn first.

PART ONE

The theoretical context

CHAPTER I

Churchgoing and the bias of virtue ethicists

The rise and growing dominance of virtue ethics within Christian ethics has brought with it a new emphasis upon the moral importance of churchgoing. Church communities and the stories, beliefs and virtues that they contain within their worship and liturgies have received renewed attention. As a result there is now a clear bias towards churchgoing and active membership of church communities amongst many Christian ethicists. However, with this bias has come a less congruent bias – a bias towards idealised rather than actual church communities. Perhaps this latter bias was inevitable given such a theoretical emphasis upon communities that, in both the past and the present, have often appeared fragile and ambiguous. Yet idealised communities ill fit a virtue ethic whether Christian or secular. The latter primarily requires actual communities to mediate virtues and to shape moral character.

This chapter will set out these claims in detail by taking an overview of the work of Stanley Hauerwas. Amongst Christian ethicists in North America today Hauerwas is outstanding. He has more influence and polarises more opinions than any other Christian ethicist of his generation. Within the discipline, Alasdair MacIntyre and Charles Taylor have both been highly influential as sympathetic philosophers. Yet, especially in North America, it is the work of Hauerwas which is widely read and discussed. In meetings of the American *Society of Christian Ethics* it is now quite usual to find several papers analysing his work, with only occasional references to MacIntyre and Taylor. Even in Britain, as early as 1985 the American James Gustafson was surprised to find so much enthusiasm for his work amongst theologians from the Church of Scotland, the Church of England and the Roman Catholic Church. At the time he suggested to them that 'some thought be given to possible incongruities between the ecclesiology that is necessary for the sectarian ethics and ecclesiologies of these churches'.[1] Hauerwas' dominance of the discipline is quite remarkable.

This dominance may, however, also be somewhat misleading. At the heart of Hauerwas' recent work there is an ambivalence about whether he is discussing actual or idealised Christian communities and an increasing exaggeration of both Christian distinctiveness and worldly secularity. In a careful and, in part, sympathetic critique of his contribution to Christian ethics, David Fergusson's book in the present series argues for 'a more ambivalent reading of the relationship between church and civil society than is suggested in Hauerwas'.[2] He is finally not convinced that churches are as distinctive as Hauerwas maintains or that all of the inheritance of secular liberalism and the Enlightenment is to be so thoroughly discarded:

> It is one thing to recognise the shortcoming and effects of liberalism, however, and another to appear to enter into wholesale condemnation. It is worth recalling in this context that the Enlightenment project did not simply spring from a misconceived epistemological programme but had its historical context in the religious wars of the seventeenth century. Liberalism was thus borne of a desire to establish a civil order which could unite competing religious factions on a moral ground which everyone could assent to independently of particular traditions.[3]

It is not necessary to rehearse the whole of Fergusson's critique of Hauerwas here since my focus is specifically upon churchgoing and Christian ethics. Within this rather narrower focus it is possible to detect changes in Hauerwas' thought over almost quarter of a century. In his earliest work Hauerwas'

[1] James Gustafson, 'The Sectarian Temptation', *Proceedings of the Catholic Theological Society of America*, 40 (1985), p. 84. I am grateful to David A. S. Fergusson's *Community, Liberalism and Christian Ethics*, Cambridge University Press, Cambridge and New York, 1998, for this reference.

[2] Fergusson, *Community*, p. 78.

[3] *Ibid.* p. 76. For a finely nuanced theological account of liberalism see Robert Song's *Christianity and Liberal Society*, Clarendon Press, Oxford, 1997.

emphasis is still upon virtue ethics, but its orientation is around individual vision and character. In the middle phase of his work there is a greater emphasis upon churches as the primary communities that are the *loci* of Christian virtues, albeit with some indications that secular communities may sometimes embed these virtues more clearly than actual churches. In his most recent work, churches (idealised if not actual) are seen as the sole repositories of Christian virtues, and Christians are viewed as aliens in an increasingly hostile world.

The earliest phase is seen clearly in Hauerwas' first book *Vision and Virtue*, published in 1974. There he depicts the task of Christian ethics as follows:

> Once ethics is focused on the nature and moral determination of the self, vision and virtue again become morally significant categories. We are as we come to see and as that seeing becomes enduring in our intentionality. We do not come to see, however, just by looking but by training our vision through the metaphors and symbols that constitute our central convictions. How we come to see therefore is a function of how we come to be since our seeing necessarily is determined by how our basic images are embodied by the self – i.e., in our character. Christian ethics is the conceptual discipline that analyses and imaginatively tests the images most appropriate to score the Christian life in accordance with the central conviction that the world has been redeemed by the work and person of Christ.[4]

He sets out this understanding of Christian ethics more fully the following year in *Character and the Christian Life*.[5] It already contains some of the enduring features of his thought, as well as some clear elements which he later modifies. Enduring features include an emphasis upon virtue, character and moral training as crucial for Christian ethics rather than upon moral decision-making as such. There is a stress upon the Christian life and the centrality of Christology and Atonement for this life. The concept of moral vision does not altogether disappear in his later work, but it does receive less emphasis. At this stage the influence of Iris Murdoch is openly acknowledged and, indeed, some of her Platonism may be evident in his language. Writing

[4] Stanley Hauerwas, *Vision and Virtue*, Fides, Notre Dame, Indiana, 1974, p. 2.
[5] Trinity University Press, San Antonio, 1975.

at the time I noted that Hauerwas tended to use philosophy in addition to theology to illuminate his understanding of the task of Christian ethics, but that he might also have used sociology since 'the latter could analyse the images actually used by Christians in their moral lives and suggest ways in which these images are determined or determinative'.[6]

A decade later he recognises that 'though I had stressed the relational character of the self, this is not sufficient to indicate the centrality of a particular community called the church for the development of the kind of character required of Christians'.[7] From this point onwards in his writings he repeatedly makes reference to the church as the Christian community from which individual Christians learn and are shaped by Christian virtues. So at the outset of his important theoretical book *A Community of Character: Toward a Constructive Christian Social Ethic* he now depicts Christian ethics as follows:

> The justification for calling this book 'social ethics' is that I wish to show why any consideration of the truth of Christian convictions cannot be divorced from the kind of community the church is and should be . . . my primary interest is to challenge the church to regain a sense of the significance of the polity that derives from convictions peculiar to Christians . . . if the church is to serve our liberal society or any society, it is crucial for Christians to regain an appropriate sense of separateness from that society . . . such a 'separateness' may involve nothing more nor less than the Christian community's willingness to provide hospitality for the stranger – particularly when that stranger so often comes in the form of our own children.[8]

With the focus evident here upon the role of the church in Christian ethics, there is also a conviction that church polity should derive from distinctively Christian beliefs. In turn, this suggests that the church should have a sense of 'separateness' from the world. It is precisely this new element of 'separateness' in his thought which soon gave rise to the charge of 'sectarianism', evident in the quotation from Gustafson. David

[6] See my *Theology and Social Structure*, Mowbrays, Oxford, 1977, p. 117.

[7] From the introduction to the 1985 re-issue of *Character and the Christian Life*, p.xxxi. I am grateful again to David Fergusson (*Community*) for this quotation.

[8] Stanley Hauerwas, *A Community of Character: Toward a Constructive Christian Social Ethic*, University of Notre Dame, Indiana, 1981, pp. 1–2.

Fergusson is not convinced about this charge, pointing out that Hauerwas, unlike a radical sectarian, is still concerned 'to serve our liberal society'.[9] Hauerwas is not, for example, suggesting that the church should simply withdraw wholly from the world as the Exclusive Brethren have done or even denounce the world totally as the Jehovah's Witnesses have done. At this stage 'separateness' seems to require a resolute distinctiveness but not the radical exclusivity of some sects (although, even here, many sociologists have followed Bryan Wilson's influential classification of sects[10] which includes many less radical positions). The fact that Hauerwas continues to write in such areas as medical ethics and to speak to professionals within these areas might support Fergusson. The final chapter will return to some of these issues in more detail.

Nonetheless, the language of 'the stranger' now emerges in his writings, as well as an increasing dichotomy between the church and what he views (and decries) as 'liberal society'. Accompanying this dichotomy is also an ambivalence about whether or not he is talking about the church as it is or the church as it ought to be. Sometimes it does appear to be the former. This allows him to suggest what almost looks like an empirical test of his understanding of Christian ethics. So he writes:

> All politics should be judged by the character of the people it produces. The depth and variety of character which a polity sustains is a correlative of the narrative that provides its identity and purpose. The contention and witness of the church is that the story of Jesus provides a flourishing of gifts which other politics cannot know. It does so because Christians have been nourished on the story of a savior who insisted on being nothing else than what he was. By being the son of God he provided us with the confidence that insofar as we become his disciples our particularity and our regard for the particularity of our brothers and sisters in Christ contribute to his Kingdom. Our stories become part of the story of the Kingdom.[11]

9 Fergusson, *Community*, pp. 76f. Cf. Oliver O'Donovan, *The Desire of Nations: Rediscovering the Roots of Political Theology*, Cambridge University Press, Cambridge, 1996.

10 E.g. Bryan Wilson, *Religion in Sociological Perspective*, Clarendon Press, Oxford, 1987, and *The Social Dimension of Sectarianism*, Clarendon Press, Oxford, 1990.

11 Hauerwas, *A Community of Character*, p. 51.

Only the words 'insofar as we become his disciples' in this quotation raise doubts. Otherwise this does seem to be a statement about the empirical church. It is this church which carries the Christian narrative which, in turn, can nourish Christians and provide evidence to the world at large of the Christian character. Sociology might well have an important role in assessing the fruits of such nourishing. Yet even here Hauerwas leaves this escape clause. It could just be that an analysis of actual churchgoers would be flawed because some of them had not truly 'become his disciples'.

Herein lies the problem for Hauerwas now. He sees the church as the locus of Christian community, as the bearer of the unique Christian story, and thus as the agent of Christian socialisation. It should, then, be possible for others outside the church to see clearly the fruits of this socialisation. Yet he is aware of the obvious limitations and fragilities of actual church congregations:

But we must admit the church has not been a society of trust and virtue. At most, people identify the church as a place where the young learn 'morals', but the 'morals' often prove to be little more than conventional pieties coupled with a few unintelligible 'don'ts'. Therefore any radical critique of our secular polity requires an equally radical critique of the church.[12]

In *The Peaceable Kingdom*, written two years later, his criticisms of the church as it is are far more trenchant. Here he insists that 'what makes the church the church is its faithful manifestation of the peaceable kingdom in the world . . . the church must never cease from being a community of peace and truth in a world of mendacity and fear'.[13] Given such a high understanding of the church, it is hardly surprising that Hauerwas immediately sees that the empirical church, past or present, can hardly be depicted in such terms. Instead he adds:

The scandal of the disunity of the church is even more painful when we recognize this social task. For we who have been called to be the foretaste of the peaceable kingdom cannot, it seems, maintain unity

[12] *Ibid.* p. 86.

[13] Stanley Hauerwas, *The Peaceable Kingdom: A Primer of Christian Ethics*, University of Notre Dame, Indiana, 1983, and SCM Press, London, 1984, pp. 99–100.

among ourselves . . . And the divisions I speak of in the church are not just those based on doctrine, history, or practices important though they are. No, the deep and most painful divisions afflicting the church are those based on class, race, and nationality that we have sinfully accepted as written into the nature of things.[14]

It would seem from this quotation that the church (as it is) is quite a long way away from the 'peaceable kingdom' which he regards as essential to the church (as it ought to be). He even adds that we may 'find that people who are not Christians manifest God's peace better than ourselves'.[15] Confusingly, though, in terms of virtue ethics it is presumably communities as they are which actually nourish their members. People may, of course, be inspired by depictions of how their particular community ought to be. Yet it is actual, existing communities that are their primary means of socialisation. At one point in *The Peaceable Kingdom* Hauerwas himself seems to recognise this when he argues that 'people in a community must learn to trust one another as well as trust the community itself . . . all communities require a sense of hope in the future and they witness to the necessity of love for sustaining relationships'. He adds that 'there is a profound sense in which the traditional "theological virtue" of faith, hope, and love are "natural" '. He even believes that 'as much as any institution the church is sustained by these "natural virtues" ', even though it is not the case that 'what is meant by faith, hope, and love is the same for Christians as for other people'.[16]

Hauerwas again faces an obvious dilemma. The church as it ought to be can enshrine Christian virtues properly, but unfortunately it cannot socialise Christians in the actual world. The church as it is can indeed socialise Christians, but sadly it does not enshrine Christian virtues properly. Of course there could be a church just around the corner which manages to do both . . . but after two thousand years this has yet to happen.

At times Hauerwas is painfully honest. In the introduction to *A Community of Character* he acknowledges that 'perhaps the reason I stress so strongly the significance of the church for social ethics is that I am currently not disciplined by, nor do I

[14] *Ibid.* p. 100. [15] *Ibid.* p. 101. [16] *Ibid.* p. 103.

feel the ambiguity of, any concrete church . . . I find I must think and write not only for the church that does exist but for the church that should exist if we were more courageous and faithful.'[17] Two years later in *The Peaceable Kingdom* he makes a point of noting that this issue has been resolved – dedicating the book to his new-found Methodist congregation. Despite this new community, it is difficult to imagine that even it provided him with an adequate empirical basis for his notion of the 'peaceable kingdom'. Methodists have seldom been able to unite behind the sort of radical pacifism espoused by Hauerwas. Even the ideas expressed in some of his medically related books, such as the finely nuanced *Suffering Presence*[18] or *Naming the Silences*,[19] still seem to imply a more alienated church context than Methodism typically provides.

By the time the third phase of his writing is reached it is difficult to avoid David Fergusson's suggestion that:

> this church advocated by Hauerwas nowhere exists. It is a fantasy community, the conception of which fails to reflect the ways in which the members of the church are also positioned within civil society. It does not correspond to any visible communities within the *oekumene*.[20]

The publication, with William H. Willimon, of *Resident Aliens: Life in the Christian Colony*[21] in 1989 decisively marks the start of this phase. Subsequent publications, including *Against the Nations*,[22] *Dispatches from the Front*[23] and *Where Resident Aliens Live*,[24] have re-enforced it. Characteristic of this phase is an increase in hyperbole in Hauerwas' writing. Even the titles of these books reflect this hyperbole – a feature which is only very occasionally acknowledged by Hauerwas himself.[25]

It is this increase in hyperbole which may tend to polarise other Christian ethicists. It coincided with Hauerwas' move from the Catholic University of Notre Dame to the Methodist Duke University. Perhaps he felt less constrained within this

[17] Hauerwas, *A Community of Character*, p. 6.
[18] University of Notre Dame, Indiana, 1986, and T. & T. Clark, Edinburgh, 1988.
[19] Eerdmans, Grand Rapids, Michigan, 1990. [20] Fergusson, *Community*, p. 66.
[21] Abingdon, Nashville, 1989. [22] University of Notre Dame, Indiana, 1992.
[23] Duke University Press, 1995.
[24] Abingdon, Nashville, 1996 (again with William H. Willimon).
[25] E.g. Hauerwas and Willimon, *Resident Aliens*, p. 165.

new environment or perhaps he had fewer colleagues to remind him of continuities between Christian and secular communities (as a natural law approach would suggest). Perhaps his increasing fame encouraged him to heighten his theories. Or perhaps it was a natural, polemical response to the criticism of sectarianism that was gaining currency.[26] Whatever the reason, his theories become increasingly exaggerated and distorted and less subject to any kind of empirical check.

A careful reading of *Resident Aliens* makes this clear. Of course it is written in a more popular format than his other books and it is also co-authored. Nevertheless it accurately represents Hauerwas' views in this third phase. The dichotomy between the church and the world has become sharper, with the church increasingly idealised and the world demonised. Liberal theologians are reminded at length about the liberal accommodation with the Nazis, with strong warnings to 'those who take the same path, hoping to update the church, to recover some of the scandal of Jesus by identifying the church with the newest secular solution: Marxism, Feminism, the Sexual Revolution'.[27] In earlier books Hauerwas praises the work of H. Richard Niebuhr,[28] but now *Resident Aliens* states that 'we have come to believe that few books have been a greater hindrance to an accurate assessment of our situation than *Christ and Culture*'.[29] Pastors are told that 'if we live as a colony of resident aliens within a hostile environment, which, in the most subtle but deadly of ways, corrupts and coopts us as Christians, then the pastor is called to help us gather the resources we need to be the colony of God's righteousness'.[30] The dichotomy is indeed sharp:

> Life in the colony is not a settled affair. Subject to constant attacks upon and sedition against its most cherished virtues, always in danger of losing its young, regarded as a threat by an atheistic culture, which in the name of freedom and equality subjugates everyone – the Christian colony can be appreciated by its members as a challenge.[31]

26 E.g. see the introduction to Hauerwas, *Against the Nations.*

27 Hauerwas and Willimon, *Resident Aliens*, p. 27.

28 E.g. in Hauerwas, *The Peaceable Kingdom.*

29 Hauerwas and Willimon, *Resident Aliens*, p. 40.

30 *Ibid.* pp. 139–40.

31 *Ibid.* p. 51.

The image of 'resident aliens' was doubtless chosen for its impact and may have been responsible more than anything else for its sales. Yet it is an image which effectively removes the church from reality. Augustine's image of the 'pilgrim' church would have been distinctly less sensational and would have allowed some check against the church as it is. There is a sense in which the church is properly seen as being in this world but not of this world. Pilgrims are clearly still part of this world, yet they have their sight set steadily beyond this world. At certain periods of history pilgrims have even dressed distinctively and travelled to dangerous and distant places, whilst leaving home and work for long periods of time. Even then they have typically relied upon the charity and hospitality of those who are not pilgrims. However 'aliens', whether in the older American form of resident foreigners or in the newer film form of visitors from other galaxies, are radical outsiders. They may take our guise but this is just a veneer, since in reality they are unlike us.

In the chapters that follow it will be seen that such a depiction simply does not match detailed empirical data about churchgoers as they are. Even though it will become evident that churchgoers do have distinctive beliefs, values and practices, their distinctiveness is relative not absolute. Many nonchurchgoers share their beliefs, values and practices (apart from churchgoing itself), even though these are found more amongst churchgoers than amongst nonchurchgoers. This detailed empirical evidence helps to settle a theoretical debate which I have outlined elsewhere.[32] There I suggested that three distinct positions have been adopted, within both philosophical and theological discussions, about the status of moral communities in relation to postmodernism. The first is the most radical. It argues that legitimation is only possible within cultural-linguistic communities and that such communities are incapable of mutual communication. Precisely because the independent 'planks' offered by modernism (notably autonomous rational thought and empirical demonstration) have now been deconstructed, moral values or virtues can only be known

[32] See my *Moral Leadership in a Postmodern Age*, T. & T. Clark, Edinburgh, 1997, pp. 67f.

within specific communities. This seems increasingly to be the position taken by Hauerwas. The second maintains that communities can communicate with each other precisely because individuals in the West today typically belong to more than one community. In his writings since *After Virtue* MacIntyre has sought to trace ways in which communities overlap and in which legitimation may sometimes decline in one at the expense of another. Jonathan Sacks is also an able theological exponent of the moral implications of simultaneously belonging to two communities – in his case those of a pluralist society and a traditional Jewish community.[33] A third response to postmodernism accepts the general position that moral values and virtues are shaped, sustained and carried in communities, but argues that there *are* some moral 'planks' that apply across cultures. It is possible that MacIntyre's own thought is developing in this direction.[34] In chapter nine it will be seen that several contributors to this series also take the third position seriously. Whether the second or third position is finally adopted, the first does seem to run contrary to the churchgoing data that follow.

The combination of hyperbole, an idealised church and a demonised secular culture – all of which feature strongly in the first position – can be found in the writings of a number of theologians influenced by Hauerwas' writing. It is now quite common to hear theologians talking with disdain about 'the Enlightenment project' or about 'liberal culture' and contrasting this with '*the* radical Christian alternative'. Such a perspective received powerful expression in John Milbank's magnum opus *Theology and Social Theory*. Elsewhere again I have criticised this challenging work for its hyperbole.[35] For example, at one point Milbank claims that 'I am going to show how all twentieth-century sociology of religion can be exposed as a

[33] Jonathan Sacks, *The Persistence of Faith*, Weidenfeld & Nicolson, London, 1992, and *Faith in the Future*, Darton, Longman & Todd, London, 1995.

[34] See his response in John Horton and Susan Mendus (eds.), *After MacIntyre: Critical Perspectives on the Work of Alasdair MacIntyre*, Polity Press, Oxford, and University of Notre Dame, Indiana, 1994.

[35] See my *Christian Ethics in Secular Worlds*, T. & T. Clark, Edinburgh, 1991, and David Martin's *Reflections on Sociology and Theology*, Clarendon Press, Oxford, 1996.

secular policing of the sublime . . . deconstructed in this fashion, the entire subject evaporates into the pure ether of the secular will-to-power.'[36]

Others have criticised Milbank's *Theology and Social Theory* precisely because the central picture of the church that it presents is idealised and even misleading. So, Rowan Williams recognises the power of Milbank's book whilst regarding its idealisation as less than helpful. For Williams 'the insistence on thinking Christ in inseparable relation with the Church is . . . one of the most important constructive elements of the book', whilst at the same time 'the risk Milbank's exposition runs is, rather paradoxically, of slipping into a picture of history as the battlefield of ideal types'.[37] More specifically, he believes that Milbank's account of the 'peace of the Church' (sharing many similarities with Hauerwas' *The Peaceable Kingdom*) pays too little attention to how this peace is historically and socially constructed.[38]

Aidan Nichols is less gentle in his criticism:

> Despite the numerous true judgments, good maxims and beautiful insights to be found scattered through this book, its overall message is deplorable. My objections can be summed up in two words: 'hermeticism' and 'theocracy'. By 'hermeticism' I mean the enclosure of Christian discourse and practice within a wholly separate universe of thought and action, a universe constituted by the prior 'mythos' of Christianity . . . For Milbank there can be no such thing as an intellectual indebtedness of the Church to natural wisdom. Every putative thought of such wisdom as can be named is not extraneous to the Christian *mythos*, and without a role in the dramatic narrative, from Genesis to Apocalypse, in which that *mythos* is expressed. Also, all natural wisdom is legitimately liable to deconstruction . . . Only the Christian *mythos*, the Christian narrative, the Christian (ecclesial) community, can secure the human good – the beautiful pattern of living – which always eludes the secular ruler's grasp. Milbank's social programme is . . . theocratic in that . . . it seeks to restore Christendom

36 John Milbank, *Theology and Social Theory: Beyond Secular Reason*, Blackwell, Oxford, 1990, p. 106.

37 Rowan Williams, 'Saving Time: Thoughts on Practice, Patience and Vision', *New Blackfriars*, vol. 73, no. 861, June 1992, pp. 319–26.

38 See also Duncan Forrester, *Christian Justice and Public Policy*, Cambridge University Press, Cambridge, 1997, p. 244.

. . . Unfortunately Milbank goes too far: in attempting to persuade to the faith of the Great Church it damages it, and not with some light scar but a grave wound.[39]

In his response to these two critics, Milbank agrees that 'between my "formal" or ideal descriptions of the Church (of an "ideal" happening, and "ideal" yet real, if vestigial transmission) and rather minimal attempts at "judicious narrative", there may exist a certain tension'.[40]

This admission raises again the issue of whether the focus in virtue ethics is primarily upon the church and churchgoers as they are or as they should be. For much of the time in both Milbank's *Theology and Social Theory* and in Hauerwas and Willimon's *Resident Aliens* it seems to be upon the latter. Nevertheless there are occasional indications in *Resident Aliens* that virtue theory does require a depiction of churchgoers as they are. Christian 'discipling' of the young, for example, does seem to need the presence of actual, rather than idealised, 'saints':

Christian ethics is, in the Aristotelian sense, an aristocratic ethic. It is not something that comes naturally. It can be learned. We are claiming, then, that a primary way of learning to be disciples is by being in contact with others who are disciples. So an essential role of the church is to put us in contact with those ethical aristocrats who are good at living the Christian faith. One role of any colony is to keep the young very close to the leaders – people who live aright the traditions of home. There is no substitute for living around other Christians.[41]

In line with virtue ethics, *Resident Aliens* recognises that 'all ethics, even non-Christian ethics, makes sense only when embodied in sets of social practices that constitute a community... such communities support a sense of right and wrong'.[42] Manifestly these must be actual and not purely idealised communities. Doubtless utopian images do have an important

[39] Aidan Nichols, 'Non Tali Auxilio: John Milbank's Suasion to Orthodoxy', *New Blackfriars*, vol. 73, no. 861, June 1992, pp. 326–32. See also Gregory Baum, *Essays in Critical Theology*, Sheed and Ward, Kansas City, 1994, p. 70, and Ian S. Markham, *Plurality and Christian Ethics*, Cambridge University Press, Cambridge and New York, 1994, p. 146.

[40] John Milbank, 'Enclaves, or Where is the Church?', *New Blackfriars*, vol. 73, no. 861, June 1992, pp. 341–52.

[41] Hauerwas and Willimon, *Resident Aliens*, p. 102.

[42] *Ibid.* p. 79.

correcting and visionary function in many communities,[43] but it is difficult to see how they can act as primary means of socialisation. In *Resident Aliens* there is also a clear recognition that actual communities can be dysfunctional: 'in a world like ours, people will be attracted to communities that promise them an easy way out of loneliness, togetherness based on common tastes, racial or ethnic traits, or mutual self-interest ... there is then little check on community becoming as tyrannical as the individual ego'. In contrast, Christian community is 'about disciplining our wants and needs in congruence with a true story, which gives us the resources to lead truthful lives'.[44] Both in Christian and in non-Christian contexts here, a process of socialisation seems to be envisaged which involves empirical communities.

Now, of course, there is a proper theological concern with the church as it ought to be. All thoughtful theologians, from the beginning of Christianity, have recognised as much. This is not my point. Rather it is that the specific insight of virtue ethics, which is especially relevant to a study of churchgoing and Christian ethics, is that the moral life is shaped by particular communities despite their actual frailties and ambiguities. Whereas there has been a tendency for moral philosophy to focus upon ethical decision-making as if individuals could act solely on the basis of autonomous reasoning, virtue ethics is more distinctly sociological in character. If MacIntyre has drawn particular attention to virtues as they are carried and nurtured within overlapping communities, Charles Taylor focuses more upon the tradition and community based antecedents of apparently autonomous choices. However, both philosophers have, in effect, a strong sense of the sociology of knowledge. Moral notions are socially generated and – even when this is not realised by the participants themselves – rely upon specific communities for their support. Given this understanding, a sociological examination of specific moral communities becomes possible – unless these communities are so

43 Cf. Karl Mannheim's classic *Ideology and Utopia*, Routledge and Kegan Paul, London, 1936.

44 Hauerwas and Willimon, *Resident Aliens*, p. 78.

idealised that they bear little relationship to empirical communities. Whereas many moral philosophers are interested in little other than the rational criteria used within ethical decision-making, virtue ethicists such as MacIntyre have an additional interest in social structures. Within virtue ethics, properly understood, the mechanisms of socialisation become at least as important as formal rational criteria.

In part *Resident Aliens* recognises this. For example, a whole chapter is devoted to theological education. In this the authors criticise their fellow theologians for being too preoccupied with their own interests and insufficiently attentive to the realities of church life. At one point they even suggest that different fashions within academic theology may have more to do with keeping up the interests of theologians themselves than with equipping students for parish life and effective ministry. There is nothing new about this particular charge – it could have been levelled just as effectively at Augustine or Aquinas – but it does serve to underline the incongruity of their own focus upon an idealised rather than an actual church.

This incongruity continues in *Where Resident Aliens Live*, the sequel to *Resident Aliens*. At more than one point Hauerwas and Willimon disarmingly admit that mainstream Methodism really does not seem to fit their seemingly 'sectarian' approach to theology and ethics. Hauerwas readily admits that his own approach has been much influenced by the Mennonites through the theology of John Howard Yoder. Nonetheless they write:

> One can understand why someone might wonder where we get our ecclesiology. After all, we are both United Methodists, in varying degrees of happiness. Mainstream United Methodism is about as far from some of the views of resident aliens as night is from day. Yet in its stress on sanctification, on the importance of the practical, practiced embodiment of the faith by the laity, we thought that our resident aliens are a very Methodist people.[45]

Behind this admission there is an obvious tension. On the one hand the two authors do not believe in a sectarian withdrawal from the world. They point out that 'the accusation that

[45] Hauerwas and Willimon, *Where Resident Aliens Live*, p. 22; see also p. 40.

we are "sectarian" strikes us as especially strange . . . because both of us work at a large, secular university'.[46] On the other, they are not sure why the term 'sectarian' should be a term of theological abuse at all and argue that it is only certain individuals within mainstream denominations who actually embody the virtues that they believe are distinctively Christian. They provide repeated practical examples of individuals who do embody these virtues, but in doing so they underline their conviction that most denominational Christians, at least for much of the time, do not.

Ironically, one of the many merits of virtue ethics for a theologian is that it does invite us to be more attentive to the specific ways that those involved in Christian communities are in reality shaped by these communities. In places Hauerwas and Willimon do seem to recognise this. For example, they commend Episcopalians for their support of the ideas in *Resident Aliens*:

> They are one of the few church families in the North American context who stress ecclesiology and can therefore see that Christian theology begins in ecclesiology, in church practices, not in something called 'Systematic Theology'. Theology begins in church and works its way out, rather than beginning in a university department of religion and dribbling back to the church as the practical application of great thoughts. Most seminary curricula embody this mistake. For example, we teach systematic theology as something that is necessary to do prior to teaching ethics. This presupposes that you have to get your ideas systematized before you talk about practices. As a result, we fail to see that theology itself is a practice in service to the church, which is in service to the world. Resident aliens challenge the presumption that theology is about ideas.[47]

There is an important insight here which I will develop further in the final part of this book. It *is* a feature of much recent Anglican theology[48] that worship is regarded as central

[46] *Ibid.* p. 29. [47] *Ibid.* pp. 57–8.

[48] E.g. Stephen Sykes, *The Identity of Christianity: Theologians and the Essence of Christianity from Schleiermacher to Barth*, SPCK, London, 1984; David Ford and Daniel Hardy, *Jubilate: Theology in Praise*, Darton, Longman & Todd, London, 1984 (American title *Praising and Knowing God*, Westminster Press, Philadelphia, 1985); and Harmon L. Smith, *Where Two or Three are Gathered Together: Liturgy and the Moral Life*, Pilgrim Press, Cleveland, 1995.

to both theology and ethics. However, for the most part, Anglican theology has tended to be more inclusive than *Resident Aliens* appears to be. The writings of Stephen Sykes exemplify this. In a warning that Hauerwas and Willimon might have heeded, he notes:

The hyperbole at the heart of Christian discipleship occasionally commits itself to an unguarded affirmation of the absolute incommensurability of Jesus' teaching with any previous example of religious teaching. But irrespective of what may be stated about Jesus' own person, in respect of what he taught we are dealing with the relative novelties of a process of religious change. Under no other circumstances could what he said have been intelligible to his contemporaries. Those who have new things to communicate do so by means of modifications of previously held beliefs. The modifications may be slight, or they may be far-reaching; but they can never be total.[49]

The connection between worship, on the one hand, and theology and ethics, on the other, is not unique to Anglicans,[50] but it does seem to be characteristically Anglican. It is also an insight which might encourage theologians to look more attentively at worshipping communities as they actually are and not just as they might in theory be.

Yet perhaps there is a fear amongst theologians that there is no empirical evidence to support claims about the actual distinctiveness of Christian communities. Perhaps they fear that, in practice, churches do not have significant influence upon their members. Citing Milbank with approval, Hauerwas and Willimon mention sociology only to dismiss it. For instance, in what itself looks like an empirical assertion, they claim that 'the American church has suffered under sociological determinism for so long, it is difficult to get the church to believe that our theological convictions could possibly be as determinative of our lives as "sociological reality" '.[51] Or perhaps theologians (including Hauerwas and Willimon at times) fear that churches *do* have an influence but that it is a far from beneficial influence. If they have such fears, it is possible that they may have

[49] *Ibid.* p. 18.
[50] See Geoffrey Wainwright, *Doxology: The Praise of God in Worship, Doctrine and Life: A Systematic Theology*, Clarendon Press, Oxford and New York, 1980.
[51] Hauerwas and Willimon, *Where Resident Aliens Live*, p. 67.

acquired them from sociologists. In the next chapter I will show that there is a long-standing bias amongst sociologists of religion that churchgoing is either without social significance or that it has significance but is dysfunctional. Until recently few sociologists have challenged this bias. In the last few years a few have begun to note new evidence which contradicts it, although even they have seldom spotted earlier data suggesting a radically different picture.[52] A fuller sociological account of churchgoing is long overdue. To this end, later chapters will examine in detail a rich and largely unexplored source of data on churchgoing as it relates to Christian beliefs, values and practices.

All of this depicts the moral significance of churchgoing as it is rather than as it ought to be. It could just be that actual churchgoing is more interesting than some exponents of virtue ethics have allowed. By focusing too quickly upon some idealised church, they may not have allowed us to see clearly the actual patterns of Christian socialisation that have carried Christian faith, values and practice from one generation to another across two millennia. In the circumstances it might be helpful to gain a more accurate picture of churchgoing as it is before deciding what it should be.

[52] A striking, but polemical, exception is Rodney Stark and William Sims Bainbridge, *Religion, Deviance and Social Control*, Routledge, New York and London, 1996.

CHAPTER 2

Churchgoing and the bias of sociologists

A curious double bias has been noted especially amongst those Christian ethicists who have been most influenced by virtue ethics. One side of the bias is to take the concept of Christian communities seriously, but the other side is to be deeply distrustful of actual Christian communities. Within Christian versions of virtue ethics, worshipping communities are seen as essential for an adequate understanding of theology and ethics. Nevertheless the frailties and inadequacies of churchgoers themselves are regarded as all too obvious. As a result, amongst a number of recent theologians a high doctrine of worship is often combined with a low estimate of worshippers.

Now it could be that this second bias has been reinforced by sociologists, who, in turn, may have unwittingly echoed a widely held popular bias. A review of literature within the sociology of religion over the last few decades does seem to confirm a widespread conviction that the beliefs and behaviour of churchgoers are little different from those of nonchurchgoers. Indeed, there has long been a sociological assumption that churchgoing lacks social significance. Whatever religious or theological significance it has, churchgoing is seldom thought to be an activity that has an appreciable effect upon moral/social attitudes or behaviour. In contrast to age, social class or gender, churchgoing is basically a dependent rather than an independent social variable. Moreover, since churchgoers are predominantly elderly, middle class and female, differences between them and nonchurchgoers are typically regarded as attributable to these variables rather than to their regularity of churchgoing.

The bulk of the empirical evidence examined in this book

will be entirely new, processing and testing for the first time recent British religious attitudes and behaviour and, then, comparing them extensively with a wide range of evidence from elsewhere in Europe, Australia and North America. However, the present chapter will review long-standing, yet often ignored, data suggesting that the beliefs of churchgoers are more distinctive than has often been realised by theologians, by sociologists, or even by the public at large. Later chapters will set out the new data generated from the two most substantial British sources of recent attitude surveys, namely the British Household Panel Survey and British Social Attitudes. Despite the inclusion of churchgoing as a regular variable in both sets of surveys, there has until now been very little analysis done upon it. Yet taken together they offer a remarkably detailed picture of the culture of churchgoing – a picture which might even have more theological implications than is sometimes realised.

EARLY SURVEYS OF THE BELIEFS OF CHURCHGOERS

The bias about churchgoing takes both a popular and a sociological form. The popular form was until recently often expressed in the following way: 'You do not have to go to church to be a good Christian.' In an age which is less confident about the merits of being a Christian at all, it might now be phrased somewhat differently: 'Churchgoers are no better than anyone else.' Yet whichever way it is expressed, it does appear to be assumed by many people that churchgoing is not a morally significant activity in the sense that there is a perceived moral 'improvement' arising from churchgoing. Churchgoers themselves usually believe that there is such an improvement; the population at large is less convinced. This finding can be traced consistently through opinion polls over four decades. In the 1954 BBC poll[1] only 25% of the whole sample thought that churchgoers 'are more trustworthy than other people' and 'are better citizens than other people', whereas 51% of those going to church 'most Sundays' agreed with the first and 52% with the

[1] British Broadcasting Corporation, *Religious Broadcasts and the Public*, Audience Research Department, BBC, 1955.

second. In the ABC TV 1964 poll[2] only 15% of the whole sample thought that 'churchgoers lead better lives than non-churchgoers', as distinct from 39% of monthly churchgoers. Widening the question to belief, the ITC 1993 poll[3] found that only 40% of the whole sample regarded religious beliefs as 'necessary to lead a good life', as distinct from 55% of general churchgoers, 78% of Black Pentecostals and 96% of Muslims.

The sociological form of this assumption may well owe much to the dominant Enlightenment principle that morality is autonomous and *sui generis*, owing nothing essential to religious tradition, revelation or faith. However it was strongly reinforced by data from the earliest opinion polls available to sociologists of religion. Even someone like David Martin, not instinctively inclined to assume that churchgoing is morally and socially insignificant, in practice relied in his classic *A Sociology of English Religion*[4] upon polls which appeared to suggest that it is. In depicting the social characteristics of churchgoers in the 1960s, he relied heavily upon the 1947 Mass-Observation study *Puzzled People*,[5] Geoffrey Gorer's remarkable 1955 study *Exploring English Character*,[6] and, to a lesser extent, early Gallup Polls. He did use the ABC TV 1964 poll, which, as will be seen, presented some contrary evidence, but had he been able to use the BBC's 1954 survey *Religious Broadcasts and the Public*, he might have been able to mount a more robust critique of the churchgoing-as-epiphenomenon position that Bryan Wilson articulated so brilliantly in his *Religion in Secular Society*.[7]

In words that have often been quoted by sociologists, and which clearly reinforce the epiphenomenal understanding of churchgoing, *Puzzled People* summarised the Mass-Observation findings as follows:

Of the doubters, agnostics and atheists ... Over a quarter say they

2 ABC Television, *Television and Religion*, London University Press, London, 1965.

3 Independent Television Commission, *Seeing is Believing: Religion and Television in the 1990s*, (ed. Barry Gunter and Rachel Viney), John Libbey, London, 1994.

4 David Martin, *A Sociology of English Religion*, Heinemann, London, 1967.

5 Mass-Observation, *Puzzled People: A Study of Popular Attitudes to Religion, Ethics, Progress and Politics in a London Borough*, Victor Gollancz, London, 1947.

6 Geoffrey Gorer, *Exploring English Character*, Cresset Press, London, 1955.

7 Bryan Wilson, *Religion in Secular Society*, C. A. Watt, London, 1966.

pray on occasions to the God whose existence they doubt. One in twelve went to church within the past six months, compared with one in three of those who say they believe in God. Over half the non-believers consider that there should be religious education in schools. Of those who say they believe in a Deity, one in five are definite in their assertion that they do not believe in a life after death; one half say they never go to church, or only go for weddings, funerals and such like. A quarter never pray or pray only in church. Of those who attend Church of England services regularly or intermittently, one-quarter do not believe in an after-life; on the other hand, one-fifth of those who don't go to church at all do believe. Of those who don't believe in a Deity or are agnostic, nearly a quarter tend to think that Christ was 'something more than a man'; on the other hand, a rather larger proportion of Church of England churchgoers say he was *only* a man. Of those who say he was only a man, one in five may also believe that he was born of a virgin. But of those who attend Church of England services, one in four doubt the doctrine of the Virgin Birth and only one in three give quite definite assent to it.[8]

It is not difficult to see how this passage soon became a crucial text for sociologists maintaining that there is little difference in belief (let alone behaviour) between churchgoers and nonchurchgoers. Having quoted it himself, David Martin wrote that in 'a general common-sense way it can be assumed that on all points women are more religious than men, the old than the young, the upper than the lower social strata, the north and west more than the south, and that churchgoers are more "orthodox" than non-churchgoers, particularly churchgoers of the Roman Catholic faith'.[9] At most, it was considered that some Christian belief is fostered amongst churchgoers and even this primarily amongst Catholics. Conversely, Christian belief is to be found amongst nonchurchgoers and its absence amongst churchgoers. For Grace Davie this means that 'belief' and 'belonging' in the modern world are relatively independent of each other.[10] Interestingly this thesis has proved popular with professional religious broadcasters, since it allows them to convince sceptical colleagues that their programmes are rele-

8 Mass-Observation, *Puzzled People*, p. 18.

9 Martin, *A Sociology of English Religion*, pp. 53–5.

10 Grace Davie, *Religion in Britain Since 1945: Believing Without Belonging*, Blackwell, Oxford, 1994.

vant not simply to the minority of the population that still attends church on a regular basis. Religious programmes, on this basis, can also be just as relevant to the many who still 'believe' but no longer formally 'belong'. Furthermore, religious broadcasters have tended to argue this despite evidence clearly established in the BBC 1954 survey, and re-enforced many times since,[11] that churchgoers are much greater users of religious broadcasts than nonchurchgoers.

Unfortunately the empirical distinction between churchgoers and nonchurchgoers that *Puzzled People* adopted was extremely weak. To qualify as a churchgoer an individual needed to attend church just twice a year. Significant differences of attitude or stated behaviour may require additional distinctions between weekly and monthly attendance. This can be illustrated by taking two of the items mentioned in the *Puzzled People* summary just quoted. In this report 44% of the whole sample believed in after-life. Gallup Polls for 1939 and 1947 offered a fairly similar general level of popular belief, namely 49% at both dates. Amongst the (occasional) churchgoers reported in *Puzzled People* this rose only to 54%. However in the ABC TV 1964 poll belief in after-life amongst those attending church at least once a month rose to 84% (as distinct from 50% in the whole sample) and in the MORI 1993 poll[12] for BBC it was 85%. Again in *Puzzled People* 52% of the whole sample expressed a belief in Jesus as Son of God, but amongst churchgoers this rose only to 55%. However, given a tighter understanding of churchgoers, a Gallup Poll in 1979 recorded 88% of monthly churchgoers expressing this belief and the MORI 1993 poll for BBC recorded 87% amongst weekly churchgoers and 76% amongst fortnightly churchgoers. It seems likely that a tighter definition of churchgoers in 1947 might have yielded similar results.

There is also indirect evidence that such a tighter definition might have given different results on the moral questions asked in *Puzzled People*. Comparing different groups who criticised or

[11] E.g. ABC TV, *Television and Religion*.

[12] MORI, *Christian Beliefs*, Research Study Conducted for BBC Songs of Praise, Nov. 1993.

gave, at best, only 'qualified praise to Christ's life and teaching', they found that 21% of nonchurchgoers came into this category, as distinct from 16% of Church of England churchgoers. However the smallest group was Roman Catholic churchgoers at 7%. *Puzzled People* tended to think of the Roman Catholics in the sample as distinct because they were Roman Catholics. The Preface written by H. J. Blackham, General Secretary of the Ethic Union which sponsored the survey, even talked disparagingly about 'the triumph of Roman Catholic indoctrination' and 'the ignorance and confusion of those who call themselves Christians'.[13] Yet it is possible that Roman Catholics may have been distinct mainly because the majority of them were in fact regular churchgoers.

Another question in *Puzzled People* asked respondents what they thought 'the most important thing in life'. They then attempted to depict two broad groups on the basis of replies given: an interdependent group which mentioned such issues as love, marriage, the family, doing good, righteousness and faith, and an independent group which mentioned, rather, such issues as pleasure, money and independence itself. On the basis of this very broad distinction the report found that 38% of the sample as whole (and some 36% of nonchurchgoers) belonged to the interdependent group, and 15% to the independent group (some 18% of nonchurchgoers). Church of England churchgoers once again differed only slightly (40% interdependent and 9% independent), whereas Roman Catholic churchgoers were indeed different (53% interdependent and 7% independent). Here too the differences evident amongst Roman Catholics might have resulted more from the effect of churchgoing than of denomination. Yet this was a possibility never discussed by the authors of *Puzzled People* and seldom entertained by subsequent sociologists of religion.

The rich set of data revealed in Geoffrey Gorer's *Exploring English Character* strongly reinforced the assumption that churchgoing is a dependent rather than an independent social and moral variable. With a sample of some 5000 respondents, Gorer

[13] Mass-Observation, *Puzzled People*, p. 7.

was the first to demonstrate in such detail the age, gender, social class and location differences between churchgoers and non-churchgoers. These have been confirmed in many subsequent surveys.[14] However, Gorer employed churchgoing as an independent variable on only four items, three of which he did not find particularly convincing and one of which he did (premarital sex) but failed to record the results. One item looked at the correlation between regularity of churchgoing and sending one's children to Sunday school. At a time just before the collapse of Sunday school going, 54% of the whole responded that their children did go, as did 41% of adults who themselves never went to church. Amongst adults attending once or twice a year it rose to 59%, to those attending monthly 65% and to those attending more than once a week 69%. Gorer remarked that 'greater devoutness makes very little difference in the proportion of children who go to Sunday school'.[15] Similarly, at a time when the teaching of children to say prayers was still so widespread, Gorer found that the children of adults who never went to church were just as likely to say prayers before going to bed as the children of adults who went regularly (although less inclined to say grace).

It is, however, the correlation between churchgoing and a moral question on personal honesty in Gorer which is the most indicative of the churchgoing-as-epiphenomenon assumption. The question itself was rather vague:

> There's a lot of talk about 'fiddling' nowadays. Please mark which of the following statements most nearly represents your opinion: nearly everybody fiddles nowadays; most people fiddle occasionally but not many do regularly; with all the rules and regulations one can't help breaking a rule sometimes; it is unpatriotic to fiddle; none of my family has ever got anything 'off the ration'; it is wrong to break the law under any circumstances; most fiddling is done by profiteers; it is unfair to try to get more than others; most fiddling is done by foreigners.

[14] See further, Clive D. Field, 'Non-Recurrent Christian Data', *Reviews of United Kingdom Statistical Sources*, vol. xx, *Religion*, Royal Statistical Society and Economic and Social Research Council, Pergamon Press 1987.

[15] Gorer, *Exploring English Character*, p. 247.

Gorer comments on the results:

Membership of a religious denomination does not appear to make any significant difference. Those who go to church once a week or more often are slightly more inclined to choose one of the ethical rejection sentences than those who never go, or only for weddings and funerals; but there is only 10 per cent difference in admissions between the most fervent church-goers and the total abstainers (52 and 62 per cent respectively) . . . The active practice of religion does make a slight difference in the attitudes towards minor law-breaking, but the influence is negligible compared to the influence on pre-marital chastity. . . if the whole population were suddenly to become extremely devout, the reduction in fiddling and similar petty offences would only be in the neighbourhood of 10 per cent.[16]

But the problem with Gorer's original question is that it mixed empirical and moral statements and, in the process, may have blurred moral differences between churchgoers and non-churchgoers. It was perfectly possible for respondents who themselves believed that 'fiddling' was wrong nevertheless to see the ubiquity of fiddling ('nearly everybody fiddles nowadays') as the most evident feature of life in the immediate post-war era. Those opposed to pre-marital sex today (a majority, albeit a declining majority, of weekly churchgoers in the 1990s) might respond in a similar way given such a confusing choice.

Once again the BBC 1954 survey suggested a rather different picture. In contrast to the data from Gorer and *Puzzled People* which served to reinforce the churchgoing-as-epiphenomenon assumption, the BBC survey showed that there was in fact *a process* on a scale of frequent churchgoing, occasional churchgoing and nonchurchgoing in relation to a variety of religious and moral questions. Like Gorer, the BBC survey found that churchgoing is related to age, gender and social class, and that it is positively correlated with Sunday school attendance. However it found that not only did frequent churchgoers themselves once go for several years to Sunday school (87% as distinct from 73% of nonchurchgoers), but they also thought that 'children should go to Sunday school' (93% of frequent churchgoers, 86% of occasional churchgoers, and 62% of non-

[16] *Ibid.* pp. 233–4.

churchgoers). In addition, a clear process was evident amongst those giving unqualified approval that 'it is a good thing for children to have religious instruction in day school' (84% of frequent churchgoers, 73% of occasional churchgoers and 52% of nonchurchgoers). A similar process was also evident amongst those claiming to have looked at the Bible within the last fortnight (71% of frequent churchgoers, 28% of occasional churchgoers and 14% of nonchurchgoers) and amongst those giving unqualified support to the belief that God answers prayer (75%, 57% and 36% respectively).

Another clear process was evident in the same BBC 1954 survey on the issue of divorce reform. Whereas 30% of the whole sample thought that divorce 'should be harder', this rose to 53% amongst frequent churchgoers, dropping to 27% amongst occasional churchgoers and to just 19% amongst nonchurchgoers. Denominational differences were also evident, yet (in contrast to *Puzzled People*) a high proportion of frequent churchgoers across denominations believed that divorce 'should be harder'. Amongst Roman Catholics this rose to 73%, but even amongst Anglicans it was still 45% and amongst other denominations combined it was 48%. Again, like *Puzzled People*, the BBC survey found that a fifth of frequent churchgoers were undecided about after-life. Nevertheless it detected much sharper differences than *Puzzled People* when it asked whether or not one's behaviour affects one's destiny after death: 76% of frequent churchgoers thought that it did, as distinct from 42% of occasional churchgoers and just 23% of nonchurchgoers.

Finally, a rather complicated question in the BBC 1954 survey sought to explore the reasons people gave for trying 'to be honest, truthful and kind', seeking both unprompted and prompted responses. The results were analysed in terms of a number of categories: enlightened self-interest, authoritarian, altruistic, hedonistic and religious. Not surprisingly, the 'religious' category showed a clear process between frequent churchgoers, occasional churchgoers and nonchurchgoers (76%, 41% and 24% respectively). However, two other categories also suggested a similar, even if less pronounced, process

– authoritarian (76%, 72% and 56%) and altruistic (72%, 68% and 61%) – as did the number of reasons endorsed by each informant (3.6, 3.1 and 2.7 respectively).

What this remarkable BBC survey suggested about churchgoing as an independent variable was quite distinct from the two better known surveys, *Puzzled People* and Gorer, that informed sociological opinion in the 1960s. The 1964 ABC survey published as *Television and Religion* did note a number of important ways in which churchgoers appeared to differ from non-churchgoers. Yet even this survey did not demonstrate *a process* since it offered no intermediate categories of less than frequent churchgoers. It did, however, note that those attending church at least once a month did differ from the sample at large in being more convinced of the veracity of specific Christian beliefs (belief in a personal God, in Jesus as Son of God, in after-life, and in the existence of the devil), but they were also more inclined to believe that the 'influence of religion in Britain is increasing' and that churchgoers lead 'better' and 'happier' lives than others. To a lesser extent Gallup Polls have also noted that churchgoers have distinctive beliefs in God (1979: 96% of churchgoers believed as distinct from 76% of the whole sample), in Jesus as Son of God (1979: 88% as distinct from 55%) and in heaven (1979: 78% as distinct from 57%; and 1981: 86% as distinct from 53%). Analysing Anglican churchgoers against the general population, successive Gallup polls have also detected different levels of belief in the Virgin Birth (1984: 53% as distinct from 34%; and 1996: 53% as distinct from 27%), in the bodily resurrection of Jesus (1979: 52% as distinct from 34%; and 1996: 49% as distinct from 29%), in Gospel miracles as 'historical facts' (1984: 31% as distinct from 25%; and 1996: 34% as distinct from 20%), in the Bible as 'absolute divine authority' (1984: 26% as distinct from 22%; and 1996: 35% as distinct from 16%) and in personal prayer (1985: 94% as distinct from 74%).

EUROPEAN SURVEYS

By the 1980s a number of other surveys had begun to notice that different levels of churchgoing do correlate with differences of belief (and sometimes behaviour) amongst respondents. The two sets of European Value Systems Study Group surveys[17] in the early 1980s and 1990s both noted a number of significant differences between churchgoers and nonchurchgoers across Europe. Mainline churches have not always been given much attention by professional sociologists in the past, so in this context these surveys have acted as very important stimulants for further research. Together these surveys have begun to shift the long-standing bias of many sociologists of religion to the effect that churchgoing is a largely epiphenomenal activity.

For example, EVSSG data 1981–3 for ten European countries suggested that 32% of the whole large sample (12,463) believed in a personal God. This dropped to 27% amongst nonchurchgoing Catholics, to 18% amongst nonchurchgoing Protestants, and to just 3% of those in the no-religion group. However, amongst weekly churchgoing Catholics it rose to 60% and amongst weekly churchgoing Protestants to 73%. Similarly, belief in after-life: 43% whole sample, 34% nonchurchgoing Catholics, 29% nonchurchgoing Protestants and 13% no-religion, in contrast to 77% weekly churchgoing Catholics and Protestants. And belief in sin: 57% whole sample, 44% nonchurchgoing Catholics, 56% nonchurchgoing Protestants and 20% no-religion, in contrast to 86% weekly churchgoing Catholics and 85% of weekly churchgoing Protestants. Belief in God, heaven and hell showed very similar patterns.

The British MORI 1993 poll[18] for BBC strongly confirmed these European findings, correlating Christian beliefs with different levels of churchgoing. It tested a sample of churchgoers, distinguishing between those going at least once a week and those going at least twice a month, albeit ignoring those going less often or almost never. Higher levels were recorded amongst weekly churchgoers on every other item of religious

[17] See Jan Kerkhofs, 'Between "Christendom" and "Christianity"', *Journal of Empirical Theology*, 1:2, 1988, pp. 88–101. For specifically British EVSSG data see Mark Abrams, David Gerard and Noel Timms (eds.), *Values and Social Change in Britain: Studies in the Contemporary Values of Modern Society*, Macmillan, London, 1985, and Noel Timms, *Family and Citizenship: Values in Contemporary Britain*, Dartmouth, Aldershot, 1992.

[18] MORI, *Christian Beliefs*.

belief which this survey tested – namely, belief in a personal God (80% weekly churchgoers/71% fortnightly churchgoers), in Jesus as Divine (85%/77%), in heaven (93%/76%), hell (69%/51%), the devil 75%/52%), sin (96%/88%), the Virgin Birth (81%/55%), the resurrection of Jesus Christ (95%/79%) survival of the soul after death (87%/76%), albeit together, somewhat uncomfortably, with physical resurrection of the body after death (51%/40%), miracles (88%/69%), the Bible as 'the complete Word of God' (70%/41%), and, reversing the order, in astrology (18%/31%) and ghosts (26%/31%). Perhaps not surprisingly, 79% of weekly churchgoers considered it very important 'for Christians to regularly attend a church' as distinct from just 27% of fortnightly churchgoers. They were also more inclined to read the Bible every day (33%/7%), to pray every day (80%/30%), and to be able to 'think of an instance when after praying ... something happened as a direct result of [my] prayers' (80%/30%). Taken as a whole this is impressive evidence for the existence of a *process* amongst churchgoers themselves on specifically religious beliefs and behaviour.

But can this process be detected more broadly in moral areas and using a wider range of degrees of regularity of churchgoing? The EVSSG surveys offer some initial suggestions that it can. However, there are two research projects which take these suggestions considerably further: the first of these is Australian and looks at adults and the second British and looks at teenagers.

Before turning to these two research projects, it is worth noting the important moral difference between churchgoers and nonchurchgoers detected in the EVSSG data. In the 1980s across Europe 19% of the whole sample was involved in voluntary work of one sort or another (EVSSG defined 'voluntary work' very broadly). Amongst nonchurchgoing Catholics this level dropped to 12%, but rose to 28% amongst weekly churchgoing Catholics. However amongst Protestants this difference was even more marked: 10% nonchurchgoing Protestants, in contrast to 58% weekly churchgoing Protestants. The British 1981 EVSSG data showed a very similar pattern: 19% of the whole sample in contrast to 50% of weekly churchgoers. The British 1990 EVSSG comparable figures were 23% and 48% respectively. Rosalie Osmond's British 1993 survey[19] also suggested a number of moral ways in which churchgoers appear distinctive: 91% believed that 'life forms a meaningful pattern (as distinct from 58% of the whole sample); only 4% of them thought that 'sin is a meaningless concept' (others = 24%); 57% believed that 'there are absolute moral guidelines' (others = 35%); and only 15% thought that 'the main purpose of life is to fulfil yourself' (others = 35%).

All of this suggests that there may indeed be a measurable process, correlating different levels of churchgoing with different levels of belief and moral behaviour. It is important to recognise what is at stake here. By looking for a *measurable* process, attention inevitably focuses upon data which have been and can be collected. Of course there are many features of the religious life which can never be reduced adequately to collectable data. In this book it will be noted at key moments that there is indeed something very crude about reducing beliefs and moral attitudes to such collectable and measurable forms. The point of this is not to pretend that that is all there is to know or say about these beliefs, but rather to be able to compare their relative strengths as objectively as possible and their possible connections with other beliefs and forms of behaviour. That is exactly what quantitative research is good at doing. It should never displace qualitative research (including theological research). Properly used, it should complement such research by allowing a broader series of tests than would otherwise be possible of the interaction between different variables. Both the following Australian research on adults and the British research on teenagers do precisely that. As it happens, in both instances this is sociological research conducted by individuals who are themselves theologically trained and who are usually aware – despite occasional lapses – of the theological nuances of their data.

[19] Rosalie Osmond, *Changing Perspectives: Christian Culture and Morals in England Today*, Darton, Longman & Todd, London, 1993.

AUSTRALIAN SURVEYS

In Australia the work of both the Christian Research Association and the National Church Life Survey has established an invaluable empirical resource on churchgoing over the last decade. There are clear links in this research with that first generated in Europe by EVSSG. The World Value Survey formed the basis of the initial work of the Christian Research Association in the 1980s and there is a continuing connection between it, the National Church Life Survey and MARC Europe. This does allow an examination of similarities and differences between churchgoers and nonchurchgoers in both Britain and Australia.

The churchgoing rates, patterns of churchgoing decline, and even the relative distribution of the denominations, are very similar in Australia to those in Britain. Australian survey data between 1950 and 1993 suggest that those claiming to attend church at least once a month have halved (47% declining to 24%),[20] that of these only about half attend every week, that particularly sharp declines can be seen amongst Uniting Church, Anglican and Roman Catholic churchgoers, and that no denomination can claim a majority of overall churchgoers.[21] Of course there are some differences – the Roman Catholic population is somewhat larger in Australia and the Anglican population slightly smaller[22] than in Britain – yet the similarities outweigh them.

These similarities allow some important comparisons to be made. At several points in the chapters that follow Australian data relating churchgoing to moral attitudes will be compared with British data. Together they suggest that churchgoing really is socially and morally significant. It is the research in 1986 of Gary D. Bouma and Beverly R. Dixon in *The Religious*

[20] See Philip J. Hughes, Craig Thompson, Rohan Pryor and Gary D. Bouma, *Believe It or Not: Australian Spirituality and the Churches in the 90s*, Christian Research Association, Kew, Victoria, Australia, 1995, p. 6.

[21] See Peter Kaldor, *Who Goes Where? Who Doesn't Care?*, Lancer, Homebush, NSW, Australia, 1987, p. 23.

[22] See Philip J. Hughes, *Religion in Australia: Facts and Figures*, Christian Research Association, Kew, Victoria, Australia, 1997.

Factor in Australian Life[23] that presents the fullest set of comparable data. In this study the two authors establish four levels of churchgoing: 'never' (38% of the sample); 'rarely', consisting of those going once or twice a year (26%); 'occasionally', consisting of those going every two or three months (10%); and 'regularly', consisting of those going at least once a month (27%). They then show that on a range of moral issues statistically significant[24] differences are apparent in these four levels. Some of these issues relate specifically to Australia: different levels are apparent amongst those agreeing that 'Australia has a duty to accept a lower standard of living for the benefit of poor nations' ('never' 21%, 'rarely' 27%, 'occasionally' 21%, 'regularly 42%), that 'People should accept a lower standard of living for the benefit of the whole of the Australian economy' (46%, 52%, 44%, 59%), and that 'Australia should remain a monarchy' rather than 'become a republic with an elected president' (60%, 66%, 69%, 76%). However other issues have wider application. So a range of issues is explored on the issues of family and sexuality, showing the following levels of agreement:

Marriage is outdated (19%, 11%, 11%, 7%)
Divorce is too easy (55%, 71%, 73%, 82%)
Divorce is *never* justified (10%, 12%, 9%, 30%)
Must limit free sex by moral rules (44%, 58%, 55%, 69%)
Approve of free sex (39%, 26%, 29%, 12%)
Sex under legal age is *never* justified (54%, 63%, 66%, 76%)
Extramarital sex is *never* justified (42%, 46%, 46%, 66%)
Approve of single mums (45%, 40%, 39%, 17%)
Homosexuality is *never* justified (31%, 39%, 40%, 57%)
Prostitution is *never* justified (25%, 32%, 33%, 53%)

There is a range of issues concerned with the sanctity of life, which again shows very clear differences of agreement in the four levels of nonchurchgoing to 'regular' churchgoing:

Abortion is *never* justified (17%, 26%, 26%, 51%)

23 Gary D. Bouma and Beverly R. Dixon, *The Religious Factor in Australian Life*, MARC Australia, World Vision and the Zadok Centre, 1986.

24 They give a gamma value and a Chi Square value and a statement of probability for each item (0.00 for all items cited here).

Approve of abortion if . . .

Mother's health threatened (91%, 90%, 89%, 71%)

Baby will be handicapped (78%, 75%, 74%, 53%)

Woman not married (42%, 34%, 36%, 16%)

Couple wants no more children (44%, 31%, 30%, 10%)

Killing in self-defence is *never* justified (7%, 10%, 9%, 17%)

Political assassination is *never* justified (66%, 64%, 65%, 81%)

Suicide is *never* justified (43%, 42%, 43%, 62%)

Euthanasia is *never* justified (17%, 16%, 17%, 43%)

Now, of course, there may well be other factors involved in these differences. For example, responses to the first range of issues have probably been influenced by the fact that churchgoers are disproportionately elderly and female, and those to the second range may reflect the relatively high level of Roman Catholics amongst the 'regular' churchgoers in the sample (45%). Churchgoers are also more 'conventional' than others in believing that 'taking marijuana or hashish' is *never* justified (49%, 54%, 53%, 69%) and that 'Possession of small amounts of marijuana should be a criminal offence' (34%, 45%, 43%, 54%): it is nonchurchgoers who are more likely to believe that marijuana should be made legal (41%, 30%, 34%, 17%). Regular churchgoers are also about twice as likely as other people to be total abstainers from alcohol (14%, 18%, 15%, 31%). Nevertheless a range of issues concerned with personal honesty does suggest a wider significance of churchgoing:

Lying in your own interest is *never* justified (38%, 43%, 41%, 64%)

Failing to report damage done is *never* justified (47%, 49%, 48%, 65%)

Buying something you know is stolen is *never* justified (68%, 69%, 66%, 82%)

Avoiding transport fares is *never* justified (54%, 55%, 54%, 71%)

Cheating on taxes is *never* justified (41%, 46%, 36%, 65%)

Churchgoers also appear distinctive in that most of them 'never think life is meaningless' (42%, 39%, 44%, 64%) and very few respond that they never think about the meaning of life (12%, 6%, 9%, 4%) or that they never think about death

(16%, 15%, 12%, 7%). They are also less inclined than others to give a negative response to the question: 'Apart from your family, in your opinion, is there anything worth sacrificing everything for, even risking your life if necessary?' (63%, 67%, 65%, 50%).

All of this does suggest that there may indeed be a *process* here, with different regularities of churchgoing being associated with different moral attitudes. However there are some weaknesses in this study. A technical weakness is that the statistical tests used on the data do not specifically test directionality – that is, they do not test whether or not the more often, level-by-level, people go to church the more they hold specific moral views. A less technical weakness is that Bouma and Dixon defined 'regular' churchgoing as attendance at least once a month. The British MORI 1993 just cited suggests that this may elide important differences between monthly and weekly churchgoers. In the chapters that follow these two levels of church attendance will be kept separate. This should also allow a clearer pattern of directionality, with monthly churchgoers acting as an intermediate level between occasional and weekly churchgoers.

Other Australian sources of data will also be used for comparison in later chapters. The Christian Research Association's analysis of the religious questions in the 1993 and 1994 Australian National Social Science Survey is particularly helpful. In one CRA study[25] sharp differences in their beliefs about God are reported between weekly churchgoers and those who 'never' attend. For example, asked in 1993 whether they believe that 'there is a God who concerns himself personally with every human being', 91% of weekly churchgoers agreed but only 12% of non-attenders. A similar contrast is reported in those who believe 'God created the world' (91% and 21% respectively). In another CRA study of these data[26] three groups are identified with distinctive religious and moral views: 'attenders' (22% of the sample), 'religious non-attenders' (29%),

[25] Peter Bentley and Philip J. Hughes, *Australian Life and the Christian Faith: Facts and Figures*, Christian Research Association, Kew, Victoria, Australia, 1998.

[26] Hughes, et al., *Believe It or Not.*

and 'non-religious' (42%). Unfortunately for present purposes these three groups are defined by a mixture of answers to questions about the strength of respondents' beliefs in God and subjective religiosity as well as by their frequency of churchgoing and practice of prayer. As a result there is a strong element of tautology in the findings. For example, there are clear differences between 'attenders', 'religious non-attenders' and 'non-religious' in their beliefs in 'God without doubts' (74%, 39%, 1%), 'Life after death' (89%, 65%, 25%), 'God created the world' (87%, 59%, 13%), 'Life is meaningful because God exists' (63%, 22%, 1%) and 'Feel close to God most of the time' (92%, 29%, 9%). Correlates and defining criteria have become thoroughly confused in these findings. Yet if nothing else, they do at least carry a warning for Christian ethics: the large size of the non-religious group points up the difficulty of using theistic language in public moral debates.

Another source is the Australian National Church Life Survey.[27] This massive ongoing study of Protestant and Anglican denominations in Australia is generating a wealth of information about churchgoers. On some issues the NCLS 1991 sample consists of 90,628 respondents, although on specifically moral issues the sample size is reduced to 2,408. This is a survey of churchgoers, so it does not provide comparative data about nonchurchgoers. In its initial phase it also excludes Roman Catholics. Yet, despite these limitations, it can still be used judiciously with other data to add nuances about churchgoers.

A SURVEY OF BRITISH TEENAGERS

Alongside this Australian research, the work of Leslie Francis and William Kay in the 1990s, especially in their *Teenage Religion and Values*,[28] is also invaluable for any exploration of a possible relationship between different regularities of churchgoing and

[27] See Peter Kaldor and Ruth Powell, *Views from the Pews: Australian Church Attenders Speak Out*, Openbook Publishers, Sydney, 1995, and Peter Kaldor, John Bellamy and Ruth Powell, *Shaping a Future: Characteristics of Vital Congregations*, Openbook Publishers, Sydney, 1996.

[28] Leslie J. Francis and William K. Kay, *Teenage Religion and Values*, Gracewing, Fowler Wright Books, Herefordshire, 1995.

moral attitudes. Using a sample of just over 13,000 young people aged 13 to 15, they show that, amongst early teenagers at least, there are many differences of religious and moral belief between churchgoers and nonchurchgoers. They also divide their sample into three groups, but in this case based solely upon three levels of church attendance: those who attend 'nearly every week' (11% of the sample), those who attend 'sometimes' (35%), and those who 'never' attend (54%). These groups are very similar to those used by the BBC 1954 survey of adults, but, as table 4 suggests, the proportions of those going regularly to church four decades later are very much smaller. However, regular churchgoers apparently remain distinctive over a surprisingly varied set of beliefs and attitudes.

Compared with the adult averages for the 1990s in table 1, the young people in the Francis–Kay survey are generally more sceptical. Nevertheless those young people attending 'most weeks' show patterns of belief very similar to those recorded in the MORI 1993 poll of adults. Thus, taken as a whole only 39% of the teenagers respond positively to the statement 'I believe in God' (in table 1 the 1990s adult mean is 67%), whereas amongst weekly churchgoers this rises to 84%, dropping to 50% amongst occasional churchgoers and to just 23% amongst nonchurchgoers. In response to the statement 'I believe that Jesus Christ is the Son of God' 85% of weekly churchgoers, 58% of occasional churchgoers and 32% of nonchurchgoers agree; to the statement 'I believe that Jesus Christ really rose from the dead' positive responses are 75%, 37% and 16%; and to the statement 'I believe in life after death' the proportions are 60%, 43% and 35% respectively. Adding contrast, this survey also includes literalist and exclusive statements which, whilst they are supported more strongly amongst churchgoers, still do not gain majority support amongst them. So in response to the statement 'I believe that God made the world in six days and rested on the seventh', 47% of weekly churchgoers respond positively, as do 20% of occasional churchgoers and 9% of nonchurchgoers; to the statement 'I think Christianity is the only true religion' positive responses are 36%, 18% and 11%; and in response to 'I believe God punishes people who do wrong' they are 30%, 22%

and 13% respectively. Belief in the devil also appears to be a minority belief amongst all groups – being supported only by 34% of weekly churchgoers, 18% of occasional churchgoers and 17% of nonchurchgoers.

In response to each of these statements about Christian belief churchgoers appear distinctive and their beliefs correspond broadly to their frequency of churchgoing. Thus it makes a clear difference to the findings about Christian belief whether the teenagers questioned go to church regularly, occasionally or never. Of course there are exceptions. Of the weekly churchgoers 2% give atheist responses, 3% apparently disbelieve in the divinity of Christ and 9% in life after death. Full consistency is rare in surveys – as *Puzzled People* indicated half a century earlier. For example, in the Francis–Kay survey 4% of those stating that they do not believe in God nonetheless agree that God punishes people who do wrong and 10% that Jesus Christ is the Son of God! Yet, on average, weekly churchgoers give more positive responses to Christian belief statements than do occasional churchgoers and, in turn, the latter give more positive responses than do nonchurchgoers. Negative responses to such a statement as 'The bible seems irrelevant to life today' show a similar pattern (weekly churchgoers 17%, occasional churchgoers 24% and nonchurchgoers 36%). In addition, as was found in the BBC 1954 survey, weekly churchgoers are much more likely than occasional or nonchurchgoers to support the statement that 'Religious education should be taught in school' (61%, 40% and 22% respectively). But such support is not static, since only 17% of weekly churchgoers amongst the young people today agree that 'Schools should hold a religious assembly every day.' Francis and Kay note, 'the vast majority of pupils, of whatever age group or sex, do not want such gatherings'.[29]

Francis and Kay also ask for responses to statements about 'new age' beliefs. Whilst none of these are supported by a majority of young people in any of the three groups, the direction of the responses is different from those on Christian

[29] *Ibid.* p. 197.

beliefs. So, whilst 12% of weekly churchgoers express a belief in black magic, this increases to 17% amongst occasional churchgoers and to 19% amongst nonchurchgoers. Belief that 'it is possible to contact the spirits of the dead' is apparently held by 23% of weekly churchgoers and by 32% of the other two groups; belief in horoscopes by 23%, 38% and 36% respectively; and belief that 'fortune-tellers can tell the future' by 12% of weekly churchgoers and by 20% of the others. Belief in ghosts has an overall response rate of 37%, which is slightly higher than the adult mean of 32% for the 1990s in table 1, but this belief too has less support amongst weekly churchgoers (31%) than amongst either occasional churchgoers (39%) or nonchurchgoers (36%).

Included in this remarkable survey are responses to a wide variety of moral and social attitude statements, most of which show significant correlations with churchgoing. Of course this *is* a survey of teenagers. Later chapters must test whether or not such correlations can be established amongst adult British churchgoers. For the moment Francis and Kay offer a very effective contrast to much of the literature in the sociology of religion in the previous generation. The effect of their data is to suggest that, amongst young people, churchgoing is a highly significant variable affecting moral and social attitudes which, taken as a whole, depict a distinctive culture within modern Britain.

The focus of my book is upon Christian ethics and upon the distinctively Christian values held by churchgoers. Some regrouping of the data that Francis and Kay present is necessary in this context. Two values amongst churchgoers appear to be especially prominent, the first altruistic and the second teleological. In terms of the first, the young people who go regularly to church in Britain, like their adult counterparts in Australia, express more concern about the vulnerable and needy than those who do not go regularly. In terms of the second, they are distinctly more inclined than others to see purpose in life and to support both moral and social order. Conversely those who never go to church are relatively unconcerned about the needy and vulnerable and are more inclined to be cynical about changing the world or about supporting established order.

A number of statements in the Francis–Kay survey test altruistic attitudes, showing clear differences between the three groups of weekly churchgoers, occasional churchgoers and nonchurchgoers. Responses to the following statements demonstrate this:

'I am concerned about the poverty of the Third World' (79%, 67%, 51%)

'I am concerned about the risk of pollution to the environment' (74%, 73%, 59%)

'I am concerned about the risk of nuclear war' (69%, 68%, 59%)

'There are too many black people living in this country' (11%, 16%, 24%)

'I think that immigration into Britain should be restricted' (27%, 32%, 34%)

'There is nothing I can do to solve the world's problems' (15%, 21%, 30%).

It is sometimes claimed that Christians/churchgoers are less concerned about the environment and more racist than others. The evidence here does not seem to support this. If anything the opposite may be the case. It could be that the greater environmental and racial awareness of many congregations is creating a culture which is distinct from society at large. Francis and Kay seem to support such a cultural interpretation at this point:

> Churchgoers, of whichever denominational group, demonstrate far fewer racist attitudes than non-churchgoers. Whatever else may be said about the church, it is apparent that it is an international and multi-racial community or collection of communities with social opinions, in many respects, quite separate from those of the surrounding society.[30]

The next chapters will need to examine similar data carefully in relation to adult churchgoers.

Perhaps less surprisingly, teenage churchgoers are more

[30] *Ibid.* p. 218.

inclined to condemn pornography and television violence than others. The responses to the statements 'Pornography is too readily available' (41%, 33%, 28%) and 'There is too much violence on television' (27%, 21%, 15%) show this. These differences may also reflect a greater concern amongst churchgoers for the vulnerable. These teenage churchgoers, like the adults in Australia, are more inclined to believe that 'Abortion is wrong' (50%, 36%, 35%) and 'Divorce is wrong' (27%, 20%, 19%). Here too it seems that on most sexual issues churchgoers are more inclined to hold 'conventional' beliefs than non-churchgoers. Nevertheless, remarkably, only a minority of teenagers support these beliefs even amongst weekly churchgoers. In response to 'Contraception is wrong' only one in twenty agree, even amongst churchgoing Roman Catholics. Evidently young Roman Catholics make distinctions within official Catholic teaching, since two-thirds of them still think abortion to be wrong. Since abortion arguably involves the taking of life of one who is vulnerable, whereas (hormonal) contraception does not, this difference may owe more to altruism than to convention. Indeed, only 22% of Roman Catholic churchgoers believe that 'It is wrong to have sexual intercourse outside marriage', 32% that 'It is wrong to have sexual intercourse under the legal age', and 35% that 'Homosexuality is wrong'. From a perspective of official Roman Catholicism this is scarcely a 'conventional' group.

These findings on altruistic attitudes suggest an important point for further investigation. As the authors note, 'church attendance is associated with . . . a greater sense of concern on a wide range of issues and a greater sense of being able to make a positive contribution to world problems'.[31] There are some obvious gaps in their data as well as some fairly crude measures. For example, although the attitudes of the young people are tested, their stated behaviour is not. Unlike the European Value Systems Study Group surveys, there is no attempt to discover whether or not they belong to other caring organisations or groups or about whether or not they are involved in voluntary

[31] *Ibid.* p. 80.

work within the community. And some of the attitude measures, such as that on racism, lack sophistication. Despite these weaknesses, which must be investigated more thoroughly in subsequent chapters, Francis and Kay provide an important starting point for this investigation.

If altruism is one key virtue held by churchgoers in the Francis–Kay survey, teleology is the other. Young churchgoers apparently have a stronger sense of purpose and order than others. They report higher positive responses to the statement 'I feel my life has a sense of purpose' (68%, 60%, 49%) and lower responses to the alarming 'I have sometimes considered taking my own life' (23%, 26%, 28%). They report that 'I am happy at school' (78%, 74%, 67%) and they are less inclined than others to respond that 'School is boring' (25%, 29%, 41%) or 'My youth centre is boring' (25%, 33%, 37%). They also have a higher respect for those in authority: 'The police do a good job' (70%, 66%, 57%), 'Teachers do a good job' (52%, 46%, 36%) and, perhaps less surprisingly, 'Christian ministers/vicars/priests do a good job' (69%, 44%, 24%).

The young churchgoers also seem to have a stronger sense of moral order. On each of the individualist moral situations presented to them, weekly churchgoers differed from others, being distinctly less inclined to moral relativism:

'There is nothing wrong in . . . '
playing truant from school (10%, 14%, 22%)
buying alcoholic drinks under the legal age (27%, 35%, 44%)
buying cigarettes under the legal age (16%, 23%, 31%)
writing graffiti wherever you like (10%, 13%, 19%)
cycling after dark without lights (8%, 11%, 20%)
travelling without a ticket (11%, 15%, 23%)
shop-lifting (3%, 5%, 9%).

As in the Australian research, there are also differences evident in responses here to statements on substance use:
It is wrong to use heroin (85%, 81%, 76%)
It is wrong to use marijuana (65%, 61%, 55%)
It is wrong to sniff glue (85%, 82%, 79%)
It is wrong to sniff butane gas (80%, 76%, 72%)

Clearly a majority of the young people in all of the groups expressed moral disapproval of these forms of substance use – with rather less disapproval of marijuana – yet the differences between the groups are still evident. Only a minority apparently believed that 'It is wrong to become drunk' (30%, 22%, 19%) or that 'It is wrong to smoke cigarettes' (53%, 46%, 42%), although the same direction is evident between churchgoers and others. Francis and Kay conclude:

> Certainly churchgoing is associated with respect for rules and law which implies that the nature of teenage religion, fostered by churchgoing has an element within it conducive to legal or moral restraint. We may be correct in seeing teenage religion as a manifestation of a desire for order or, alternatively, a recognition of an order whose existence depends on God . . . Those who attend church weekly have a clearer idea of right and wrong than do non-attenders.[32]

There is a judicious choice of words in this conclusion which leaves the issue of causation ambiguous. On the one hand, this sense of order is 'fostered by churchgoing' but, on the other, religion may be a response to 'a desire for order'. Using regression analysis on the data it is possible to establish that the variables here are significantly correlated. Francis and Kay use this form of statistical analysis carefully at every point in their study, establishing in the process that there is a causal link, in one direction or the other, between belief/values and churchgoing. It is also possible to use a specifically directional form of analysis to test whether or not a step-by-step increase in churchgoing is matched by a corresponding increase in belief/values. If more distinctions are made than the three levels of churchgoing offered by Francis and Kay, then it should be possible to apply such a directional test more rigorously. Both forms of statistical analysis will in fact be used on the new data in later chapters.

Yet is it really churchgoing which finally shapes morality? It might simply be that people with 'conventional' moral attitudes are more likely to go to church. In the case of the teenagers in the Francis–Kay survey, it might be that those young people who are already predisposed to be altruistic and teleological are

[32] *Ibid.* pp. 110–11.

most likely to remain churchgoers. Or, to express this in the opposite direction, amongst those brought up to go to church the egoistic and cynical may be the first to abandon churchgoing. There may be some truth in this suggestion which will need to be taken seriously in later chapters. Nevertheless, there are some early indications that it is not the whole of the truth. The evidence from surveys such as John Finney's 1992 *Finding Faith Today*,[33] as well as the Mass-Observation research reported in the January 1949 *British Weekly*,[34] suggests that most adults initially go back to church as a result of having Christian friends, partners or spouses rather than because they have a change of belief. The *British Weekly* argued that 'comparatively few churchgoers maintain the practice unbroken throughout their lives . . . people who return to church are generally won back as the result of personal contact, and at least as often by personal friends or lay visitors as by ministers'.[35] Conversely, they stop going to church because they move house, lose interest, or change life-style, rather than because they experience some change of religious or moral beliefs.[36]

The 1949 *British Weekly* report unambiguously saw early churchgoing as the necessary precondition for belief later in life, arguing:

> Churchgoing in childhood and youth, even though not marked by personal and deeply emotional religious conviction, can predispose people to a later and positive acceptance of the religious attitude. Other people, of course, may never become conscious of personal religious convictions, but may continue to go to church as a habit. On the whole it is our contention, however, that the churchgoing 'habit' . . . precedes in many cases a genuine religious conviction and that throughout life churchgoing depends both on religious belief *and* habit. The two reasons are interlinked throughout, but usually maintain a separate existence.[37]

33 John Finney, *Finding Faith Today*, British and Foreign Bible Society, Swindon, 1992.

34 Mass-Observation, 'Why Do People Come to Church?', *British Weekly*, 13 January 1949.

35 *Ibid.*

36 See my *The Myth of the Empty Church*, SPCK, London, 1993, pp. 213f., and Philip Richter and Leslie J. Francis, *Gone But Not Forgotten: Church Leaving and Returning*, Darton, Longman & Todd, London, 1998.

37 Mass-Observation, 'Why Do People Come to Church?'.

This observation is important for the much disputed sociological issue which will be discussed in the next chapter, namely the conceptual relationship of churchgoing to belief. What seems to be implied here is that, although Christian beliefs and values may be retained by lapsed churchgoers for many years, they may not be passed on so readily to their children unless they become churchgoers again themselves. Churchgoing may nurture and sustain Christian beliefs and values (and perhaps attracts and retains those particularly responsive to them). In addition, those brought up as churchgoers, even though they subsequently lapse, are more likely to hold these beliefs and values than those who have never been churchgoers (this will be seen most clearly in table 11). So, while it is of course possible that churchgoing may attract and retain those who already have high levels of Christian belief, altruism and teleology, there do seem to be initial indications that exposure to regular worship does at the very least reinforce them. Data in the coming chapters must test these early indications more rigorously.

One final point needs to be made. My analysis of the Francis–Kay survey highlights Christian belief, altruism and teleology as being the three most distinctive features of teenage churchgoers. Together these provide a framework for analysing the new adult data that follows, albeit filling out some of the gaps noted in this survey. Slightly re-ordered, these three features might be seen as the measurable aspects of St Paul's key virtues – namely Faith, Hope and Love. Of course there are many, subtle ways in which Faith, Hope and Love go quite beyond any possible measurement. It would be ridiculous to claim that the Christian life can be captured by the crudities of social attitude surveys. From a theological perspective Faith is not simply about expressed belief, Hope is not simply about expressed purpose or order, and Love is not simply about expressed concern for the vulnerable and needy. All three also involve trust, commitment, application and depth – none of which is readily measurable. Without reducing theological concepts to sociological variables, the Francis–Kay survey does suggest that there are some aspects of the Christian life which can be measured meaningfully. Such measurement might actually be more relevant to Christian ethics than is usually recognised:

> Now we see only puzzling reflections in the mirror, but then we shall see face to face. My knowledge now is partial; then it will be whole, like God's knowledge of me. In a word, there are three things that last for ever: Faith, Hope and Love . . . [38]

In short, Faith, Hope and Love may still leave puzzling, yet discernible, reflections amongst churchgoers.

[38] 1 Cor. 13.12–13 (NEB).

CHAPTER 3

Four theories of churchgoing

Emerging at the end of the previous chapter is a new interest amongst some sociologists of religion in churchgoing and, especially, in the relationship between churchgoing and religious belief. There are at least three main rival theories – secularisation, persistence and separation – which must be taken into account. In this chapter I will argue that there is now a need for a fourth sociological theory – a cultural theory of churchgoing – which offers predictions about when rates of churchgoing are likely to increase or decline and about how these changing rates affect Christian beliefs and values.

A generation ago the choice was between only two of these theories, namely secularisation and persistence. Crudely expressed, secularisation theories typically hold that in the modern world religious beliefs become increasingly implausible and decline. As a result of this decline, religious practices, especially in the form of regular churchgoing, also decline. An activity which was once sustained by deeply held religious beliefs becomes largely pointless without these beliefs and slowly withers. In this understanding of the relationship between churchgoing and religious belief, it is belief which is the independent variable. That is to say, churchgoing depends upon religious belief for its sustenance. Of course it is not difficult to imagine a few individuals who might continue to go to church – out of habit or nostalgia – even though they have personally lost any distinctively religious belief. Nonetheless, secularisation theories typically predict that, taken as a whole, within a modern society in which belief has become largely implausible, churchgoing will inevitably decline.

Persistence theories present a radical alternative, holding that even in the modern world religious beliefs and practices remain abiding features. There may well be relative shifts from one form of religious belief or practice to another, yet, viewed as a whole, religion persists today as it always has in every society. Those who support a persistence theory tend to be suspicious of what they regard as the secularist ideological commitments of many secularisation theorists. The latter tend to present a sociological analysis of religion which too readily fits their own personal religious scepticism. Persistence theorists contend that secularisation theorists tend to present their own bias as if it were simply detached observation, assuming in the process that because religious belief is implausible to them it must also be so to anyone else who is truly modern. In contrast, persistence theorists usually hold that religious beliefs result from ubiquitous human aspirations and needs which cannot adequately be met in any other way. Religious beliefs and practices in one form or another are part and parcel of the human condition and will abide for as long as humanity abides.

Depicted in this unnuanced way these two theories are more characteristic of the sociological debate in the 1960s and 1970s than of that of today. The early writings of Bryan Wilson[1] and S. S. Acquaviva[2] typify secularisation theory at this stage and those of Andrew Greeley[3] and the early writings of David Martin[4] typify persistence theory. After a generation of sociological debate on this issue it is perhaps not surprising that the distinction between these two positions has become more blurred. So, whereas secularisation theorists tended once to see

1 E.g. Bryan Wilson, *Religion in Secular Society*, C. A. Watt, London, 1966, and *Contemporary Transformations of Religion*, Clarendon Press, Oxford, 1974; see also: Will Herberg, 'Religion in a Secularized Society', *Review of Religious Research*, 3:4, 1962; Anthony F. C. Wallace, *Religion: An Anthropological View*, Random House, New York, 1966; Peter L. Berger, *The Social Reality of Religion*, Faber & Faber, London, 1969; and N. J. Demerath, *A Tottering Transcendence*, Bobbs-Merrill, New York, 1974.

2 S. S. Acquaviva, *The Decline of the Sacred in Industrial Society*, 1966, trans. P. Lipscomb, Harper & Row, New York, 1979.

3 Andrew M. Greeley, *Unsecular Man: The Persistence of Religion*, Schocken Books, New York, 1972, and SCM Press, London, 1973.

4 David Martin, *The Religious and the Secular*, Routledge and Kegan Paul, London, 1969, and 'The Secularisation Question', *Theology*, vol. 76, no. 630, Feb. 1973.

secularisation as the *inevitable* product of modernity, today they tend to be more agnostic about this.[5] Likewise persistence theorists tended once to deny that European churchgoing is generally in decline, whereas today some might admit this but regard it as an exception to trends elsewhere in the world and compensated by the increase of other forms of religious practice even in Europe.[6] Of course sociologists of religion read each others' works and, over time, it becomes difficult to maintain polarised theories when so much of the evidence appears to be ambiguous. In this respect the recent work of José Casanova is particularly important. In his influential book *Public Religions in the Modern World*[7] he accepts that churchgoing is declining in most parts of Europe and that a process of separation or differentiation of church and state has happened or is likely to happen everywhere. Nevertheless he maintains that there is evidence, even within Europe and certainly elsewhere in the world, of a deprivatisation of religion, that is of religion taking on a significant public role. Religious resurgence, sometimes in the form of sharp fundamentalism but sometimes in a more sophisticated political form, is as much a feature of modern societies as is religious decline.

This more nuanced approach does not altogether eliminate genuine differences between secularisation and persistence theories of churchgoing. Even though recent secularisation theorists are usually less dogmatic today than in the past, they do still tend to see churchgoing as the dependent variable and religious belief as the independent but declining variable. For them, in so far as people in the modern world are becoming increasingly sceptical, then it is likely that churchgoing will continue to decline. Of course, there could be an unforeseen event which might increase faith at some point in the future. If that happens then churchgoing may well increase. Yet, in modern Britain, this seems to be unlikely. On balance, churchgoing will

[5] See Steve Bruce, *Religion in the Modern World*, Oxford University Press, Oxford, 1996.

[6] See Rodney Stark and Laurence R. Iannaccone, 'A Supply-Side Reinterpretation of the "Secularization" of Europe', *Journal for the Scientific Study of Religion*, 33, 1994, pp. 230–52.

[7] José Casanova, *Public Religions in the Modern World*, University of Chicago Press, Chicago, 1994.

probably continue to decline, at least amongst mainstream churches, precisely because religious belief is implausible to so many people today.

Many persistence theorists also hold that religious belief is the independent variable. Yet unlike even modified secularisation theorists, they tend to argue that religious beliefs may change but not disappear even in the modern world. Since religious beliefs abide, they are likely to find expression in ritual form at some point in the lives even of apparently secularised individuals. Faced with evidence about the apparent decline of churchgoing in modern Britain, persistence theorists today tend to argue either that the evidence is deceptive or that it takes no account of alternative forms of ritual practice. Using the first of these arguments, Peter Brierley,[8] for example, points out that many 'regular' churchgoers today no longer go to church every Sunday (let alone twice on a Sunday) but may go either during the week or, say, once a month. Even if they go to church less often than previous generations of churchgoers they may still regard *themselves* as regular churchgoers. The theoretical work of Thomas Luckmann[9] and the practical work of Edward Bailey,[10] on forms of religious belief and practice which owe little to formal religious institutions, have both been used to support the second argument. For example, there is growing sociological interest in the public rituals that developed around the funeral of Princess Diana. Here, it is argued, is evidence that a nonchurchgoing public needs to ritualise public grief and still finds innovative religious ways to do this. Religious belief in some form persists and will, if necessary, foster new forms of religious practice.

In the last few years a third theory of churchgoing, termed here separation theory, has begun to develop. An important

[8] See Peter Brierley's research for MARC Europe reported in successive volumes of *UK Christian Handbook*, his *Prospects for the Nineties: Trends and Tables from the English Church Census*, MARC Europe, London, 1991, and his *'Christian' England: What the English Church Census Reveals*, MARC Europe, London, 1991.

[9] Thomas Luckmann, *The Invisible Religion*, Macmillan, London, 1967, and 'Shrinking Transcendence, Expanding Religion?', *Sociological Analysis*, 50, 1990, pp. 127–38.

[10] Edward Bailey, Centre for the Study of Implicit Religion and Contemporary Spirituality, Middlesex University, White Hart Lane, London N17 8HR.

feature of this theory is a conviction that late modernity, or postmodernity, is characterised by growing fragmentation and religious pluralism.[11] Unlike the other two theories, separation theory does not presume that religious belief is the independent variable and religious practice the dependent variable. Rather, religious beliefs and practices are treated as variables which can be quite independent of each other. Separation theory is also less inclined to make overarching claims about whether or not religion in modern society is declining or persisting. It is quite consistent with this theory to see decline in some modern societies and persistence in others. There is thus no need to claim, as persistence theory often does, that European decline is the exception, or conversely to claim with secularisation theory that it is American persistence which is the exception. Separation theory can cope with both European and American data because it usually avoids such overall predictions about the fate of religion in modern societies.

The work of Grace Davie[12] has been particularly influential in shaping this third theory as it relates specifically to data about churchgoing in Britain today. She argues that these data suggest a remarkable separation between churchgoing and religious beliefs. There are now many people who hold conventional Christian beliefs but never go to church and there are other people who go regularly to church but hold few of these beliefs. For her, believing and belonging have become increasingly separated in modern Britain. In separating 'believing' and 'belonging', Davie's position depends upon two empirically testable propositions. The first of these is that whilst Christian 'belonging' has evidently declined in Britain, Christian beliefs nonetheless persist. Thus she claims that:

> Regarding practice or active membership of religious organizations, the findings are unequivocal. Such activities involve a relatively small proportion of the population (just under 15 per cent on average). But

[11] See Reginald Bibby, *Fragmented Gods*, Irwin Publishing, Toronto, 1987; Anthony Giddens, *Modernity and Self-Identity*, Stanford University Press, Stanford, 1991; and Peter L. Berger, *A Far Glory: The Quest for Faith in an Age of Credulity*, Anchor Books, New York, 1992.

[12] Grace Davie, *Religion in Britain Since 1945: Believing Without Belonging*, Blackwell, Oxford, 1994.

it is equally evident that between two-thirds and three-quarters of British people indicate fairly consistently that they believe in some sort of God.[13]

The second claim made by Davie is that, as traditional Christian practice has been declining in Britain, so non-traditional beliefs have been growing. For example:

> New Age ideas have become increasingly prevalent as the twentieth century draws to a close . . . the New Age provides yet further evidence that the British are far from being – or becoming – a secular society in a strict sense of the term.[14]

In this chapter I will argue that empirical data about religious beliefs and practices in Britain do not quite fit any of these three theories. Instead, I will suggest a fourth theory, to be termed a cultural theory of churchgoing. In outline this new theory suggests that it is churchgoing more than religious belief which is the independent variable, that is to say, it is churchgoing which fosters and sustains a distinctive culture of beliefs and values. This culture is not static over time: it does change in relation to broader changes within societies and particularly in relation to global changes across societies. Furthermore, churchgoing culture does show some variation between different denominations, especially on personal moral issues. Nonetheless, distinctive patterns of belief and value can be measured amongst the generality of churchgoers compared with non-churchgoers. Taken as a whole these patterns represent a distinctive culture which is shared by most churchgoers and which is fostered and sustained through churchgoing.

Precisely because churchgoing fosters and sustains a distinctive culture it can be an important means of individual identity. The practice of regular churchgoing, with church congregations acting as moral communities, reinforces distinctive beliefs and values which, in turn, sustain individual identity. Through churchgoing an individual acquires a broad and distinctive pattern of beliefs and values that can sustain a sense of personal identity.

Those changes in physical context which challenge personal

[13] *Ibid.* pp. 74–5. [14] *Ibid.* pp. 83–4.

identity act as important predictors of churchgoing decline and increase. These changes can be either at an individual life-cycle level or at a corporate level of major physical change. At the first level, changing rates of churchgoing are particularly associated with life-cycle changes such as puberty, becoming a parent, retirement, serious illness and bereavement. At the second level, they are characteristically associated with population changes, immigration and rapid urbanisation. It is at such moments that people, individually and corporately, tend to search for identity and may find this by joining churches, changing churches or even by leaving churches for other moral communities.

In contrast to persistence theory, a cultural theory does not claim that there are abiding levels of religious belief and belonging in societies. To control data properly, British data about belief and belonging will form the primary focus of this book, although the EVSSG, Australian and Francis–Kay surveys described in chapter two will be particularly useful for comparisons at many points. Since I have analysed the data on the decline of British churchgoing at length elsewhere,[15] it is unnecessary to repeat the evidence for this again here. Urban churchgoing within the Church of England has been declining steadily since about the 1850s, Free Church churchgoing since about the 1870s, and Roman Catholic churchgoing since the 1960s. There can now be little doubt that, taken as a whole, adult churchgoing in Britain has been declining throughout the twentieth century. In addition, Sunday school attendances have been declining since at least the middle of the century. What needs to be tested now is whether or not there are data suggesting a decline in Christian beliefs in Britain, and, if there is such a decline, to see whether there are compensating data about a corresponding increase in other forms of religious belief. A cultural theory predicts that a decline in specifically

15 See my *The Myth of the Empty Church*, SPCK, London, 1993. For an analysis of the connection between international immigration and identity, see R. Stephen Warner, 'Religion and Migration in the United States', *Social Compass*, 45:1, 1998, pp. 123–34 and 'Religion, Boundaries and Bridges', *Sociology of Religion*, 58:3, 1997, pp. 217–38.

Christian beliefs will follow rather than precede a decline in churchgoing and Sunday school attendance.

In contrast to secularisation theory, a cultural theory does not see a decline in churchgoing (and/or active church membership) as a linear process. Rather, fluctuations in churchgoing can be expected at both an individual and a corporate level depending upon changes in physical context. Again in contrast to secularisation theory, decline in churchgoing is not seen as typically preceded by a decline in Christian beliefs and/or values. The latter may be sustained for a generation after churchgoing has ceased.

In contrast to separation theory, a cultural theory does regard believing and belonging as causally related. It claims that the culture of churchgoing fosters and sustains beliefs/values, so a decline in churchgoing will over time result in their demise unless they are sustained by an alternative moral community. Empirical evidence of apparent separation (i.e. believing without belonging) is largely a result of an older generation with residual beliefs and values fostered by earlier churchgoing/ Sunday school attendance. A younger generation which has little direct experience of churchgoing culture is less likely to hold these Christian beliefs and values – although its beliefs and values may not be purely secular.

This new cultural theory of churchgoing is clearly contentious. However this chapter will show how British longitudinal attitude survey data, as well as comparative data from Northern Ireland, Europe, North America and Australia, are consonant with it. The first set of data, based upon research published jointly with C. Kirk Hadaway and Penny Long Marler,[16] demonstrates that support in Britain for distinctively Christian beliefs does appear to be declining and disbelief increasing. This evidence could, of course, fit a secularisation theory, although it does count against a straightforward persistence theory (and a version of separation theory which assumes persistence). More awkward for most forms of secularisation theory is evidence of persisting and even slightly increasing

[16] Robin Gill, C. Kirk Hadaway and Penny Long Marler, 'Is Religious Belief Declining in Britain?', *Journal for the Scientific Study of Religion*, 37:3, 1998, pp. 507–16.

'new age' beliefs. A second set of data counts against a secularisation theory since it suggests that churchgoing typically declines earlier than belief. Since it also suggests that there is a long-term connection between churchgoing and belief it also counts against a longitudinal separation theory. The third and largest set of data, which will be the concern of chapters four to seven, supports a cultural theory more directly. This shows that, despite some changes in attitude towards personal morality, Christian beliefs and values are significantly more distinctive amongst regular churchgoers than amongst other people. The more regularly individuals go to church, the more likely they are to hold these beliefs and values. Instructively, some of the values held are either invisible to churchgoers themselves or are visible but probably not derived directly from Christian beliefs. For example, it will be found that regular churchgoers are much more likely to be nonsmokers than nonchurchgoers – churchgoing is largely a nonsmoking culture. Finally, crucial differences of belief between adult nonchurchgoers who went regularly to church as children and nonchurchgoers who never went, provides some of the most convincing evidence for a cultural theory suggesting that it really is churchgoing which fosters religious beliefs.

Once the broad characteristics of this culture have been established through detailed analysis of survey data, the issue of Christian identity must be discussed in more depth. What is it about worshipping communities that might enable them to shape a distinctively Christian moral identity amongst regular churchgoers? This is the question that will be explored in chapter eight. Yet an obvious problem still remains. Church congregations appear to be characterised as much by moral disagreements as by any common moral identity. The final chapter will consider this paradox and its implications for Christian ethics.

TRENDS IN RELIGIOUS BELIEFS IN BRITAIN

By piecing together data from attitude surveys over the last fifty years it is at last possible to map longitudinal trends in some religious beliefs. A central weakness of many accounts of secularisation, as well as persistence, theories is that either they ignore much of the data or they compare it over too short a time-span. The new public availability of survey data makes a more serious analysis possible. Table 1 gives the weighted means for data for five periods from the 1940s/1950s through to the 1990s, mapped in conjunction with Hadaway and Marler. Data from at least two surveys, and in some instances up to ten, were required for each period. Scarcity of data for the 1940s and 1950s makes the combination of these two decades more reliable than recording them separately. All data have been weighted in proportion to the size of the samples used. Taken together they suggest a decline in several traditional Christian beliefs, a confusing pattern of persistence and some slight increase in 'new age' beliefs, and a general increase in scepticism about both forms of religious belief.

In response to broad questions about whether or not they believed in God, table 1 shows a decline of those answering positively from 79% in the 1960s to 67% in the 1990s and an increase of those answering negatively from 10% to 27%. One interpretation of a part of this difference is that agnostics (i.e. those responding 'don't know') have declined from 11% to 6%: people have become more polarised in their beliefs. Another explanation is that some people have simply become more prepared to give negative rather than evasive answers. Whichever explanation is adopted, atheist responses do seem to have increased very considerably, at the expense of both theist and agnostic responses. Similarly, table 3 suggests that those responding negatively to the British Social Attitudes[17] question 'Do you regard yourself as belonging to any particular religion?' increased from 33% in the combined 1983 and 1984 polls[18] to 39% in 1994 (and to 43% in 1996). The similar Gorer[19] question

[17] The data used here (both for BSA and BHPS) were made available through Data Archive. The data were originally collected by the ESRC Research Centre on Micro-social Change at the University of Essex. Neither the original collectors of the data nor the Archive bear any responsibility for the analyses or interpretations presented here.

[18] Combined to give a more comparable sample to 1994.

[19] From Geoffrey Gorer, *Exploring English Character*, Cresset Press, London, 1955.

in 1950 'Would you describe yourself as being of any religion or denomination?' recorded a negative response rate of just 23%. The simpler, but more directive, Gallup Poll[20] question 'What is your religious denomination?' showed an increase in nil responses from 9% in 1957 to 18% in 1993 – with very similar increases evident in both the United States and Australia.

A comparison of those surveys which asked people to differentiate between belief in a personal God and belief in a more impersonal 'spirit' or 'life force' suggests that it is the first type of belief which has declined. In five decades those professing belief in an impersonal God have fluctuated only between 38% and 40%. However those professing belief in a personal God have declined from 43% in the 1940s/1950s to 31% in the 1990s. Comparing earliest and most recent Gallup Poll data alone, this shift becomes very clear: 45% in 1947 apparently held a personal belief and 39% an impersonal belief, whereas by 1993 this balance had shifted to 30% and 40% respectively. A rather less reliable, but still instructive, way of showing changes here is to take those polls which asked people simply whether or not they believed in a personal God. A weighted mean for the two large, but unscientific, newspaper surveys carried out on readers of *The Daily News* and *The Nation*[21] in 1926 suggested a positive response of 68%; a Harris Poll[22] for 1970 recorded 48%; and a BSA survey for 1991 just 32%.

The Independent Television surveys[23] of 1968 and 1987 make possible a number of short longitudinal comparisons, which again indicate a general decline in traditional Christian belief. For example, given the statement that 'God created the universe', 80% in 1968 responded that they thought it to be true,

[20] For Gallup Poll data, see George H. Gallup (ed.), *The Gallup International Public Opinion Polls: Great Britain 1937–1975*, Random House, New York, 1976; Gordon Heald and Robert J. Wybrow (eds.), *The Gallup Survey of Britain*, Croom Helm, London, 1986; *The International Gallup Polls* (1978); and *Gallup Political and Economic Index* (annual).

[21] Reported in C. E. M. Joad, *The Present and Future of Religion*, Ernest Benn, London, 1930.

[22] Reported in *Daily Express*, 13 May 1970, p. 10.

[23] *Religion in Britain and Northern Ireland: A Survey of Popular Attitudes*, Independent Television Authority, London, 1970; and Michael Svennevig, Ian Haldane, Sharon Spiers and Barrie Gunter (eds.), *Godwatching: Viewers, Religion and Television*, John Libbey/IBA, London, 1988.

Table 1 *Traditional religious belief in Britain*

	Percentage of British population				
	1940s/50s	1960s	1970s	1980s	1990s
Belief					
God	–	79	74	72	67
God as personal	43	39	32	32	31
God as spirit or life force	38	39	38	39	40
Jesus as Son of God	68	62	–	49	–
Life after death	49	49	37	43	44
Heaven	–	–	52	55	52
Hell	–	–	21	26	25
Devil	24	28	20	24	26
Disbelief					
God	–	10	15	18	27
Jesus as just a man/story	18	22	–	38	–
Life after death	21	23	42	40	42
Heaven	–	–	33	35	39
Hell	–	–	68	65	66
Devil	54	52	70	64	67

Non-traditional religious belief in Britain

	1940s/50s	1960s	1970s	1980s	1990s
Belief					
Reincarnation	–	–	24	26	25
Horoscopes	–	–	23	26	26
Foretelling future	–	–	48	54	47
Lucky charms	–	–	17	19	18
Black magic	–	–	11	13	10
Exchange messages with dead	15	–	11	14	14
Ghosts	15	–	19	28	32
Disbelief					
Reincarnation	–	–	53	57	59
Horoscopes	–	–	72	69	67
Foretelling future	–	–	41	40	46
Lucky charms	–	–	79	78	78
Black magic	–	–	82	82	86
Exchange messages with dead	59	–	79	77	80
Ghosts	64	–	73	65	58

Table 1 (*cont.*)

Note: A dash represents 'insufficient data available'.
Source: Table 1 updated from that first published in Robin Gill, C. Kirk Hadaway and Penny Long Marler, 'Is Religious Belief Declining in Britain?', *Journal for the Scientific Study of Religion*, 37:3, 1998.

Sources: *God*: [Mass Observation 1947]; ITA 1968; Gallup 1968, 1973, 1975, 1979, 1981, 1986, 1989, 1993, 1995; NOP 1980; EVSSG 1981, 1990; STV 1985; MORI 1985, 1989 (2 surveys) 1998; IBA 1987; BSA 1991, 1993. *God as personal/spirit*: Gallup 1947, 1957, 1963, 1979, 1981, 1986, 1989, 1993; ABC 1964; ITA 1968; Harris 1974; EVSSG 1981, 1990. *Jesus*: Mass Observation 1947; Gallup 1957, 1963, [1979], 1981, 1986, 1989, [1993]; ABC 1964. *Life after death*: Gallup [1939], 1947, 1957, 1960, 1963, 1968, 1973 (3 surveys), 1975, 1978, 1981, 1986, 1988, 1986, 1993, 1995; Mass Observation 1947; Gorer 1950, 1963, ABC 1964, Harris 1970, 1974; NOP 1980; EVSSG 1981, 1990; STV 1985, 1989; BSA 1991; MORI 1985, 1989, 1998. *Heaven*: Gallup [1968], 1973, 1975, 1979, 1981, 1986, 1989, 1993, 1995, EVSSG 1981, 1990; STV 1985; MORI 1985, 1989, 1998; BSA 1991. *Hell*: [Gorer 1950]; [Gallup 1968], 1973, 1975, 1979, 1981, 1986, 1989, 1993, 1995; EVSSG 1981, 1990; STV 1985. *Devil*: Gorer 1950, 1963; Gallup 1957, 1963, 1968, 1973, 1975, 1979, 1981, 1986, 1989, 1993, 1995; ABC 1964; EVSSG 1981, 1990; STV 1985; MORI 1985, 1989; BSA 1991. *Reincarnation*: Gallup [1968], 1973, 1975, 1979, 1981, 1986, 1989, 1993, 1995; EVSSG 1981, 1990; STV 1985; MORI 1998. *Horoscopes*: [Gorer 1950]; Gallup 1973, 1975, 1978, 1981, 1986, 1988, 1989, 1993, 1995; STV 1985; MORI 1989, 1997, 1998; BSA 1991. *Foretelling*: Gallup 1973, 1975, 1978, 1981, 1986, 1988, 1989, 1993, 1995. *Lucky charms*: [Gorer 1950]; Gallup 1973, 1975, 1978, 1981, 1986, 1988, 1989, 1993, 1995, BSA 1991. *Black magic*: Gallup 1973, 1975, 1978, 1981, 1986, 1988, 1989, 1993, 1995. *Exchange message with dead*: Gallup 1940, 1957, 1973, 1975, 1978, 1981, 1986, 1988, 1989, 1993, 1995. *Belief in ghosts*: Gorer 1950; Gallup 1950, 1973, 1975, 1978, 1981, 1986, 1988, 1989, 1993, 1995; MORI 1997, 1998.

Notes: since a minimum of two surveys was required for each period, data in [ ] were not used. Southern Television (STV) see Gordon Heald and Robert J. Wybrow (eds.), *The Gallup Survey of Britain*, Croom Helm, London, 1986; Harris 1974 reported in *The Times* 14 Oct. 1974; ABC Television, *Television and Religion*, London University Press, London, 1965. Local surveys consulted but not used here: Longhill local survey see Peter G. Forster, *Church and People on Longhill Estate*, University of Hull, 1989; Leeds local survey reported in Grace Davie, *Religion in Britain Since 1945*, Blackwell, Oxford 1994.

whereas in 1987 only 62% did. Rather less change was suggested by a decline of support from 49% to 47% for the statement that 'God watches what each person does and thinks'. Sharper declines were suggested in response to the statement that 'Without belief in God life is meaningless' with a decline from 68% to 44%, and in response to the statement that 'You can be a good Christian without often thinking about God and religion' with a decline from 80% to 72%. The 1993 Independent Television survey[24] statement that 'Without religious beliefs life is meaningless' was slightly different, but it does suggest further decline since it was supported by just 36% of respondents.

Questions about belief in God are notoriously difficult to frame and assess. If they become too complex they are difficult to compare, but if they are too simple they risk being too simplistic. More sophisticated questions which can be compared over time were asked both by the two Independent Television surveys and by BSA in 1991 and 1995. The Independent Television surveys offered respondents five options: 'I am certain there is a God' which showed a decline between 1968 and 1987 of 50% to 42%; 'I believe there is a God, but I am not certain' showed a decline from 30% to 27%; 'I am really not sure there is a God or not' showed an increase from 10% to 15%; 'I do not believe that there is a God but I may be wrong' showed an increase from 7% to 10%; and 'I am certain there is no God' showed an increase from 2% to 4%. Thus this nineteen year interval was apparently characterised by a consistent decline in theistic belief and an increase in scepticism.

BSA respondents were given self-completion surveys in which they were instructed 'Please tick one box below to show which statement comes closest to expressing what you believe about God' and were then given six options. Of the respondents 24% in 1991 and 26% in 1995 ticked either 'I don't believe in God' or 'I don't know whether there is a God and I don't believe there is any way to find out'; 25% and 24% respectively ticked either 'I don't believe in a personal God, but I do believe in a Higher Power of some kind' or 'I find myself believing in

[24] Barry Gunter and Rachel Viney (eds.), *Seeing is Believing: Religion and Television in the 1990s*, John Libbey/ITC, London, 1994.

God some of the time, but not at others.' And a more striking 49% in 1991 reducing to 44% in 1995 ticked either 'While I have doubts, I feel that I do believe in God' or 'I know God really exists and I have no doubts about it.' Of course the time difference here is short and even these questions, although more sophisticated than many others, including those of the Independent Television surveys, still allow respondents considerable latitude in the meaning they give to the word 'God'. Nonetheless, these results do cohere with the broad pattern suggested by the longer-term data derived from blunter questions. Together they suggest that atheism, albeit still professed by a minority of the general public in Britain, is increasing and that theism is decreasing.

Although the data are more limited, several surveys over the last 70 years have asked respondents about their christological beliefs. Table 1 shows that, in those periods that can be compared reliably, a decrease from 68% in the 1940s/1950s to 49% in the 1980s can be seen in those professing a belief in Jesus as 'the Son of God' and an increase from 18% to 38% respectively in those responding that Jesus was 'just a man' or 'just a story'. Taking Gallup Poll data alone, 71% of the respondents in 1957 chose the option 'Son of God', whereas in 1993 only 46% did. In addition, 9% in 1957 chose 'just a man' and 6% 'just a story', whereas in 1993 these responses increased to 34% and 9% respectively.

An alternative way of comparing longitudinal responses in this area is to look at those responding positively to the statement 'Jesus is the Son of God'. In the 1968 and 1987 Independent Television surveys this reduced from 85% to 74% and in the 1989 MORI survey[25] to 69%. Again, support for a statement in the Independent Television surveys that 'People who believe in Jesus as the Son of God can expect salvation' reduced from 66% to 47%. Without pretending that these questions are particularly sophisticated, data from them still point in the same general direction as data from the theistic

25 For MORI data, see Eric Jacobs and Robert Worcester, *We British: Britain Under the MORIscope*, Weidenfeld and Nicolson, London, 1990; and *British Public Opinion* (monthly).

questions. Traditional Christian beliefs do appear to be declining and scepticism to be increasing.

Responses to questions about the existence of life after death show a very similar pattern. Questions on this topic have proved to be particularly popular and enduring in attitude surveys. The results in table 1 are the product of comparing data from thirty-one separate surveys over half a century. Because of the richness of the data here, this issue may offer quite a reliable guide to longitudinal trends about Christian beliefs in Britain. In the 1940s/1950s and the 1960s almost half of the population (49%) responded that they did believe in a life after death and less than a quarter (21% and 23% respectively) that they did not. By the 1980s and 1990s positive belief had apparently declined somewhat to 44% whilst active disbelief had increased very considerably (to 40% and 42% respectively). As a result the population now appears very polarised on this issue. An additional feature, which will emerge soon on other questions, is that respondents in the 1970s became more sceptical. Perhaps this period of public theological debate really did have an influence upon popular attitudes. Whether or not this is the case, respondents in the 1980s and the 1990s remained distinctly more sceptical than in the periods before the 1970s.

Another way to make longitudinal comparisons here is again to take the earliest and most recent Gallup Polls. In this case such a comparison makes possible a remarkable 56-year interval. In 1939 a Gallup Poll found that 49% of respondents professed a belief in life after death and 33% responded negatively; by 1995 these proportions had changed to 39% and 44% respectively. If the weighted means for the two surveys carried out on readers of *The Daily News* and *The Nation* in 1926 are allowed (and there must be some doubt about whether they should), an even more remarkable 69-year comparison becomes possible. In 1926 69% of readers surveyed responded positively to a question about the existence of life after death and 26% negatively. On this basis, positive belief appears to have more than halved over the seven decades and negative belief increased by two-thirds. The even earlier survey, *The Army and Religion*, based upon questionnaires given to British troops by their chaplains at the end of the First World War, also suggested that 'the marked drift of the evidence is that, taken as a whole, the men, though vaguely, believe in the life to come'.[26] Even taking the less dramatic Gallup 1939 and 1995 results, a clear shift away from traditional Christian belief and an increase in scepticism seem to have taken place in the second half of the twentieth century.

Comparing again the results of statements made in the two Independent Television surveys of 1968 and 1987 confirms this conclusion. So, apparently support for the statement 'A person who lives a good life will be rewarded in a future life' declined from 67% to 48%. The first of these figures is particularly striking since, apart from the 1926 (and probably 1919) survey, data in none of the other surveys suggest a level of belief in life after death higher than 56%. Again, support for the statement 'To lead a good life it is necessary to have some religious belief' declined from 69% to 48%; and support for the statement that 'Religious beliefs help make it easier to face up to dying' declined from 89% to 82%. Although not conclusive evidence on their own, since they mix faith and empirical statements, they are more convincing when set alongside the other data.

Questions about belief in heaven were asked first in the 1960s, but the pattern of data that they suggest compares interestingly with belief in life after death. In both there was apparently a slight increase in positive belief between the 1970s and 1980s. However in the case of belief in heaven the 1990s saw a decline in positive belief and the whole period shows a steady increase in active disbelief. By the 1990s levels of disbelief in both areas were very similar, but positive belief in heaven was higher than belief in life after death. Taking the Gallup Polls alone, in 1968 positive belief in heaven was apparently 54% reducing to 50% in 1995: negative belief was 27% increasing to 40%. So even though half of the population still appear to believe in heaven, two-fifths disbelieve in it.

Where they can be measured, beliefs in the existence of hell and the devil have remained minority beliefs throughout the

[26] D. S. Cairns (ed.), *The Army and Religion: An Enquiry and its Bearing upon the Religious Life of the Nation*, Macmillan, London, 1919, p. 16.

second half of the twentieth century. By the 1990s two-thirds of the population apparently disbelieve in both and only about a quarter express active belief in either. Both also show a slight increase between the 1970s and 1980s in positive belief and a slight decline in active disbelief. Gorer's 1950 survey gives the earliest reliable reference point for both beliefs, suggesting that only 18% of respondents actively believed in the existence of hell, 20% in the existence of the devil, and 60% disbelieved in both. Taking Gallup Polls alone, in 1968 it appeared that 23% believed in the existence of hell and 58% disbelieved, whereas by 1995 these figures had changed to 24% and 68% respectively. Gallup Polls on the existence of the devil suggest a change in 1957 from belief at 34% and disbelief at 42% to 24% and 69% respectively in 1995. Taken together these findings suggest that there has been a rise in scepticism in both areas, accompanied by a persisting minority of the population professing belief.

Surveys of religious beliefs have often been sponsored by lobby groups with firm views on the inspiration and authority of the Bible. Although this does mean that questions on this issue are quite frequent, they often reflect the different views of the sponsoring groups and are thus notoriously difficult to compare. For example, the standard Gallup Poll procedure is to ask separate questions about the Old Testament and the New Testament giving the first option for both as 'It is of divine authority and its commands should be followed without question' (in 1986 10% agreed to this option on the Old Testament and 13% on the New Testament); the Church of Scotland's 1987 *Lifestyle Survey*[27] asked only about the Bible as a whole wording the first option more simply as 'God's word – true in every detail' (19% of C of S members agreed and 11% of non-church-members); the 1987 IBA survey worded the first option as 'The Bible is the actual word of God and is to be taken literally, word by word' (14% agreed); the 1991 BSA first option 'The Bible is the actual word of God and it is to be taken literally word for word' changed only the preposition (6% agreed); but a variant Gallup question on the Bible as a whole commissioned by the

27 *Lifestyle Survey*, Church of Scotland Board of Social Responsibility, 121 George Street, Edinburgh, 1987.

Protestant Reformation Society[28] in 1996 gave the first option as 'It is of divine authority and its teachings are absolutely reliable' (16% agreed). Comparison across such a range of questions is clearly risky.

Probably the only safe procedure is strictly to compare like with like. On this basis only the Gallup data qualify and within this data separate questions about Old and New Testaments give six points of comparison between 1960 and 1993. These suggest once again that the sharpest changes took place between the 1960s and 1970s. Between 1960 and 1979 support for the first option on the Old Testament declined from 19% to 12% and then to 10% in 1993. Support for this option on the New Testament declined from 25% to 13% and then remained at that level in 1993. The second option for both was 'It is mostly of divine authority but some of it needs interpretation'. This gained the support of 41% of respondents in 1960, 39% in 1979, and 34% in 1993. On the New Testament, levels of support for this second option were 43%, 42% and 36% respectively. However, the third option 'It is mostly a collection of stories and fables' showed sharp changes. For the Old Testament it was supported by 22% in 1960, by 33% in 1979, and by 45% in 1993. For the New Testament, support for this option was 13%, 28% and 40% respectively.

This pattern closely matches that found in other data on Christian beliefs: scepticism increases and most forms of belief decrease over the whole period but especially around the 1970s. However the sharpness of the increase in scepticism in this area is particularly consonant with a cultural theory. The latter suggests that churchgoing is a distinctive culture which shapes beliefs and values. If this is so, then attitudes towards a Bible which plays such a central role in most forms of Christian worship are likely to be particularly affected by a decline in churchgoing. Outside a context of worship it may not be too surprising that the Bible, and especially the Old Testament, comes to be regarded as 'mostly a collection of stories and fables'.

Sponsored initially by the Protestant Reformation Society,

[28] The two Gallup Polls of Church of England Laity and Clergy (1984 and 1996) sponsored by the Protestant Reformation Society are reproduced with permission.

rather stark questions were asked by Gallup Polls on gospel miracles and the Virgin Birth in 1984 and 1996. Responses to both suggest some possible evidence of declining Christian belief. Back in 1947 Mass-Observation's study *Puzzled People*[29] reported that only a third of those questioned believed in the Virgin Birth, with an equal proportion disbelieving it. In 1984 in response to the question 'Turning to the belief that Christ was born of a virgin, do you believe that this is an historical fact or do you believe it to be a legend?', a similar 35% agreed that it was 'an historical fact', but by 1996 this had declined to 27%. Those opting for 'a legend' were 46% in 1984 and 56% in 1996. Yet since 41% of Anglican monthly church attenders in 1996 and 20% of Anglican full-time clergy also agreed with the 'legend' option, it would be debatable to interpret this change as simply a decline in Christian belief. A rather more sophisticated set of options on the question 'Thinking about the gospel miracles, do you believe that they are mostly historical facts, mostly the gospel writers' interpretations of certain events, or mostly legends?' suggested a more static situation. The general population opting for 'historical facts' declined from 25% in 1984 to 20% in 1996, but those opting for 'gospel writers' interpretations' increased from 38% to 42%, and those opting for 'legends' changed little from 26% to 27%. Of Anglican monthly attenders 56% in 1996 chose the second option and only 9% the third: amongst Anglican clergy 31% chose the second and only 1% the third. Again there appears to be some ambiguity about whether or not the second option here represents a decline in Christian belief as such. Perhaps in this case the statement rather than question of the 1968 and 1987 Independent Television surveys – 'The miracles of the Bible really happened' (suggesting a decline in popular support for it from 70% to 54%) – is less ambiguous. Much will depend upon the theological position of the interpreter.

This last point offers a warning against too simplistic an interpretation of all the survey data on Christian belief reviewed here. The rise of hermeneutics and biblical interpretation

[29] Mass-Observation, *Puzzled People: A Study of Popular Attitudes to Religion, Ethics, Progress and Politics in a London Borough*, Victor Gollancz, London, 1947.

within academic theology over the last two decades should guard against simplicities. Without claiming that quantitative survey data can ever uncover the subtleties of Christian belief, it is nevertheless difficult to avoid the force of the data taken as a whole. In each of the areas surveyed there is evidence of an increase of disbelief in the second half of the twentieth century in Britain. This does seem to fit the predictions of a secularisation theory quite closely.

However, the persistence and even increase of what has loosely been termed 'new age' or non-traditional religious beliefs count against most forms of secularisation theory (unless, of course, such a theory refers only to the decline of specifically Christian beliefs). The data on belief in reincarnation illustrate this clearly. Some of the earliest attitude surveys noted that a belief in reincarnation was held by some respondents. However, they tended not to ask people directly whether they believed in reincarnation but simply noted occasions when respondents spontaneously mentioned reincarnation when discussing life after death. On this basis both Mass-Observation and BIPO[30] in 1947 noted those holding this belief (4% and 3% respectively), as did Gorer's two surveys[31] in 1950 and 1963 (11% and 4% respectively). However, since 1968 Gallup Polls have asked a direct question about belief in reincarnation. Comparing data from this date with Gallup data from 1995 it appears that positive belief has increased from 18% to 26% and disbelief more slightly from 52% to 58%. Table 1 compares weighted data from twelve different surveys between the 1970s and 1990s. This suggests that about a quarter of the population still persist with this belief even while sceptics slightly increase (53% to 59%). Evidently this is a minority belief, but it does not appear to be a disappearing belief. If anything, respondents here are becoming more polarised.

The clearest increase seems to be in belief in ghosts. Table 1 suggests that those believing in the existence of ghosts have increased consistently from 15% in the 1950s to 32% in the

[30] Early Gallup Poll data reported in Gorer, *Exploring English Character.*

[31] *Ibid.* See also Gorer, *Death, Grief and Mourning in Contemporary Britain*, Cresset Press, London, 1965.

1990s. Disbelief in the existence of ghosts, whilst it reached a high point of 73% in the 1970s is now lower at 58% in the 1990s than it was in the 1950s (64%). Data from the earliest and most recent Gallup Polls again illustrate this: in 1950 apparently only 10% of respondents believed in the existence of ghosts and 80% actively disbelieved, whereas by 1995 these figures had changed to 31% and 62% respectively. Ironically this change seems to have occurred despite the fact that less than half of those believing in ghosts claim actually to have seen one. The 1950 Gallup Poll found that the 10% of believers were matched by only 2% of those claiming to have seen a ghost. Gorer in the same year found 17% believers and 7% seers; Gallup 1989 found 32% and 14%; and MORI 1998 found 40% and 15% respectively.

Since 1973 Gallup Polls have consistently asked people whether or not they believe in 'Being able to forecast that something is going to happen before it actually happens'. Asked on its own this might be interpreted as a straightforward empirical question. However, it is typically asked alongside other questions about the paranormal. Table 1 suggests that approximately half of the respondents express belief in this phenomenon and that believers outnumber disbelievers. The gap between the two may be getting narrower, but at this stage it is difficult to discern a clear trend. In contrast, only a quarter express belief in horoscopes and almost two-thirds express disbelief. Yet in this area too it is difficult to see a clear sceptical trend. A minority belief here seems to have persisted from the 1970s to the 1990s. If Gorer's 1950 data is taken as an early benchmark, suggesting that 17% believed that 'there is something in horoscopes' and 60% definitely did not, then both belief and disbelief may have grown in this area. Gorer also found that although almost three-quarters of respondents reported 'regularly' or 'occasionally' reading horoscopes in a newspaper or magazine, only one in twenty of this group admitted regularly following the advice given in them. Table 1 also suggests that a persisting minority from the 1970s to the 1990s has believed in lucky charms and black magic, whilst a large majority of respondents remain sceptical of both. Using

Gorer again as an early bench mark, the 15% who believed in lucky charms in 1950 and the 82% who disbelieved appear little different from the 15% who believed and the 83% who disbelieved in the Gallup Poll of 1995.

For fifty-five years Gallup Polls have uniquely asked people whether or not they believe in 'exchanging messages with the dead'. Given the decline in public attention given to spiritualism, it might be thought that this minority belief would also decline over this period of time. However the weighted means in table 1 suggest little change in positive belief (15% in the 1940s/1950s and 14% in the 1990s). Rather it is disbelief which appeared to increase sharply from 59% in the 1940s/1950s to 79% in the 1970s. According to MORI Poll 1997 data, 17% believe in spiritualism, 16% in clairvoyance, and 20% in out-of-body experiences. MORI 1998 found, in addition, that 64% believe in premonitions/ESP, 18% in fortune-telling/tarot, and 30% (despite David Hume) that dreams can predict the future.

Reviewing this data on 'new age' beliefs as a whole, there is some evidence of growing scepticism, which in turn would seem to support a secularisation theory. Yet there is also other evidence of persisting minority beliefs and even tentative evidence of some increase. Whilst specifically Christian beliefs across the board show signs of decline accompanied by a growth in scepticism, the pattern of 'new age' beliefs appears different. If beliefs which are held in common by both Christians and 'new age' believers are examined, a process of secularisation is less clear. So the pattern of belief in faith healing suggests large proportions of both believers and sceptics with no clear trend yet evident: a Gallup Poll in 1973 found that there were 38% believers and 48% disbelievers, yet a Gallup Poll in 1995 found that these proportions had changed only to 39% and 52% respectively.

Similarly Gallup Polls on belief in personal prayer suggest that 69% of respondents in 1950 were believers in this and 19% disbelievers, changing very little to 74% believers and 18% disbelievers in 1985. The 1919 survey *The Army and Religion* also reported that the men of the British armies, however dim their faith may be, do in the hour of danger, at least, believe in God, 'the great and terrible God'. Most men we are told pray before they go over the parapet, or advance in the face of machine guns, and they thank God when they have come through the battle.[32]

Even the small indications of declining subjective religiosity are hardly conclusive. Data can be clustered together in two groups: the first consisting of individuals who saw themselves as 'very' or 'fairly' religious and the second of those responding 'not very' or 'not' religious. Comparing the earliest survey to ask about this, the 1968 ITA survey, and the most recent, a 1993 Gallup Poll, the decline in the 'very' and 'fairly' group is from 58% to 52% and the increase in the second, 'not very' and 'not', group is from 41% to 46%. Set alongside the evidence of declines in both religious belonging evident in table 3 and churchgoing in table 4 and table 5, these are not dramatic changes.

BELIEVING AND BELONGING COMPARED

At the start of this chapter it was seen that secularisation theory typically assumes that a decline in religious belonging is preceded by a decline in religious belief. The forces of secularity – whether in the form of the Enlightenment, rationality, science, or just modernity – persuade individuals that their belief is groundless. Once convinced that this is the case they can then see little point in continuing religious practice. There are important elements here, which could be tested against longitudinal survey data, yet which never have been adequately tested. The alternative wisdom of a separation theory is that believing and belonging are distinct: individuals can believe without belonging and a few belong without believing. Stated in this simple form there is indeed empirical evidence in Britain today to support it. However, if it is turned into a longitudinal theory to act as an alternative to secularisation theory, then it too could be tested against longitudinal survey data.

Table 2 suggests how this longitudinal testing might be

[32] Cairns, *The Army and Religion*, p. 7.

Table 2 *Belief and belonging compared* (in percentages)

	Belief in a personal God	Belief in life after death	Belief in Jesus as divine	Church regular attendance
1926 *Daily News/Nation* weighted mean	68	69	64	68
1947 Gallup	45	49	–	30
1964 ABC	42	50	64	25
1981 Gallup	36	40[a]	52	22[a]
1991 BSA	32	47	–	20
1993 Gallup	30	42	–	46
1991 BSA N. Ireland	74	69	–	64
1964 ABC Monthly churchgoers	79	86	–	100
1993 MORI Monthly churchgoers	78	85	82	100

Note: [a] Separate Gallup surveys.

achieved. It sets out a longitudinal selection of those surveys which allow a comparison to be made between expressed Christian beliefs and stated church attendance. The earliest set of data is a weighted mean from the two newspaper surveys carried out in 1926 by *The Daily News* and *The Nation.* In this context, the relative accuracy of these surveys (they relied upon the self-selection of readers rather than upon a stratified randomised sample) matters less. Even if they somewhat exaggerate the levels of belief and belonging in the community at large, it is the internal relationship between the items reported by the respondents themselves that matters. It can be seen that the levels of belief in a personal God (68%), in a life after death (69%) and in Jesus as divine (64%) match very closely the stated high level of 'regular' church attendance (68%). These correspond in a remarkable way to the two items of belief – (in a personal God at 74% and in life after death at 69%) and of high monthly attendance (64%) in the BSA 1991 survey of Northern Ireland. Compare the latter with the BSA 1991 British survey: just 20% monthly attendance and beliefs in a personal God at

32% and in life after death at 47%. As might be expected even higher levels of belief than any of these are reported amongst monthly churchgoers in the 1964 ABC survey and the 1993 MORI survey. When all of these results are compared with the general population surveys of 1947 Gallup Poll, 1964 ABC, and 1981 and 1993 Gallup, then it becomes clear that both beliefs and belonging decline, but that the latter declines faster than the former. Even belief in a personal God, which declines the fastest of all three beliefs, does not decline as fast as churchgoing.

What these diachronic and synchronic comparisons suggest is that – *contra* a separation theory – there is a relationship between decline in Christian belief and a decline in belonging measured in terms of churchgoing. However, the relationship is not in the order typically predicted by secularisation theory. Decline in churchgoing is faster than decline in Christian belief – exactly as a cultural theory of churchgoing predicts.

This also fits an interesting piece of evidence from West Germany. *Der Spiegel* commissioned a survey[33] in 1967 which was repeated in 1992. This suggests that those attending church 'every or almost every Sunday' declined sharply in the twenty-five years from 25% to 10%. There was a corresponding decline in belief in God (from 68% to 56%), in Jesus as the son of God (42% to 29%), in the Virgin Birth (36% to 22%) in Jesus' bodily resurrection (39% to 33%), in Jesus raising people from the dead (53% to 42%), in Jesus feeding the 5000 (50% to 40%), in human descent from Adam and Eve (49% to 32%), in hell (34% to 24%) and in the Last Judgment (59% to 50%). Only belief in life after death showed persistence (48% and 50%). Of course some of these declines may indicate a shift away from literalistic belief rather than a decline in Christian belief as such. Nonetheless, none is as sharp as the decline in regular churchgoing.

Using a narrower time frame but a broader brush, the European Value Systems Study Group data for ten European countries measured in the early 1980s and again in the early

[33] Reported in Jack D. Shand, 'The Decline of Traditional Christian Beliefs in Germany', *Sociology of Religion*, 59:2, 1998, pp. 179–84.

1990s suggest a similar pattern.[34] The mean weekly churchgoing rates in these ten countries declined dramatically from 49% to 29%. The decline in the youngest age-groups was particularly sharp – from 43% to just 18% in the 18–24 age-group and from 37% to 16% in the 25–34 age-group. However, even those aged 65 and over showed a decline in weekly churchgoing from 63% to 50%. Declines in Christian belief were also evident in the mean for the ten countries, but again they were not nearly so sharp. For example, belief in God declined from 85% to 79%; in heaven from 53% to 49%; in hell from 32% to 27%; and belief in the soul was static at 71%. Early analysis of the EVSSG 1980s data alone suggested that Christian belief and churchgoing are 'quite strongly intercorrelated'.[35] Now a comparison of the 1980s and 1990s data suggests that the decline in churchgoing precedes that in belief.

A cultural theory also predicts that Christian belief will be higher amongst an older generation whether or not individuals currently go to church. Most people born before the Second World War will have been to church and/or Sunday school in their youth, whereas most of those currently at school will not. In other words, the latter will have little experience of the culture that nurtures Christian beliefs and are, thus, less likely than an older generation to share them. Only those young people who do go to church are likely to hold high levels of Christian belief. Others will show increasing signs of scepticism. Precisely because the collapse in any form of church participation has been so swift amongst young people, it should be possible to find unambiguous evidence of corresponding falling levels of Christian belief.

Now there are, of course, long-standing data suggesting that the old are more inclined to profess traditional Christian beliefs than the young, as well as women more than men. For example a Gallup Poll for *The Humanist*[36] noted that 54% of women in

[34] Reported in Sheena Ashford and Noel Timms, *What Europe Thinks: A Study of European Values*, Dartmouth, Aldershot, 1992.

[35] Stephen Harding, David Phillips and Michael Fogarty, *Contrasting Values in Western Europe: Unity, Diversity and Change*, Macmillan, Basingstoke, 1986, p. 62.

[36] *The Humanist*, vol. 76, 1961, pp. 161–71.

1947 and only 32% of men, and 62% of women and 49% of men in 1960, believed in life after death. It also noted that in the 1947 survey, 46% of those aged 21–29 believed, compared with 52% of those aged 50-and-over. A Gallup Poll commissioned by the *News Chronicle*[37] in 1957 also found that belief in a personal God was held by 44% of those aged 30-and-over but only by 32% of those aged 16–29. An NOP survey[38] in 1980 found that 81% of women compared with 65% of men believed in 'God' or a 'Supreme Being', as well as 56% of those age 15–24 compared with 81% of those aged 65-and-over. And a Gallup Poll, this time commissioned by The *Sunday Telegraph* in 1981, found very similar differences of belief in God: 82% women compared with 64% men, and 60% aged 16–24 and 84% aged 65-and-over. Secularisation theorists have often noted these differences and offered them as further evidence of a process of secularisation. A rather awkward assumption may lie behind this interpretation of the data: namely, that women are less 'rational' or 'enlightened' than men and the old less than the young. However, in terms of a cultural theory, it merely confirms the relationship between belief and belonging: since it is women and older people who go more regularly to church, and/or went more regularly in their youth, it is not surprising that the relative strength of their Christian beliefs will also differ from those of men and the young.

But what of the suggestion that, since churchgoing amongst the young is declining so fast, belief may also be declining faster amongst them than amongst other groups? This is exactly what is suggested in the EVSSG data across the ten European countries. Just taking the two British EVSSG surveys,[39] the 1990 survey found that only 31% of the 18–24 age-group reported that they had been 'brought up religiously at home', compared with 58% of the 35–44 age-group and 82% of the 65-and-over age-group. The sharpest declines in Christian belief

37 *News Chronicle*, 17 April 1957, p. 4.

38 Reported in *Political Social Economic Review*, August 1980, p. 33.

39 See Mark Abrams, David Gerard and Noel Timms (eds.), *Values and Social Change in Britain: Studies in the Contemporary Values of Modern Society*, Macmillan, London, 1985, and Noel Timms, *Family and Citizenship: Values in Contemporary Britain*, Dartmouth, Aldershot, 1992.

were noted between the 1981 and 1990 surveys in the youngest age-group: belief in God declining from 59% to 45%, in a personal God from 23% to 18%, in life after death from 44% to 36%, in heaven from 46% to 41%, and in sin from 58% to 49%. Disbelief also increased sharply in this age-group: professed atheism rising from 28% to 38% and disbelief in life after death from 39% to 52%. So, although levels of belief in most of these areas are still higher than the 31% level of those 'brought up religiously at home', Christian belief amongst the young does seem to be declining sharply and disbelief growing – exactly as a cultural theory would predict. Indeed, amongst those over 55 years old in 1990, some of these beliefs remain relatively strong: 83% believe in God, 48% in life after death, 62% in heaven and 70% in sin. Amongst this older group there is not a considerable difference from those levels of belief in the oldest age-group recorded three or four decades earlier.

This sharp decline in Christian beliefs amongst the young is also what Leslie Francis' twenty-year study[40] of religious attitudes amongst 11–15 year-olds helps to establish. Testing attitudes on twenty-four questions on six samples of school children between 1974 and 1994 he shows changes in all but one area. Some of the changes are very sharp indeed. For example the statement 'I know that Jesus helps me' was supported by 42% in 1974 but only by 22% in 1994; support for the statement 'God is very real to me' fell from 41% to 25%; support for 'The idea of God means much to me' fell from 40% to 24%; for 'God helps me to live a better life' fell from 39% to 22%; for 'Prayer helps me a lot' fell from 36% to 20%; and for 'I know that God helps me' fell from 42% to 25%. The mean score of the churchgoers was some 50% higher than that of the nonchurchgoers. And the mean score for each year-group declined over the twenty-year period.

40 Reported in William K. Kay and Leslie J. Francis, *Drift from the Churches: Attitude Toward Christianity During Childhood and Adolescence*, University of Wales Press, Cardiff, 1996. For a similar longitudinal study of university students, see G. W. Pilkington, P. K. Poppleton, J. B. Gould and M. M. McCourt, 'Changes in Religious Beliefs, Practices and Attitudes Among University Students over an Eleven-year Period in Relation to Sex Differences, Denominational Differences and Differences Between Faculties and Years of Study', *British Journal of Social and Clinical Psychology*, 15, 1976, pp. 1–9.

Table 3 *No-religion compared* (in percentages)

	Gorer 1950 (n = 4983)	BSA 1983–4 (n = 3280)	BSA 1994 (n = 3315)
Age Group			
18–24	22	61	66
25–34	22	44	54
35–44	24	35	49
45–54	22[a]	25	31
55–64	22[a]	22	26
65+	24	15	21
All	23	33	39

[a] Groups combined.
n = Number (sample size).

No-religion = those responding negatively to the question:
Would you describe yourself as being of any religion or denomination?' (Gorer)
or
'Do you regard yourself as belonging to any particular religion?' (BSA)

The question 'Do you consider yourself as belonging to a particular religion? If yes, which one?' gave a negative response rate of 33% (*Times/Mirror* Poll 1991).

Note: lower no-religion responses were recorded for questions suggesting a positive response, such as 'What is your religious denomination?' (e.g. 9% Gallup 1957; 7% BIPO 1963; 9% Gallup 1971; 8% Gallup 1973; 10% Gallup 1976; 8% Gallup 1979; 9% Gallup 1981; 9% Gallup 1984; 13% Gallup 1988; 18% Gallup 1993); 'What religious denomination do you belong to?' (6% ABC/Gallup 1964); or 'Which religious group would you say you came into, in terms of your beliefs?' (10% atheist/agnostic and don't know/none NOP 1978 and *ibid.* 1981). Gallup data for the USA suggest a no-religion increase of 2% to 11% from the 1950s to the 1990s. Those opting for the specific 'no religion' option in the Australian national censuses increased from 6.7% in 1971 to 16.6% in 1996 (Hughes, *Religion in Australia*).

In table 3 a comparison of recent BSA data with data from Gorer's 1950 survey shows the rapid rate of decline in church-going and affiliation amongst British young adults. The general increase between 1950 and 1994 of those giving a response of 'no religion' from 23% to 39% (and 1996 to 43%) has already been noted. A comparison of this change in terms of age cohorts is very revealing. In Gorer there was very little variation between the age-groups in the percentage of those giving this 'no religion' response. Amongst 18–24 year-olds it was 22% and amongst those aged 65-and-over it was 24%. However, since its inception BSA has always found very sharp differences. In 1983–4 the youngest group recorded 61% and the oldest only 15%. In 1994 the youngest group had increased to 66%. A comparison of these two BSA sets of data suggests that as a cohort gets older so individuals in it tend to be somewhat less likely to give a 'no religion' response. Nonetheless successive generations also appear more secular. Thus, the 18–24 group in the 1980s had a 'no religion' level of 61% but a decade later it had dropped to 54%. Yet they were still more secular than the 44% level of the 25–34 group in the 1980s.

All of this corresponds closely to observations by Philip Hughes on data from recent censuses of the whole population of Australia:

> The percent of all 40 to 49 year olds stating 'no religion' grew from 14.2 percent in 1991 to 16.2 percent in 1996. The percentage of 20 year olds claiming 'no religion' grew from 19.7 to 21.7 percent in the period 1991 to 1996. This suggests that 'no religion' is not age related, but reflects changes in culture. It is likely then that the percentage claiming 'no religion' will continue to grow.[41]

European sociologists working in this area have often used the more ecclesiastical concept of the 'unchurched'. Nevertheless, Frank Lechner's report on the Netherlands is very similar:

> The single most significant fact about organized religion in the Netherlands is its precipitous decline in recent decades. To be sure, members of the Dutch Reformed church had begun to depart as early as the 1920s, but surveys conducted since the 1950s display a further, more general decline, notably among Catholics . . . an increase in the proportion of unchurched from 24% to 57%, and a first indication of a strong generational effect reinforcing this decline . . . since the 1950s each new generation has started adult life more unchurched, the decline is more rapid among the young.[42]

[41] Philip J. Hughes, *Religion in Australia: Facts and Figures*, Christian Research Association, Kew, Victoria, Australia, 1997, p. 74.

[42] Frank J. Lechner, 'Secularization in the Netherlands?', *Journal for the Scientific Study of Religion*, 35:3, 1996, p. 254.

Table 4 *Monthly churchgoing compared* (in percentages)

	Gorer 1950 (n = 4983)	BSA 1983–4 (n = 3280)	BHPS 1991 (n = 9260)	BSA 1994 (n = 3315)
Men	18	15	14	15
Women	29	25	24	22
Age Group				
15–17	–	–	16	–
18–24	29	12	13	9
25–34	16	12	13	13
35–44	20	20	17	17
45–54	25[a]	22	22	22
55–64	25[a]	25	22	23
65+	30	27	29	28
All	23	20	19	19

[a] Groups combined.
See also: BBC 1954 'frequent churchgoers' ('most Sundays') = 25% (n = 1859); men = 19, women = 29; aged 16–20 = 41; 21–29 = 18; 30–49 = 19; 50–64 = 31; 65+ = 37.

In the youngest age group, aged 21–30, the 'unchurched' in the Netherlands amounted to 20% in 1958 (compared with 23% in the 51–70 year old group). Yet by 1991 they had dramatically increased to 72% (compared with 41% in the 51–70 year old group).

Table 4 offers a similar comparison of different cohorts of monthly churchgoers in Britain compared over the same period of time. This confirms Francis' finding that the drift from churchgoing is happening at a younger and younger age. Thus in Gorer's 1950 data monthly churchgoing remained relatively high at 29% amongst the 18–24 age-group, almost matching the oldest age-group at 30%, but declined sharply to 16% in the 25–34 age-group. Using somewhat different age-groupings, the BBC 1954 data reported a similar pattern, albeit recording a very high 41% 'frequent' churchgoers in the 16–20 age-group – the highest rate for any age-group (a slight health warning is necessary here since the sample for this group was rather small). The BSA data suggest that by the 1980s churchgoing was already low amongst the 18–24 age-group and is now the lowest

Table 5 *Churchgoing compared by denominations*

	Roman Catholic	Free Church	Anglican	Total
Percentage of churchgoers				
Once a week				
1983–4	37	39	24	100
1994	34	35	31	100
At least once a month				
1983–4	29	37	34	100
1994	29	34	37	100
Percentage of population				
Once a week				
1983–4	4.6	4.9	2.9	12.4
1994	3.8	4.0	3.5	11.3
At least once a month				
1983–4	5.9	7.4	6.9	20.1
1994	5.4	6.5	6.9	18.9

1983–4 n = 3282; 1994 n = 3311
Source: BSA data.

of all of the age-groups in the 1990s. The British Household Panel Survey data for 1991 gives additional information on the 15–17 age-group, suggesting that churchgoing is still higher at 16% in this age-group than it is in the next two age-groups at 13%, but that it is now considerably lower than the oldest age-group at 29%.

If a cultural theory of churchgoing is correct then this evidence about changing patterns of churchgoing and affiliation in a number of countries has very serious implications for the future of Christian beliefs and values there. A separation theory offers a tempting but misleading note of optimism for the Christian ethicist. Even if a secularisation theory is rejected, a serious problem remains for the churches. A cultural theory contends that Christian beliefs and values do depend upon churchgoing. Yet the evidence just reviewed suggests that churchgoing is declining fast in a number of countries, especially amongst young people.

In Britain this may well have important implications for society at large. The longitudinal data in table 2 suggests that there is quite a close similarity between the beliefs of the general population in Northern Ireland today, where churchgoing levels are high (as they possibly were in parts of Britain in 1926) and those of British churchgoers today. It seems possible that, in a society in which the culture of churchgoing is strong, Christian beliefs and values will spread well beyond the boundaries of churchgoers. Given a cultural theory of churchgoing the reason for this is not difficult to guess. An older generation in Britain was largely brought up within a culture of Sunday school and/or churchgoing, acquiring in the process Christian beliefs and values. Members of this generation shared many of the same values as churchgoers whether or not they continued to go to church themselves as adults.

There are also indications that this might be an important factor in the differences of belief between nonchurchgoers in the United States and those in Canada. Using results from the World Value Survey[43] of the early 1980s, there are close similarities amongst weekly churchgoers in the two countries on their beliefs in God (99%+), in life after death (USA 88% and Canada 86%), in the soul (98% and 97%) in heaven (98% and 95%) in sin (96% and 90%), in their taking time to pray (97% and 92%) and in their disbelief in reincarnation (78% and 73%). They differed sharply only on their belief in the devil (81% and 64%) and in hell (86% and 67%). Yet amongst those who 'rarely attend' there were sharp differences on most of these items of belief: life after death (70% and 60%), heaven (78% and 62%), sin (84% and 66%), taking time to pray (72% and 62%), and some difference on God (95% and 88%), the soul (85% and 79%) and disbelief in reincarnation (72% and 62%). Put simply, it is relatively difficult to detect differences between churchgoers and nonchurchgoers in the United States. A number of American sociologists, despite arguing that other aspects of religiosity

[43] See Samuel H. Reimer, 'A Look at Cultural Effects on Religiosity: A Comparison Between the United States and Canada', *Journal for the Scientific Study of Religion*, 34:4, 1996, p. 452.

may influence beliefs and values, have noted this.[44] Rather than concluding that churchgoing is simply epiphenomenal, a cultural theory would attribute these differences to the radically different levels of churchgoing in the two countries. As in Northern Ireland, churchgoing affects most people in America at some point in their lives. In contrast, in Britain and increasingly in Canada as well, churchgoing no longer touches the lives of a majority of the population at any age and, as a result, a general culture of churchgoing has been lost.

Yet without such a culture many young people today are likely to know or share few of the beliefs and values held by churches. Accordingly, churchgoers gradually become an enclave within an increasingly pluralistic, but not necessarily secular, society. Earlier this century in Britain, and still in Northern Ireland and the United States, a weekly churchgoing minority was set in a society that had largely been nurtured in Christian beliefs and values. Today a churchgoing minority in Britain finds itself located in a society in which only the older generations have been thoroughly nurtured in these beliefs and values. Thus, amongst the fragmentations of postmodernity, weekly churchgoing – for long a minority activity amongst British adults – may now be becoming a culturally isolated activity as well.

44 E.g. Robert Wuthnow, *Sharing the Journey: Support Groups and America's New Quest for Community*, The Free Press, New York, 1994, p. 328.

PART TWO

The evidence

CHAPTER 4

The British Household Panel Survey

So far this book has reviewed data most of which has already been published, even if much has been forgotten or hidden in archives. Taken as a whole it suggests that churchgoing has more effect upon beliefs and values than is often admitted by sociologists or even by many theologians. Three areas in particular – Christian belief, teleology and altruism – appear to be especially associated with regular churchgoing. It is time now to test this association and to measure its strength more accurately against an entirely new set of data.

The British Household Panel Survey (BHPS) was established with a grant from the Economic and Social Research Council to the Research Centre on Micro-social Change at the University of Essex in 1989. BHPS is designed as an annual survey of each member over 15 years old of a nationally representative sample of more than 5,000 households, making a total of approximately 10,000 individual interviews. The same adults are interviewed in each year and children are interviewed once they reach the age of 16. Eventually it should be possible to map longitudinal changes amongst the respondents. The survey sometimes includes an additional sample of 11–15-year-old household members. Alongside a host of other social indicators, the annual survey usually includes a question about attendance at religious services and always includes questions about whether or not respondents are members of, and/or active within, religious groups. Given its size and scope, this largely untapped religious resource offers an invaluable basis for research.[1]

[1] Please note again, the data used here were made available by Data Archive. Neither

Churchgoing in BHPS is assessed by the question, 'How often, if at all, do you attend religious services or meetings?' In the first wave of the survey, in 1991, respondents were given four options: once a week or more, at least once a month, at least once a year, and 'practically never'. In subsequent waves of the survey a fifth option was added – 'only weddings etc.'. This does make serious directional analysis of churchgoing possible. In other words, it allows for tests of whether or not more frequent churchgoing has an effect upon respondents' attitudes and/or behaviour. In the first wave alone there was an additional question, 'Do you regard yourself as belonging to any particular religion?', allowing respondents to specify to which, if any, religion or Christian denomination they belong. So only in this wave is it possible to distinguish churchgoers from those attending services or meetings in non-Christian religious traditions. The figures for BHPS in table 4 are those for Christian churchgoers alone. However, the figures given in this chapter will not be able to make this distinction since it will include data from three other waves ('churchgoers' will be used instead as a generic title). The British Social Attitudes (BSA) data given in chapter five will be able to isolate Christian churchgoers. In the event, where it can be tested, this distinction makes very little difference to the data, since the total identifying with a non-Christian religious tradition in BHPS 1991 was only 2.5% of the whole sample. In contrast, the total giving a 'no religion' response was 38.3% (a figure that fits in closely with those in table 3).

Religious membership in BHPS is assessed by the question, 'Are you currently a member: Religious group or church organisation?' In the first wave a surprisingly low 10% of the sample responded positively to this question – that is, only half of those who reported that they went at least monthly to a religious service or meeting. When asked the additional question, 'Are you currently active in: Religious group or church organisation?', again only 10% responded positively. In most other groups, when asked questions about membership, on the one

the original collectors of the data nor the Archive bear any responsibility for the analyses or interpretations presented here.

hand, and activity within a group, on the other, respondents answered very differently. So, whereas 18% were members of a trade union, only 3% reported being active within it, and whereas 3% were members of either a political party or an environmental group, only half of these were active within them. In fact only those active in a sports club (17%) showed a higher level of active membership than members of a religious group. So it seems that for BHPS respondents a question about religious membership was understood to be a question about activity within a religious group. This does suggest a group that takes religious belonging seriously. Although it obviously cannot provide a basis for directional testing, it does provide an important basis for testing differences between religious and other groups (using regression analysis).

Comparing religious attendance and membership over five years of BHPS data, there is another unexpected finding. In the light of table 4, it is hardly surprising that monthly attendance has declined from 19.9% in 1991[2] to 17.6% in 1995, but it is puzzling that stated membership has increased from 10.1% to 12.7% and active belonging from 10.1% to 13.1%. Possibly this means that more of those who already go to church recognise that they are indeed active church members. Or, perhaps more likely, the fewer people who go to church the more active those who remain have to be to maintain the churches at all. In Britain it does seem to be in the smaller denominations that there is a closer correspondence between churchgoing and church membership/activity. In 1991 in the two largest denominations – the Church of England and the Roman Catholic Church – only a minority of those attending church at least once a month identify themselves as members (44% and 29% respectively) or as active in their church (46% and 30%). Also supporting the second interpretation is the comparative evidence about attendance and giving within the Church of England. Between 1968 and 1995 usual Sunday attendance declined from 1,606,000 to 1,045,000 (3.5% of the population to

[2] Table 4 records 19%, but this excludes those attending non-Christian religious services or meetings (other years in BHPS do not give sufficient data for this to be done).

2.1%). Occasional attendance fell even more sharply: Easter Day communicants represented 6.5% of the population aged 15+ in 1960, but only 3.2% in 1995. In contrast, between 1964 and 1995 covenanted giving per subscriber rose from £0.32 per week (or £3.41 in real terms of 1995) to £5.29 and uncovenanted planned giving from £0.13 (or £1.42) to £2.22.[3]

The new data provided by BHPS are useful for testing the altruistic and teleological categories – especially for assessing the relationship between stated attitudes and behaviour. However there are also two items which relate more closely to Christian belief. One of these asked people to respond to the statement that 'The Bible is God's word and every word in it is true.' The second asked respondents 'How much difference would you say religious beliefs make to your life?' Both adults and children were tested, albeit in different waves.

Adults in 1994 were asked whether or not they agreed with the literalistic statement on the Bible. In the BHPS sample as whole 17% strongly agreed/agreed and 43% disagreed/strongly disagreed. In the BHPS youth sample (aged 11–15) those agreeing rose to 29% but those disagreeing still amounted to 34%. The wide variation of wording in questions about the Bible, noted in the previous chapter, make it difficult to compare results accurately across different surveys. Indeed, questions in other surveys usually allow for both literalistic and non-literalistic options. Nonetheless, it is clear both from the BHPS evidence and from the evidence cited earlier that only a minority of the general population is likely to support literalistic claims about the Bible however they are worded. Interestingly, the weighted mean for the surveys of *The Daily News* and *The Nation*[4] in 1926 suggests that, despite high levels of churchgoing (see table 2), even then 58% readers responded negatively and only 34% positively to the literalistic question 'Do you accept the first chapter of Genesis as historical?' Even the non-literalistic question 'Do you regard the Bible as inspired in a sense in

3 *Church Statistics: Parochial Membership and Finance Statistics for January to December 1995*, The Central Board of Finance of the Church of England, Church House, Westminster, 1997.

4 Reported in C. E. M. Joad, *The Present and Future of Religion*, Ernest Benn, London, 1930.

which the literature of your own country could not be said to be inspired?' was supported by only 60% of respondents in the 1926 surveys.

However, tested against churchgoing, a highly significant pattern, which will be examined further at the end of this chapter, is seen. The 1993 MORI poll[5] cited earlier showed that 70% of weekly churchgoers and 41% of fortnightly churchgoers supported the statement that the Bible is 'the complete Word of God'. The literalist BHPS 1994 statement reveals that 28% of weekly adult churchgoers 'strongly agree': adding 'agree', a five-stage descending pattern emerges (57% weekly, 28% monthly, 17% occasional, 16% 'practically never', 11% 'only weddings etc.'). This shows a clear and statistically significant directionality:[6] the more individuals attend, the more likely they seem to agree that 'The Bible is God's word and every word of it is true'. In the adult sample there is a tendency for this belief to be supported more by the old than by the young. Nevertheless churchgoers in all age-groups support it much more strongly than do nonchurchgoers. So directionality is as clear in the 16–24 age group (48%; 34%; 11%; 8%; 5%) as it is in the 65+ age-group (65%; 41%; 31%; 33%; 27%). Nor is gender responsible for this directionality: the pattern of men (56%, 22%, 17%, 14%, 11%) is similar to, and only very slightly lower than, that of women. It is also apparent that a sizeable proportion of weekly churchgoers in all of these groups withhold their agreement.

A rather clearer majority of weekly churchgoers strongly agreed that religious beliefs make a difference to their lives. In the whole adult sample in 1991 there were 18% who responded 'a great difference', 20% 'some difference', 21% 'a little difference' and 39% 'no difference'. The youth sample five years later was offered one less category, but was distinctly more negative – 10% 'a great difference', 40% 'some difference', and

[5] MORI, *Christian Beliefs*, Research Study Conducted for BBC Songs of Praise, Nov. 1993.

[6] Somers' ordinal by ordinal directional test in SPSS has been used on this and all subsequent directional tests in this chapter. Those referred to as 'significant' all recorded a level of statistical significance at the high level of 0.000.

50% 'no difference'. In the earlier adult sample it is possible to test responses with a four-point churchgoing scale: according to this, 67% of weekly churchgoers responded 'a great difference', 30% of monthly churchgoers, 12% of occasional churchgoers and only 6% of nonchurchgoers. There were also denominational differences fitting those already noted: 72% of weekly churchgoers in the smaller denominations responded 'a great difference', whereas amongst Anglicans this dropped to 66% and amongst Roman Catholics to 60%. Conversely the proportions of those responding 'no difference' were 4%, 10%, 31% and 61% respectively. The directionality of both sets is again highly significant. Here too this directionality occurs in all age-groups: amongst those in the 16–24 age-group the proportions responding 'a great difference' are as clear (62%, 25%, 5% and 2%) as they are in the 65+ age-group (66%, 37%, 23% and 14%). A similar pattern also occurs amongst men (64%, 30%, 10%, 5%) and women (69%, 30%, 14%, 8%). Unlike responses to the literalistic Bible statement, a clear majority of weekly churchgoers in every group agreed that religious beliefs make 'a great difference' to their lives.

It will be noted constantly in this chapter and the next that directionality is a strong and statistically significant feature of the relationship between churchgoing and beliefs/values, yet it is still a relative not an absolute process. That is, some respondents reported that they 'practically never' went to church and yet considered that religious beliefs made 'a great difference' to their lives. There were also a few who said that they went every week and yet that religious beliefs apparently made 'no difference' to their lives. It is very rare indeed to find unanimous responses in any churchgoing category. In that sense the oddities, noted earlier, which were first recorded in *Puzzled People*[7] half a century ago, still appear in present day surveys of religious and moral beliefs. However, the relative differences between churchgoers and nonchurchgoers are very much stronger and more directional than *Puzzled People* ever imagined.

[7] Mass-Observation, *Puzzled People: A Study of Popular Attitudes to Religion, Ethics, Progress and Politics in a London Borough*, Victor Gollancz, London, 1947.

But can such directionality be found on moral issues? It is scarcely remarkable that regular churchgoers are much more likely than others to give literalistic responses to statements about the Bible and to report that religious beliefs make a great difference to their lives. If that is all a cultural theory of churchgoing could establish, it would be a very meagre offering indeed. Evidence about altruism and teleology is distinctly more interesting and here BHPS data is far more helpful.

Analysing the questions asked in BHPS it is clear that churchgoers do have a significantly greater concern about moral standards than nonchurchgoers. Asked directly about 'declining moral standards', respondents in 1994 were shown a card with four options on it – 'great deal', 'fair amount',' not very much', and 'not at all' – with the instruction to give the answer 'that comes closest to how concerned you are'. 49% opted for 'great deal', 36% for 'fair amount', 13% for 'not very much', and 3% for 'not at all'. This did represent a slight increase in concern compared with the responses two years earlier (47%, 34%, 16%, 3%). Yet amongst weekly churchgoers in 1994 the level of concern was very considerably higher (71%, 21%, 5%, 1%). Testing the data against five different levels of churchgoing, there was again a significant directional relationship: a 'great deal' of concern was expressed by 71% of weekly churchgoers, 61% monthly, 54% occasional, 44% 'practically never', and 48% 'weddings etc.'. This directionality was present in all age-groups, but overall levels increased with age and amongst women. Differences can be seen clearly comparing the 16–24 age-group (35%, 35%, 18%, 19%, 17%) with the 65+ age-group (85%, 82%, 75%, 62%, 75%). However, in all but the youngest age-group a majority of weekly churchgoers expressed a 'great deal' of concern, as did a majority of weekly churchgoing men (64%).

While this does provide evidence for a directional link between churchgoing and moral concern, it does not establish altruistic attitudes as such. Evidence for this can be drawn from the responses to other questions. Immediately following the question about moral standards, the adults surveyed were given a list of five qualities and asked: 'If you had to choose, which quality on this list would you pick as the most important for a child to learn to prepare him or her for life?' Combining the first and second choices of respondents, 64% chose 'think for self', 53% 'help others', 46% 'work hard', 29% 'obey parents', and 7% 'well liked'. However, the 'help others' option again showed evidence of a significant directional relationship to churchgoing: it was given as the first or second choice by 59% of weekly churchgoers, 56% monthly, 55% occasional, 52% 'practically never', and 50% 'weddings etc.'. Once again this shows that differences between churchgoers and nonchurchgoers are relative not absolute. Many share similar concerns, even though churchgoers tend to hold these concerns more strongly.

A similar pattern is evident in the youth sample (11–15 years). Respondents were asked about a number of areas in which 'young people can get into trouble for doing' whether they were 'extremely serious, very serious, fairly serious, or not very serious'. The six areas were stealing money, young people swearing, smoking, telling lies to parents, playing truant and taking drugs. Having answered, they were then asked: 'I am going to read all six things again. Please wait until I have read them all, before you answer, and then tick the box of the thing you think is the most serious of all.' Taking drugs and stealing money were the most serious for all groups, yet the relative proportions differed. So, whereas 84% of nonchurchgoers ticked drugs and 10% stealing, amongst weekly churchgoers this changed to 67% and 18%. And 14% of the weekly churchgoers ticked 'telling lies to parents', in contrast to just 5% of nonchurchgoers. It certainly cannot be claimed that the nonchurchgoing young people in the sample lacked a sense of wrongdoing. Here too differences between churchgoers and nonchurchgoers were relative – a majority in both groups agreed about wrongdoing.

Another question to adults in 1994 provides evidence of altruistic attitudes. Those surveyed were asked to respond to the statement that 'Adult children have an obligation to look after their elderly parents.' Of the whole sample 35% agreed or strongly agreed and 32% disagreed or strongly disagreed, with

33% neither agreeing nor disagreeing. Taking the agree/strongly agree category, a significant directional relationship to churchgoing can be found: 47% of weekly churchgoers, 35% monthly, 34% occasional, 35% 'practically never', and 32% 'weddings etc.'. On this item the youngest age-groups showed the sharpest differences, especially the 16–24 age-group (55%, 44%, 35%, 34%, 33%) and the 25–34 age-group (57%, 36%, 32%, 28%, 31%). Yet amongst older people, the 65+ age-group, the pattern was more mixed (42%, 37%, 28%, 42%, 35%). Curiously both the young and the elderly responses may enshrine altruistic tendencies – the young for believing that elderly parents should be cared for and the elderly for not wishing to be a burden upon their children.

A rather sophisticated pattern of altruism begins to emerge. Altruistic attitudes do seem to be directionally related to differing regularities of churchgoing. They may also be related to the different perspectives that age brings. This evidence is impressive because of the sheer size of the BHPS sample. The ten thousand adult respondents match well the thirteen thousand teenage respondents in the Francis–Kay sample reviewed in the previous chapter. Although questions relevant here are fewer in the BHPS survey than in the Francis–Kay survey, they do allow for more sophisticated directional testing. Taken together they provide very strong evidence indeed for directionality. Yet none of the evidence rehearsed so far moves beyond attitudes. It is possible that whilst churchgoers might mouth more altruistic sentiments than others, they do not actually act differently. It has long been a jibe against churchgoers that they are more moralistic but no more moral in behaviour than nonchurchgoers. Is there evidence in BHPS to suggest otherwise?

A comparison of the membership of different groups in BHPS is helpful here. It was noted in chapter two that the European Value Systems Study Group surveys found that weekly churchgoers, both in Britain and in Europe as a whole, were two or three times more likely than others to be involved in some form of voluntary work. There is also similar evidence in Australia. One recent study there found that 45% of weekly churchgoers were involved in voluntary work, whereas only 18% of nonchurchgoers were.[8] Using BHPS data for 1995, members of religious groups were more than three times as likely to be members of voluntary service groups than others. So, whereas 3.9% of those who did not mention being members of a religious group stated that they were members of a voluntary service group, this rose to 13.6% amongst members of a religious group. The latter were also about twice as likely to belong to a parents association (7.3% as distinct from 3.5%), a community group (3.3% as distinct from 1.5%), a tenants group (19.8% as distinct from 9.7%), an environmental group (6.3% as distinct from 3.6%), and the Scouts or Guides (1.6% as distinct from 0.9%). And they were three times as likely to belong to a political party (7.8% as distinct from 2.6%) or to a pensioners group (2.4% as distinct from 0.9%).

The membership of both religious and voluntary service groups consisted of twice as many women as men. So perhaps women are simply more religious and caring than men. Perhaps in part they are, yet the ratio of religious members to non-members in the voluntary groups was similar amongst men (11.9% to 3.3%) as amongst women (14% to 4.5%). Indeed, 29% of the men who were members of a voluntary service group also belonged to a religious group (amongst women this rose to 39%).

Overall a very high 27% of members of voluntary service groups reported that they were weekly churchgoers (in the sample as a whole it was 11%) and 42% went at least once a month (it was 18% in the whole sample). And 35% of them were members of a religious group, as distinct from 13% of the whole sample. Naturally this means that a majority of members of a voluntary group, or those active within one (they were very largely the same people), were not members of a religious group or regular churchgoers. It is important not to claim too much at this point. So, without knowing more about the detailed background of volunteers, it would be an exaggeration to claim that without actively (or formerly) religious helpers voluntary service

[8] See Peter Bentley and Philip J. Hughes, *Australian Life and the Christian Faith: Facts and Figures*, Christian Research Association, Kew, Victoria, Australia, 1998, p. 66.

Table 6 *Membership comparisons – compared with religious group membership*

Group membership	Standardized coefficients Beta	t	Significance
Women's institute	0.315	15.195	0.000
Voluntary service	0.161	11.982	0.000
Tenants/residents	0.083	8.661	0.000
Women's	0.190	8.092	0.000
Political party	0.122	7.499	0.000
Parents association	0.065	4.376	0.000
Pensioners organisation	0.104	3.960	0.000
Trade union	0.017	2.175	0.030
Other community	0.019	0.844	0.399
Scouts/guides	0.015	0.563	0.573
Environmental	0.004	0.290	0.772
Professional organisation	−0.028	−1.417	0.157
Sports club	−0.020	−2.481	0.013
Social	−0.050	−5.833	0.000

Dependent variable: member of religious group.
Source: BHPS 1995.

work would collapse in Britain. It will also be seen in a moment that some forms of theological orientation appear to be less conducive to voluntary work in the wider community than others. The most that can be claimed is that there does seem to be a strong relationship between voluntary service and some forms of religious membership. Only a third of volunteers reported that they never went to church at all, whereas in the whole sample they amounted to two-thirds. On all of these measures those involved in voluntary service groups were disproportionately religious.

Another, more technical, way of testing this relationship is to do linear regression analysis on the membership of all of the different caring and leisure groups. Table 6 shows the results taking membership of religious groups as the dependent variable and table 7 takes membership of voluntary service groups as the dependent variable. The first of these suggests that membership of women's institutes and voluntary service groups

Table 7 *Membership comparisons – compared with voluntary service group membership*

Group membership	Standardized coefficients Beta	t	Significance
Other community	0.185	12.843	0.000
Religious	0.070	11.982	0.000
Women's institute	0.160	11.655	0.000
Environmental	0.111	11.229	0.000
Women's	0.103	6.669	0.000
Political party	0.071	6.642	0.000
Tenants/residents	0.036	5.659	0.000
Scouts/guides	0.096	5.503	0.000
Pensioners organisation	0.088	5.049	0.000
Sports club	0.020	3.735	0.000
Parents association	0.035	3.539	0.000
Professional organisation	0.030	2.299	0.022
Social	0.001	0.105	0.916
Trade union	−0.006	−1.067	0.286

Dependent variable: member of voluntary service group.
Source: BHPS 1995.

are the most closely linked to membership of religious groups. The second suggests that membership of community, religious, women's institutes, and environmental groups are most closely linked to voluntary service groups. It might be thought that women's institutes are rather different from the caring groups and that perhaps this particular relationship owes more to the predominantly female character of both the religious and voluntary service groups. However, it may well be that there is a more directly causal relationship as well. Many women's institutes meet in church properties and have regular talks on voluntary service in the community. They may also act as informal recruiting places both for church membership and for more active voluntary service.

The groups that are least related to religious membership, in these regression tests, are the leisure groups. So, in table 6, membership of a social group or a sports group is negatively associated with membership of a religious group. Using linear regression on the 1994 question about moral standards, it also appears that members of these two groups differ sharply from members of religious groups. Membership of a sports group does seem to be more closely related to membership of a voluntary service group, in table 7, but membership of a social group does not.

Taken together table 6 and table 7 point to clusters of caring groups within which membership of religious groups is a highly significant factor. Of course the relationship between the groups is complex and there is much evidence of overlapping concerns and membership. These are not entirely separate enclaves and causality is unlikely to be in a single direction. For members of some of these caring groups other factors appear more important than religious belonging. For example, membership of environmental groups is more closely related to membership of voluntary service and political groups than to religious groups. So, amongst voluntary service members 14.4% also belong to an environmental group, whereas amongst respondents who are not voluntary service members this drops to 3.4%. Similarly, among those belonging to a political party environmental membership is 13.7%, dropping to 3.4% among those who do not belong. These are stronger relationships than that already noted with religious membership.

While this is so, the actual membership of political groups (3.1% of the whole sample) and voluntary service groups (4.9%) is very much smaller than that of religious groups (12.7%). As a result only 12% of the members of environmental groups also belong to a political party and 19% to a voluntary service group. In contrast 21% belong to a religious group and 30% of active environmentalists report that they go to church at least once a month – a higher level of support for environmental issues amongst the religious than is sometimes maintained.

Chapter seven will return to the important issue of religion and environmentalism in more detail. Here it is worth noting that the only groups in BHPS which are as large or larger than religious groups are trade union, social and sports groups – and none of these is strongly associated with caring groups. In this respect religious groups are unique. The net result is that a sizeable section of each caring group is also religious. So, if the active membership of each of the groups is examined, 54% of those active in the women's institutes also attend church at least once a month, 42% of those in voluntary service and women's groups, 38% of those in political parties, 33% of those in parents associations and community groups, and 32% of those active in tenants/residents groups. Anglicans are much more likely than Roman Catholics to be active in political parties and environmental groups, whereas Roman Catholics are more likely to be active in trade union groups. Amongst those active in voluntary service groups the balance between churchgoers in the Anglican, Roman Catholic and Free Churches is fairly even. While few caring groups might actually collapse without the active participation of churchgoers, all would be seriously affected.

Together with this BHPS evidence of altruistic beliefs and practices amongst the religiously active, there is also evidence about teleological beliefs and practices. Here too the range of questions is more limited than that in the Francis–Kay survey, yet the size and sophistication of the survey does again make serious directional analysis possible. Adult churchgoers, like their teenage counterparts, do appear to value order and purpose more highly than nonchurchgoers.

In 1991 BHPS asked respondents: 'In politics it is not always possible to obtain everything one might wish. On this card several goals are listed [maintain order; people more say; rising prices; free speech]. If you had to choose among them, which would be your first choice?' Amongst weekly churchgoers 39% chose 'maintain order', 25% 'people more say' and 17% both 'rising prices' and 'free speech'. Amongst nonchurchgoers this order changed: 33% chose 'people more say', 31% 'maintain order', 20% rising prices' and 15% 'free speech'. So apparently order and free speech were valued more highly amongst regular churchgoers than amongst nonchurchgoers, and autonomy and finances amongst the nonchurchgoers more than churchgoers. Adding the two categories of monthly and annual churchgoers, a statistically significant direction is evident on the 'maintain order' option (39%, 36%, 35%, 31%).

A similar directional relationship can be found on questions concerned with sexuality and the bringing up of children. In 1995 BHPS asked for responses to the statement that 'Children need a father to be as closely involved in their upbringing as the mother.' Adding the fifth churchgoing category of 'weddings etc.', the 'strongly agree' responses showed a significant direction from churchgoers to nonchurchgoers (39%, 32%, 30%, 31%, 30%). What is more, amongst weekly churchgoers 'strongly agree' responses were actually higher amongst the 16–24 age-group (44%) than amongst the 65+ age-group (40%). Conversely in the fifth 'weddings etc.' category the difference between the youngest and oldest groups was much sharper (29% and 38%). A similar, but more strident, statement also showed a sharp difference between young churchgoers and nonchurchgoers, but a rather different pattern between young and old churchgoers. So, in response to 'A single parent can bring up children as well as a couple', a significant direction was apparent in the overall pattern of agree/strongly agree responses (29%, 35%, 37%, 41%, 41%). While churchgoers differed from nonchurchgoers in both the 16–25 age-group (34% as distinct from 59%) and the 65+ age-group (21% as distinct from 24%), they also clearly differed from each other.

As will be found repeatedly, most of the oldest group, whether or not they go to church now, support more traditional and ordered beliefs on sexuality. Perhaps this is not too surprising. This is after all a group that mostly went to Sunday school and/or church when young. In contrast, wider differences between churchgoers and nonchurchgoers can often be detected amongst young adults on such issues. In terms of a cultural theory of churchgoing it is precisely this group which is now the least enculturated into Christian beliefs and values.

A strong sense of traditional order is also evident in responses to the 1994 statement that 'The man should be the head of the household.' Again a statistically significant direction is apparent amongst the overall agree/strongly agree responses using the five categories of churchgoing–nonchurchgoing (37%, 22% 20%, 20%, 17%). Amongst weekly churchgoers in the youngest age-group support is surprisingly high (33%), but it soon drops amongst monthly churchgoers (8%). It is highest of all amongst weekly churchgoers in the oldest age-group (44%), ironically many of them widows or spinsters, and still high amongst nonchurchgoers in this group (32%). Least surprising of all,[9] the overall pattern amongst men (43%, 25%, 25%, 23%, 21%) shows higher support in every category than that amongst women (37%, 20%, 16%, 17%, 13%).

In the same year BHPS asked for responses to the statement, 'It is better to divorce than to continue an unhappy marriage.' Agree/strongly agree responses again showed significant directionality in relation to churchgoing–nonchurchgoing (58%, 73%, 77%, 81%, 81%). On this issue young weekly churchgoers (51%) were more traditional than 65+ weekly churchgoers (62%) and both were sharply different from nonchurchgoers in their two age-groups (80% and 81% respectively). In chapter six it will be seen that questions about divorce and remarriage allow for some fascinating longitudinal comparisons. For the moment a striking feature of these data should be noted. Although weekly churchgoers are clearly more hesitant than nonchurchgoers about agreeing that 'it is better to divorce than to continue an unhappy marriage', a majority in every age-group nonetheless does. Later it will be seen that there has been a very considerable change in belief on this issue even amongst regular churchgoers.

Attitudes towards cohabitation also provide striking evidence of changing beliefs even amongst regular churchgoers. On this issue BHPS allows for analysis of both belief and behaviour. The 1994 statement, 'Living together outside of marriage is always wrong', showed a significant directional pattern of agree/strongly agree responses in relation to churchgoing–nonchurchgoing (46%, 21%, 13%, 14%, 11%). Yet a majority supporting this statement was only found in a single category – namely weekly churchgoers in the 65+ age-group (52%). Less than a majority (46%) supported it amongst weekly churchgoers in the 16–24 age-group, and in the 35–44 age-group support dropped still further even amongst weekly churchgoers (30%).

[9] Especially from a perspective of Christian feminism – see Gloria Albrecht's response to Stanley Hauerwas' *In Good Company* in *Scottish Journal of Theology*, 50, 1997, p. 225.

There were sharp differences between churchgoers and nonchurchgoers in every age-group – most striking in the youngest group (46% dropping to 2%) but also amongst the oldest group (52% dropping to 30%). Yet it seems likely that all categories and age-groups have changed radically over the last few years.

These differences are also reflected in patterns of actual cohabitation. Those recorded in BHPS as 'living as married' are more likely to be nonchurchgoers than churchgoers. Nevertheless within each of the five categories of churchgoing–nonchurchgoing, there are some people, including weekly churchgoers, who cohabit (2%, 2%, 5%, 8%, 8%). Again this will be explored further in chapter six. Yet already there is evidence that cohabitation is not condemned by a majority of regular churchgoers and is also practised by a few of them. Amongst weekly churchgoers those most likely to agree that 'living together outside of marriage is always wrong' are the married (48%) and widowed (48%). Whereas those least likely to agree with this are weekly churchgoers who are themselves 'living as married' (12%), divorced (19%), under 16 years old (20%) or separated (22%). Clearly context and age are related to beliefs in this area. The internal culture of churchgoing does not appear to be an island. Outside cultural and social factors cannot be ignored even amongst regular churchgoers.

Order, in the shape of moral order and tradition, does seem to be a characteristic of churchgoers in the BHPS data. This data also provides some evidence amongst adults, as does the Francis–Kay amongst teenagers, that regular churchgoers tend to report that they are happier than others. Asked in 1994, 'Have you recently been feeling unhappy or depressed?', a significant 38% of weekly churchgoers responded 'not at all' as distinct from 33% of nonchurchgoers. Conversely, when asked 'Have you recently been feeling reasonably happy, all things considered?', the pattern of those responding less so/much less shows significant directionality in relation to churchgoing–nonchurchgoing (9%, 13%, 14%, 15%, 12%). The subjective happiness of individuals is notoriously difficult to capture in questionnaire surveys, so it is important not to claim too much about the evidence here. Yet it is consonant with data from the 1964 ABC survey[10] referred to in chapter two. This earlier survey suggested that, whereas 33% of the general population agreed that 'churchgoers lead happier lives than nonchurchgoers', this rose to 69% amongst those attending church at least once a month. And whereas 56% of the sample gave a response 'I am very happy', this rose to 68% amongst the churchgoers. Manifestly, churchgoing is not a panacea for subjective happiness. However it may attract and nurture a sense of purpose, and thus a feeling of wellbeing and happiness, amongst regular churchgoers.

BHPS provides striking data about significantly different levels of Christian belief, altruism and teleology between churchgoers and nonchurchgoers. Together it adds considerably to the data collected from a variety of surveys which were reviewed in the previous chapters. However it also provides one puzzling piece of evidence about the behaviour of churchgoers. As noted earlier, it turns out that churchgoing is an excellent predictor of whether or not individuals smoke. A member of a religious group is less likely to smoke than a member of any other caring or social group. And a regular churchgoer of either gender and in every age-group is significantly less likely to smoke than a nonchurchgoer. So, taking the four categories of churchgoing of BHPS 1991, the pattern of smokers was as clear amongst men (16%, 23%, 30%, 36%) as amongst women (14%, 20%, 28%, 35%). It was lower amongst Methodists (4%, 19%, 14%, 34%) than Anglicans (12%, 17%, 27%, 34%), than Presbyterians (17%, 16%, 33%, 39%) and, indeed, than Roman Catholics (24%, 29%, 42%, 49%), yet it was significantly directional in each. And overall, despite some longitudinal decline in smoking levels, it was just as directional in 1991 (14%, 21%, 29%, 36%) as in 1995 (11%, 16%, 20%, 32%, 32%).

Why is this? What on earth is the link between not smoking and going to church?

One possibility is that the link lies in Christian teaching. For some the Pauline belief that the body is a temple might preclude

[10] ABC Television, *Television and Religion*, London University Press, London, 1965.

them from smoking. It would, though, be quite difficult to establish widespread support for such a theological link. It is possible to imagine sermons making this link, but, frankly, drinking alcohol has been a much more serious target of preaching and teaching especially amongst the Free Churches. Yet the evidence discussed in chapter six suggests that the link between teetotalism and churchgoing is considerably weaker than that between non-smoking and churchgoing. Indeed, in chapter two it was noted that only 30% of weekly churchgoing teenagers in the Francis–Kay survey thought that 'it is wrong to become drunk', as distinct from 53% who thought that 'it is wrong to smoke cigarettes'. And, in any case, differences between churchgoers and nonchurchgoers on smoking are just as evident amongst Roman Catholics as amongst others. It seems highly unlikely that sermons at Sunday Mass would be directed against smoking.

Another possibility is that it is linked to the teleological characteristic of churchgoers. Although I made this link in relation to the Francis–Kay data, it is less credible in relation to adults. They are not, after all, 'under age'. It may be widely held that smoking is unhealthy amongst adults, but it is not illegal. Nor is non-smoking an especially traditional attitude – if anything, the reverse might be more accurate.

Qualitative interviews reported later suggest that this difference may be largely invisible to churchgoers themselves. That is, typically they are neither aware that churchgoers smoke less than others nor are they able to provide a plausible reason themselves for the link. This makes a cultural theory of churchgoing particularly attractive. From this perspective churchgoers are simply part of a culture in which people smoke rather less than those in most other cultures. Without other people in a churchgoing culture actively moralising on the subject, there is little in this culture to encourage them to smoke. Whilst worshipping in church they will certainly be discouraged from smoking, but even at church meetings they may feel that it is inappropriate to smoke. In contrast, members of a social club are likely not just to be encouraged to smoke but to feel different if they do not. Table 8 shows that there are sharp differences –

Table 8 *Membership comparisons – compared with smokers*

Group membership	Standardized coefficients Beta	t	Significance
Religious	0.183	11.925	0.000
Other community	0.285	8.843	0.000
Sports club	0.099	7.174	0.000
Voluntary service	0.137	5.813	0.000
Environmental	0.138	5.365	0.000
Political party	0.096	3.609	0.000
Trade union	0.045	3.152	0.002
Social	0.009	0.583	0.560

Dependent variable: smokers.
Source: BHPS 1995.

using regression analysis – on smoking between various groups. Thus, in BHPS in 1995 amongst members of religious groups only 11% were smokers, amongst environmental groups this increased to 12%, to 16% in voluntary groups, to 17% amongst members of political parties, to 24% within the trade unions, and to 33% in social groups.

Smoking might act as an interesting guide to the social significance of churchgoing. Obviously some regular churchgoers do smoke. Yet on average churchgoers smoke considerably less than nonchurchgoers. Neither age nor gender appear to be responsible for most of this difference, nor does denomination. Rather it appears that the more an individual goes to church the less likely she or he is to smoke. Smoking is for the most part uncharacteristic of this particular culture. So either this culture tends to attract non-smokers, or, perhaps more likely, it makes smokers feel that their habit is less than appropriate. Without active moralising on this subject, religious groups have less smokers than any of the other groups measured in BHPS.

A largely invisible, smokeless culture surrounds churchgoers. More importantly, BHPS data does seem to provide evidence that this is a culture characterised, at least in part, by Faith, Hope and Love. There does appear to be some resemblance here to the church that Paul looked and longed for:

If our common life in Christ yields anything to stir the heart, any loving consolation, any sharing of the Spirit, any warmth of affection or compassion, fill up my cup of happiness by thinking and feeling alike, with the same love for one another, the same turn of mind, and a common care for unity.[11]

Depending upon their theological orientation, some parts of the evidence reviewed here may appeal to churchgoers more than other parts. For example, the data pointing to the high participation of the religiously active in voluntary service groups may be more welcome than those suggesting that churchgoers are more inclined than others to believe that the man should be head of the household. And, naturally, theological responses to cohabitation are likely to vary considerably from one tradition to another. The responses to the BHPS question about biblical literalism are also likely to be greeted very differently by opposed theological traditions. In chapter nine it will be seen that evidence of Christian distinctiveness does not make sharp moral disagreements amongst churchgoers less likely.

Table 9 offers an important early clue about a possible source of this moral disagreement amongst regular churchgoers. The large size of the BHPS sample makes a comparison possible of two distinct churchgoing groups, in which members hold some moral beliefs in common but also have quite wide differences. The first of these groups might be termed 'biblical literalists', consisting of 306 weekly churchgoers who 'strongly agree' with the statement that 'the Bible is God's word and every word in it is true'. The second group, 'biblical non-literalists', consists of 451 weekly churchgoers who give 'neither agree nor disagree', 'disagree' or 'strongly disagree' responses to this statement. The terms literalist and non-literalist are intended to be as neutral as possible. They are certainly preferable to value-laden terms such as 'biblical fundamentalists', 'biblical reductionists', 'biblicists' or even 'Bible Christians'. This division leaves out an intermediate group of 315 weekly churchgoers giving simply an 'agree' response, but it does allow for sharper comparisons to be made between two sizeable groups.

[11] Philippians 2.1–2 (IV).

Table 9 *Two groups of weekly churchgoers*

	Biblical literalists (n = 306)	Biblical non-literalists (n = 451)	Whole sample (n = approx. 9000)
Matters of great concern . . .			
Moral standards	76	62	49
Threat to nature	45	41	43
Ozone layer	42	39	37
Unemployment	61	66	57
Rising prices	46	29	37
Most important political issue (first/second choices combined) . . .			
Maintain order	68	65	62
People more say	49	53	61
Rising prices	40	34	41
Freedom of speech	34	46	36
Cohabitation is wrong	73	25	15
Respondents living as couple	*0.7*	*2.9*	*8.2*
Man should be head of household	66	20	20
Divorce is better than unhappy marriage	50	64	78
Children should care for elderly parents	61	37	35
Qualities which best prepare children for life (first/second choices combined) . . .			
Think for self	45	64	64
Help others	58	61	53
Work hard	34	42	46
Obey parents	57	29	29
Well liked	4	3	7
Respondents active in voluntary service group	*9*	*11*	*5*
Respondents who suffer from anxiety / depression	*10*	*7*	*6*
Respondents who smoke	*8*	*12*	*28*

In percentages.
Biblical literalists = weekly churchgoers who 'strongly agree' that 'the Bible is God's word and every word in it is true'. Non-literalists = weekly churchgoers who 'neither agree nor disagree', 'disagree' or 'strongly disagree'.
Source: BHPS: Wave 4 (1994).

Immediately it is apparent from table 9 that these two groups have a number of characteristics in common which make them distinctive from the sample as a whole. Both groups show a much greater level of concern about moral standards than the whole sample and members of both are much more likely to be active in a voluntary service group and to be non-smokers. They are also both somewhat less likely to accept divorce and cohabitation, or actually to cohabit themselves. Members of both groups are apparently as concerned about environmental issues as others, somewhat less concerned about giving people more say in politics, but somewhat more concerned about unemployment and maintaining political order than the sample as a whole. In addition, they are somewhat more reluctant to advise children that hard work and being well liked are qualities which best prepare them for life – encouraging them instead to help others.

This mixture of altruistic and teleological features is held in common by members of these two churchgoing groups. However, many of the ways that these two broad features are particularised by them differ quite considerably. Biblical literalists are generally more concerned than other people about issues – even about rising prices – and are also more likely to suffer from anxiety or depression. They are, though, most distinct from non-literalists in their concern for moral order in personal relationships rather than in socio-political issues. So, it is the literalist group which differs so sharply from the whole sample in its beliefs that it is wrong to cohabit and that the man should be head of the household. Additional evidence from the intermediate group shows these differences to be statistically highly significant. Adding this group, there is a clear directional pattern – in the literalist, intermediate and non-literalist groups – of strongly agree/agree responses that it is wrong to cohabit (73%, 50%, 25%) and that the man should be head of the household (66%, 41%, 20%). The rank ordering by literalists of qualities for children is also distinct: thinking for self and working hard are valued much less, and obeying parents (57%, 45%, 29%) and caring for parents (61%, 50%, 37%) much more. Honouring parents seems to be placed higher by this distinctive group than a principle of autonomy or hard-work (despite having a sociological reputation for individuality and hard-work).

Weekly churchgoers in the biblical non-literalist group share the values of the whole sample more closely than do the literalists. Their environmental attitudes, concern to maintain political order, belief in adults having their say and children thinking for themselves and working hard, are close to those of the whole sample. Unlike the literalists, but like the whole sample, they do not rate obedience to parents very highly. Yet they are less concerned than all others about rising prices, somewhat more concerned about unemployment and about children helping others, and distinctly more concerned about freedom of speech. Members of this group are also more likely than any others to be active in a voluntary service group. In several respects, then, this group shows a distinctive pattern of love of neighbour.

The difference noted here between these two groups of frequent churchgoers on voluntary work adds an important nuance to the connection noted earlier in the European Value Systems Study Group and Australian surveys. Noting a connection between church membership/activism and volunteer work in American surveys, John Wilson and Thomas Janoski show that this connection is actually very weak among conservative Protestants. In contrast, it is strong among middle-aged Protestants and among Catholics of all ages. These results, they argue, 'suggest caution in generalizing about the connection between religious preference or involvement and volunteering because this connection depends on the theological interpretation of volunteering and the significance attached to frequent church attendance'.[12] They suggest, for example, that conservative Protestant churches may both 'discourage more "secular" activities among their members' and that 'a greater proportion of their organizational activities cater to their own members, are aimed at maintaining the social fabric of the church, or are thinly-disguised missionary enterprises'.[13] A similar explanation

[12] John Wilson and Thomas Janoski, 'The Contribution of Religion to Volunteer Work', *Sociology of Religion*, 56:2, 1995, p. 137.

[13] *Ibid.* p. 149.

may account for the difference between the biblical literalists and non-literalists in the BHPS data. Nevertheless, the difference here is much slighter than that noted by Wilson and Janoski. And the difference between churchgoers (in either group) and nonchurchgoers on this issue is, once again, much sharper in Britain than in America.

The BHPS data suggest that these two groups of weekly churchgoers have rather different, but nonetheless distinctive, ways of expressing their altruism and teleology. Both do show distinctive patterns of concern and action for others which are higher than those to be found in the sample as a whole. They also show a higher concern about order, albeit in rather different areas. Of course these differences can be exaggerated. Neither group has a monopoly of particular concerns or actions and neither differs absolutely from the whole sample. Once again these are relative differences. Even amongst weekly churchgoers who strongly agree that 'the Bible is God's word and every word in it is true' there are two members who cohabit and there are many more who are reluctant to say that cohabiting is actually wrong. Half of this group also seems to accept divorce, despite an obvious clash with biblical literalism.

However, set within a broader context of Christian belief, altruism and teleology, the BHPS data as a whole do suggest that there are challenging and theologically relevant differences to be detected between churchgoers and nonchurchgoers. These differences will be explored next in new data from British Social Attitudes.

CHAPTER 5

Faith in British Social Attitudes surveys

In much of the New Testament there is a tension between the now and the not yet. In the Synoptic Gospels this tension takes the form of the Kingdom of God which is already present in the life and ministry of Jesus and the fulfilment of the Kingdom which still lies in the future. Appropriately, in the liturgical version of the Lord's Prayer the phrase 'your kingdom come' is balanced by 'for yours is the kingdom'. In Paul's writings also there is an oscillation between lyrical depictions of the fruits of the Spirit within the church and denunciations of the shortcomings of his fellow Christians. The trouble for Paul is that Christians 'are no better than pots of earthenware to contain this treasure'.[1] Nevertheless for him:

> The love of Christ leaves us no choice, when once we have reached the conclusion that one man died for all and therefore all humankind has died. His purpose in dying for all was that people, while still in life, should cease to live for themselves, and should live for him who for their sake died and was raised to life. With us therefore worldly standards have ceased to count in our estimate of any man; even if once they counted in our understanding of Christ, they do so now no longer. When anyone is united to Christ, there is a new world; the old order has gone, and a new order has already begun.[2]

Once again this passage depicts the three distinctive features of Christian life – namely Christian belief, altruism and teleology. It is the belief that Christ died for others that they might live in him which is fundamental to this passage. Specifically Christian theology – christology, the cross, resurrection and

[1] 2 Cor. 4.7 (IV).
[2] 2 Cor. 5.14–17 (IV).

atonement – is essential here. Altruism and teleology are the fruits of this work of Christ in humankind. As a result Christians should 'cease to live for themselves' and enter 'a new order'. The language here is still dynamic: the new order is not yet completed but it has 'already begun'. Faith, Hope and Love are already manifest amongst the Corinthian Christians, despite their being 'pots of earthenware'.

This tension between the now and the not yet has already been illustrated using data from the British Household Panel Survey. As already noted, the sheer size of this survey allows fine distinctions to be made with confidence when analysing the data. However, the range of relevant questions is fairly limited – naturally this survey is concerned with many demographic features of the households in the sample which have little or no bearing upon churchgoing. Data from eleven British Social Attitudes surveys (BSA)[3] and five Northern Ireland Social Attitudes surveys (NISA) offer a much richer choice of questions, which can sometimes be tested over a full decade. The sample size of each of these BSA and NISA surveys is much smaller than BHPS. As a result some care must be taken when making finer distinctions. Nevertheless, when set alongside BHPS, the data from BSA and NISA, sometimes amalgamated from more than one survey, do provide a remarkably rich and largely unexploited resource for analysing the moral and social characteristics of churchgoers.

The BSA surveys have been carried out annually since 1983 (and NISA since 1989), except in 1988 and 1992, and have been designed to be fielded as a series of surveys, to allow the monitoring and understanding of trends in attitudes, and to examine the relative rates at which different sorts of attitudes change. Not all questions or groups of questions are included in each fieldwork round. However, unlike BHPS, it is a great advantage of the BSA and NISA surveys that they have always contained questions about respondents' religion/denomination (used in table 3) and their attendance at 'services or meetings

[3] Please note again that the data used here were made available through Data Archive. Neither the original collectors of the data nor the Archive bear any responsibility for the analyses or interpretations presented here.

connected with your religion' (used in table 4 and table 5). Because these two questions are asked together in the BSA and NISA surveys, the small number of those attending services or meetings in non-Christian faiths can be taken out of the data (it is rather too disparate a group to be treated as a single whole). In BHPS this is only possible in the first wave (as in table 4) and, as a result, the data in chapter four always included both Christians and non-Christians. In this and chapters six and seven the term 'churchgoers' really will refer only to those going to a Christian church.

In 1991 BSA and NISA asked a series of questions specifically about religious belief and belonging. The questions were designed as part of the much wider International Social Survey Programme[4] and allow a number of important comparisons of religious belief to be made between churchgoers and non-churchgoers. They strongly support and enhance the conclusions drawn from other surveys in earlier chapters. Most questions show a clear and statistically significant directional relation[5] between the regularity of churchgoing and the strength of Christian beliefs. Thus those who go to church more regularly than others generally have higher levels of Christian belief, whereas those who never go tend to have significantly lower levels. Conversely, the less people go to church, the more they seem to be attracted to 'new age' beliefs.

As was noted in chapter two from Australian data,[6] a belief in a personal God does seem to be closely linked to churchgoing. Table 1 shows how this belief seems to have declined in the British population from 43% in the 1940s/50s to 31% in the 1990s. The latter is very similar to BSA 1991 responses to the statement, 'There is a God who concerns Himself with every human being personally', asking, 'Please tick one box on each

4 See Andrew Greeley, 'Religion in Britain, Ireland and the USA', in Roger Jowell, Lindsay Brook, Gillian Prior and Bridget Taylor (eds.), *British Social Attitudes the 9th Report*, Social and Community Planning Research, Dartmouth, 1992.

5 Somers' ordinal by ordinal directional test in SPSS has again been used on all directional tests in this chapter. The samples in BSA and NISA are smaller than those in BHPS, so those referred to as 'significant' all recorded a level of statistical significance at between 0.000 and 0.006.

6 See Peter Bentley and Philip J. Hughes, *Australian Life and the Christian Faith: Facts and Figures*, Christian Research Association, Kew, Victoria, Australia, 1998.

line' (BOXES: 'strongly agree; agree; neither agree nor disagree; disagree; strongly disagree; can't choose' – unless otherwise stated, in this chapter and the next, 'agree' will combine agree/strongly agree and 'disagree' will combine disagree/strongly disagree). Those agreeing in Britain amounted to 32%. However in Northern Ireland, with much higher levels of churchgoing, 74% agreed (see table 2). Four levels of churchgoing can be safely distinguished in the BSA and NISA surveys – weekly, monthly, seldom and never. On this basis there is a clear and statistically significant relation between those who go to church most regularly in Britain and those who agree that there is a God concerned personally with human beings (84%, 62%, 37%, 21%). The 84% of weekly churchgoers here compares closely with the MORI 1993 poll[7] noted earlier. The latter used the same response options for the similar statement 'There is a personal God who interacts with the world and its people', and found that 80% of weekly and 71% of fortnightly churchgoers agreed.

To the statement, 'The course of our lives is decided by God', BSA 1991 also found that there was a highly significant directional relation, albeit at a lower level of positive responses, amongst churchgoers–nonchurchgoers (53%, 28%, 21%, 12%). A slightly higher, but again significantly directional, level of positive responses was found to the statement, 'To me, life is meaningful only because God exists' (68%, 27%, 20%, 8%). Although weekly churchgoers undoubtedly react differently to others on all of these questions, their responses do not match those recorded for British Muslims and Black Pentecostals in the 1993 Independent Television survey[8] cited earlier. There, to the statement, 'Without religious beliefs life is meaningless', 91% of Muslims and 89% of Black Pentecostals responded positively.

How do these results compare with those in Northern Ireland? Before answering this question it is worth thinking for

[7] MORI, *Christian Beliefs*, Research Study Conducted for BBC Songs of Praise, Nov. 1993.

[8] Barry Gunter and Rachel Viney (eds.), *Seeing is Believing: Religion and Television in the 1990s*, John Libbey/ITC, London, 1994.

a moment about what differing theories of religious change might predict. Persistence, separation, secularisation and cultural theories might make very different predictions:

Persistence theories might claim that *overall* levels of religious belief and belonging will differ very little between Britain and Northern Ireland. Faced with some of the *prima facie* evidence, this would be quite difficult to establish. BSA 1991 and NISA 1991 present sharp differences of overall Christian belief and belonging at almost every point. For example, in response to the question, 'Now thinking about the present, how often do you attend religious services', in Britain 14% respond 'nearly every week' or more, whereas in Northern Ireland this reaches 53%. Asked how often they attended 'when you were around 11 or 12', in Britain 52% respond in this way, whereas 86% do in Northern Ireland. And on every item of Christian belief there are sharp differences between Britain and Northern Ireland. To give a single example, in Britain 24% respond either 'I don't believe in God' or 'I don't know whether there is a God and I don't believe there is any way to find out' and 23% that 'I know that God really exists and I have no doubts about it': in Northern Ireland the first figure reduces to just 2% and the second increases to 61%.

One argument that persistence theorists might use is that, although Christian believing and belonging are undoubtedly higher in Northern Ireland than in Britain, there are other forms of religious believing and belonging in Britain which compensate. BSA 1991 and NISA 1991 do provide some evidence to this effect. For example, in Britain 28% of the whole sample believe that 'a person's star sign at birth, or horoscope, can affect the course of their life', whereas only 17% do in Northern Ireland. There is also a small difference amongst those accepting that 'good luck charms sometimes do bring good luck' (22% and 20% respectively) and that 'some fortune tellers really can foresee the future' (40% and 31%). Conversely 74% in Northern Ireland and only 63% in Britain have never 'felt as though you were really in touch with someone who had died'. Yet these small differences hardly compensate for the wide differences on specifically Christian beliefs between the two countries, nor does the greater, but still small, presence of adherents of non-Christian faiths in Britain. Despite his long commitment to a persistence theory,[9] Andrew Greeley concludes from his review of this evidence that 'the differences need to be taken seriously', albeit adding rather optimistically that, 'the British are more religious than they think they are . . . they are also possibly more religious than they used to be'.[10] Table 1 and table 2, however, make it unlikely that they have become more religious over the last half century.

A separation theory might acknowledge differences between Britain and Northern Ireland more readily. However, since it plays down a causal link between declining levels of belief and belonging, it would not predict a directional relation between the two in both Britain and Northern Ireland. On this theory Christian belief can persist even when Christian belonging declines. In part, it will be seen, the NISA evidence does seem to support this. However, it fits less comfortably with the BSA evidence. And in both NISA and BSA 1991 there is a statistically significant direction on every item of Christian belief measured against the four levels of churchgoing–nonchurchgoing.

A secularisation theory might offer a rather different prediction, especially if it is believed that churchgoing decline results primarily from a loss of Christian belief. Evidence of churchgoing decline has already been seen in table 2. Although churchgoing rates are still much higher in Northern Ireland, there is some evidence in NISA suggesting that it is nevertheless declining there as well. Asked about their attendance now at religious services, 45% of the men claimed at least 'nearly every week' and 15% 'never'. Yet asked about the attendance of their fathers when respondents were young, 'nearly every week' increases to 53% and 'never' declines to 9%. A similar difference is evident amongst women and their mothers – 'nearly every week' increases from 59% to 65% and 'never' declines from 11% to 4%. A similar process, albeit starting at much lower levels, can be found in British statistics – men increasing

9 See Andrew Greeley, *Unsecular Man: The Persistence of Religion*, SCM Press, London, 1973.

10 Greeley, 'Religion in Britain', in Jowell et al. (eds.), *British Social Attitudes*, 1992, p. 69.

Table 10 *Faith: Britain and Northern Ireland compared*

	Weekly churchgoers		Nonchurchgoers	
	Britain (n = 149)	N. Ireland (n = 415)	Britain (n = 569)	N. Ireland (n = 122)
Strongly agree/agree that . . .				
There is a God who concerns Himself personally with every human being	84	89	21	48
To me life is only meaningful because God exists	68	66	8	20
The course of our life is decided by God	53	62	12	26
Right and wrong should be based on God's laws	77	82	27	40
The Bible is the actual word of God and it is to be taken literally, word for word	23	39	4	15
Definitely/probably believe in . . .				
Life after death	83	79	39	55
Heaven	89	93	45	69
Hell	62	77	19	53
The devil	64	73	17	48
Religious miracles	81	84	28	42
Some faith healers really do have God-given powers	68	66	41	54
A person's star sign at birth, or horoscope, can affect the course of their future	19	14	28	23
Good luck charms sometimes do bring good luck	14	17	25	26
Some fortune tellers really can foresee the future	33	25	41	42

Table 10 (*cont.*)

	Weekly churchgoers		Nonchurchgoers	
	Britain (n = 149)	N. Ireland (n = 415)	Britain (n = 569)	N. Ireland (n = 122)
Pray once or more a week	87	91	16	30
Believe definitely that there should be daily prayers in all state schools	66	65	28	34
Describe yourself as extremely or somewhat religious	86	87	29	24

In percentages.
Sources: BSA and NISA 1991.

from 10% to 18% and declining from 40% to 27%, and women increasing from 17% to 26% and declining from 34% to 16%. In both countries it seems that the present generation goes to church less than their parents did in the past.

The indications of churchgoing decline in Northern Ireland here are slight, but they do seem to fit a secularisation theory. What then about belief? If churchgoing decline does result primarily from a loss of faith, then a comparison of BSA and NISA should show that nonchurchgoers in both samples have similar low levels of belief – or at least similar low levels of Christian belief. The overall higher levels of Christian belief in Northern Ireland compared with Britain, on this theory, would result simply from a greater section of the population there going to church.

In contrast, a cultural theory would expect to find evidence of directionality in both Britain and Northern Ireland. There should be clear evidence in both countries of similar high levels of Christian belief and low levels of 'new age' belief amongst regular churchgoers compared with nonchurchgoers. It is also possible that, since churchgoing decline is so much more modest in Northern Ireland, levels of Christian belief there will be higher than in Britain amongst irregular churchgoers and nonchurchgoers. Finally a cultural theory would predict that, amongst the many nonchurchgoers in Britain today, higher levels of Christian belief will be found amongst those who went regularly to church as children than amongst those who never went. Thus a culture of Christian belief which is gradually being lost in Britain should still be detectable in Northern Ireland.

This final pattern is the one that is illustrated clearly in table 10 and in table 11. Together they really do vindicate the cultural theory of churchgoing. On every item of Christian belief in table 10 there are obvious differences between weekly churchgoers and nonchurchgoers in both Britain and Northern Ireland. If the intermediate levels of 'monthly' and 'occasional' churchgoers are added, then on every single item of Christian belief in both countries there is a decrease at each level and without exception. Again using a statistical directional test each item proves to be highly significant. There can be little doubt that Christian belief and belonging are intimately related in both countries.

In addition, whilst there is a close correspondence of Christian belief on most items amongst weekly churchgoers in the two countries, there are considerable differences amongst nonchurchgoers. Indeed, the level of Christian belief amongst nonchurchgoers in Northern Ireland exceeds any of the British weighted means recorded in table 1. Thus the 55% of nonchurchgoers in Northern Ireland who believe in life after death is higher than the 49% recorded half a century ago for the British population as a whole: and the 69% believing in heaven, 53% in hell and 48% in the devil are very considerably higher than any of the British averages. For a cultural theory this is exactly what is to be expected in a context such as Northern Ireland. NISA shows that two-thirds of these nonchurchgoers report that as children they went to church 'almost every week' (and, amongst this two-thirds, belief in life after death increases to 62%). In contrast, BSA shows that only one-third of British nonchurchgoers went regularly when young – and a quarter never went at all. Contrary to a secularisation theory which regards nonchurchgoing as a product of loss of Christian belief, the Northern Ireland evidence shows that nonchurchgoers there still continue to pray regularly and retain a surprisingly high level of Christian belief. In terms of a cultural theory, the latter derives largely from the culture of churchgoing which most nonchurchgoers in Northern Ireland, but not in Britain, experienced as children. Ironically, although the Northern Irish apparently do not seem to see themselves as any more religious than do the British, on most Christian indicators they do seem to be.

Table 11 makes it possible to take this analysis deeper still by comparing two different groups of British nonchurchgoers. Both groups consist only of those who respond that today either they 'never' go to church or they have 'no religion' and were not brought up with any religion. The first of these groups respond that, in addition, they 'never' went to church as children aged about 11 or 12, whereas the second respond that they went then 'nearly every week' or even more. On every item of faith there are differences, and sometimes very wide differences, between these two groups. As expected by a cultural theory, it is the second group which shows the higher levels, often approximating to those in the sample as a whole. The theistic responses of these two groups are quite distinct: for example, well over three times as many of the second group as the first group state, 'I believe in God now and I always have.' Apparently neither group prays very much, but the second resists saying 'I never pray' and sees itself as distinctly more 'religious'. Views on the Bible, heaven, miracles and faith healers are also clearly different. Most striking of all, more than two-thirds of the second group believe that there should be daily prayers in all state schools, whereas only about one in six of the first group do. If the strongest response to the last question is taken (i.e. those responding 'definitely'), then none of the first group yet almost a third of the second agree. It really does seem that people who never go to church now, but yet who were brought up doing so, have residual beliefs and affections for Christian belief and practice. In contrast, the never-nevers are distinctly more distant from Christian culture.

Table 11 *Faith in two groups of nonchurchgoers*

	Nonchurchgoers as children (n = 126)	Weekly churchgoers as children (n = 274)	Whole sample (n = 1206)
'I know God really exists and I have no doubts about it' *or* 'While I have doubts, I feel that I do believe in God'	19	40	49
'I don't believe in God' *or* 'I don't know whether there is a God and I don't believe there is any way to find out'	54	27	24
'I don't believe in God now and I never have'	40	6	12
'I believe in God now and I always have'	11	39	46
'The Bible is the . . . actual word of God and it is to be taken literally, word for word . . . *or* . . . inspired word of God but not everything should be taken literally, word for word'	13	32	40
Never pray	70	41	32
Pray at least every fortnight	6	13	35
Strongly agree/agree that . . .			
There is a God who concerns Himself personally with every human being	4	18	32
Definitely/probably believe in . . .			
Life after death	31	35	47
Heaven	22	40	47
Hell	12	16	25

Table 11 (*cont.*)

	Nonchurchgoers as children (n = 126)	Weekly churchgoers as children (n = 274)	Whole sample (n = 1206)
The devil	10	17	24
Religious miracles	12	26	38
Some faith healers . . .	25	42	45
Daily prayers in all state schools	17	69	64
Describe yourself as extremely or somewhat religious	7	29	41

In percentages.
Both groups of nonchurchgoers consist of those answering 'never' or 'no religion' now.
Source: BSA 1991.

It is worth noting at this stage that some (albeit smaller) differences can also be traced in responses to a variety of questions on moral issues. Chapters six and seven will examine these questions in much more depth and will see how they can be related to different regularities of churchgoing. Here only the differences between these two groups of nonchurchgoers need be noted. However, a word of warning is necessary first. Even amongst adult nonchurchgoers those who went regularly as children are more likely to be women and elderly than those adult nonchurchgoers who never went as children. Sunday school attendance, which was a much stronger feature before the Second World War than it has been since, has also long had a gender imbalance. As a result the differences between the two groups, especially on sexual issues, will owe something to gender and age differences. (It would soon become tedious in this and chapters six and seven to set out all age and gender differences in the data, so this will only be done either when they make a very large impression or, alternatively, when they make less than might be expected.)

With this caveat in mind, there do appear to be marked

moral differences between the two groups of nonchurchgoers, with the never-never nonchurchgoers being significantly different from the population at large. So, whereas 18% of the whole sample in BSA 1991 thought that it was always or almost always wrong 'if a man and a woman have sexual relations before marriage', in the never-never group only 4% responded in this way (never-once group 13%). Similarly, whereas 83% of the whole sample responded that 'a married person having sexual relations with someone other than his or her husband or wife' is wrong, in the never-never group it was 71% (never-once 83%). And 61% of the sample thought 'sexual relations between two adults of the same sex' to be wrong, yet in the never-never group it was 47% (never-once 62%). Similarly, 35% of the sample believed that divorce in Britain should be more difficult to obtain, but only 28% of the never-never group (never-once 36%). The never-once group was also much more likely than the never-never group to believe that censorship is necessary to uphold morals (59% as distinct from 33%) and that blasphemous books and films should be banned (25% as distinct from 10%).

The never-once group were also more likely than the never-nevers to respond that 'I can't refuse when someone comes to the door with a collecting tin' (62% as distinct from 34%) Most (but not all) of the questions on personal honesty also suggest differences between these two groups of adult nonchurchgoers. For example, given the situation 'A person gives the government incorrect information about himself to get government benefits that he is not entitled to', 92% of the never-onces thought this to be wrong but only 67% of the never-nevers. Using the same order of negative responses, similar differences between the two groups were found as follows:

A company employee exaggerates his claims for travel expenses over a period and makes £75 (70% and 47%)

A man gives a £5 note for goods he is buying in a big store. By mistake, he is given change for a £10 note. He notices but keeps the change (79% and 57%)

In making an insurance claim, a man whose home has been burgled exaggerates the value of what was stolen by £150 (79% and 62%)

A householder is having a repair job done by a local plumber. He is told that if he pays cash he will not be charged VAT. So he pays cash (47% and 29%)

Returning to table 10, differences between British and Northern Irish nonchurchgoers largely disappear when it comes to 'new age' beliefs – horoscopes, lucky charms and fortune tellers. In both countries weekly churchgoers hold these beliefs less strongly than do nonchurchgoers and in both they are minority beliefs. Specifically in Britain, the two nonchurchgoing groups differ little from each other on these beliefs. Contrary to a persistence theory there is no evidence here that 'new age' beliefs compensate more in Britain for a comparative loss of Christian beliefs. Contrary, also, to those forms of secularisation theory which predict an increase of rationalist belief with the demise of organised religion, nonchurchgoers in both countries seem to be more susceptible to these 'new age' beliefs than regular churchgoers.

These directional links – between regular churchgoing and Christian beliefs, on the one hand, and between nonchurchgoing and 'new age' beliefs, on the other – are confirmed by the more limited data in BSA 1993. The claim that 'astrology has scientific truth' finds stronger support amongst nonchurchgoers than amongst regular churchgoers (26%, 42%, 44%, 46%), as does a claim that religious studies in school is unimportant (6%, 16%, 21%, 43%). Indeed, two-thirds of those depicting themselves as having 'no religion' support the latter claim. Conversely the claim, 'We believe too often in science, and not enough in feelings and faith' shows significantly stronger support amongst churchgoers (64%, 51%, 51%, 50%), as does the claim, 'Human beings should respect nature because it was created by God' (86%, 75%, 66%, 61%). In contrast, they are supported by only some two-fifths of the no-religion group.

The differences between these groups are well illustrated by the BSA 1993 choice between three claims – 'nature is sacred because it is created by God'; 'nature is spiritual or sacred in itself'; and 'nature is important, but not spiritual or sacred'. Respondents were asked to choose just one of the three options. Majority support for the first option is found only amongst weekly churchgoers (54%), and has little support amongst nonchurchgoers (16%) and the no-religion group (8%). Majority support for the third option is found especially in the no-religion group (66%) and shows a clear directionality between churchgoers and nonchurchgoers (35%, 39%, 57%, 59%). The middle option finds highest support (16%) amongst no-religion and monthly groups, but little support amongst weekly churchgoers (4%). So, in theory, three distinct groups – regular churchgoers, nonchurchgoers and the no-religion group – agree that nature is to be taken seriously. In the sample as a whole only 19% actually disagreed with the claim, 'Human beings should respect nature because it was created by God.' Yet, when given a choice of these three options, God language is clearly more attractive to regular churchgoers, and secularised, or alternatively 'new age', language to the no-religion group, with nonchurchgoers responding more ambivalently.

These divisions over God language are illustrated further by the BSA question about belief in God, asked in 1991, 1993 and 1995. An earlier chapter noted that responses to this rather complicated question suggest that there has been an overall decline in theistic belief even within these four years. Those reporting, either 'While I have doubts, I feel that I do believe in God' or 'I know God really exists and I have no doubts about it', declined from 49% to 44%. A clear and statistically highly significant directionality can be found amongst churchgoers–nonchurchgoers across the data and in all age-groups. So, BSA 1993 shows a clear pattern amongst those responding 'I know God really exists . . . ': in the whole sample (76%, 33%, 28%, 18%), in the 18–34 age-group (65%, 29%, 25%, 19%), in the 35–59 age-group (75%, 30%, 27%, 15%) in the 60+ age-group (79%, 41%, 32%, 23%), amongst men (71%, 36%, 24%, 13%) and amongst women (76%, 32%, 30%, 22%). These are remarkably consistent results: churchgoers and nonchurchgoers are very different from each other even across age and gender differences. The no-religion group is different again: in no age-group and in neither gender group do more than 10% of them give this response. Conversely, 47% of the no-religion group respond, either 'I don't believe in God' or 'I don't know whether there is a God and I don't believe there is any way to find out'. The non-believing pattern amongst churchgoers–nonchurchgoers is again distinct (0%, 6%, 11%, 19%).

Behind these statistics there are some rather important implications for Christian ethics. Asked blandly, a question about attitudes towards nature which includes language about God as creator is accepted by a majority, but not an overwhelming majority, of respondents. Frequently such evidence has been taken as proof that some forms of 'public theology' are still plausible to the British. This claim is typically related to the fact that generalised questions about belief in God still show majority support in Britain (albeit declining support, as table 1 suggests). The advantage of the BSA questions is that they make it possible successfully to probe behind this apparent acceptance by the British public of theistic explanations. Given a choice of options, a majority of respondents (57%) choose the most secular, namely 'Nature is important, but not spiritual or sacred.' And given a graded set of choices about belief in God, only 23% of the whole sample opt for 'I know God really exists . . .'. This is hardly surprising since the nonchurchgoing and no-religion groups in 1993 amount to more than three-fifths of the sample. It appears, then, that given the choice, a large and increasing section of the British population avoids using theistic language and does not hold strong theistic beliefs. This section is not entirely secular – a sizeable minority within it is apparently sympathetic to 'new age' beliefs and about half agrees that 'modern science does more harm than good' – but it is becoming more distant from theistic, let alone christological, beliefs. The steep decline in churchgoing amongst young people in Britain, Europe, Australia and indeed several other Western countries, already noted in chapter three, is likely to make theistic language increasingly strange to many people in the future.

Taken as a whole the new data from BSA and NISA add considerably to that reviewed earlier. The close link between churchgoing and Christian belief is strongly confirmed and shown to be significantly directional in character. The more individuals go to church now, or in their past as children, the more likely they are to hold Christian beliefs. In addition, a loss of these beliefs does seem to follow and not precede a decline in churchgoing. Within a society which retains high levels of churchgoing amongst children, Christian beliefs are likely to remain relatively strong even amongst adult nonchurchgoers. Churchgoing does seem to be an identifiable culture which nurtures Christian beliefs.

Table 12 makes possible finer distinctions amongst regular churchgoers within this broad finding. Using BHPS data in the previous chapter a distinction was made between 'biblical literalists' and 'biblical non-literalists' amongst weekly churchgoers. Unfortunately the data did not allow for any comparisons between these two groups on Christian beliefs. They did, however, allow the important moral and social comparisons shown in table 9. An obvious weakness of this distinction is that it defines the first group rather more clearly than the second. So the first group consists of those weekly churchgoers in BHPS 1994 who 'strongly agree' with the statement, 'the Bible is God's word and every word in it is true'. Yet the second group consists of those who rather diffusely dissent from this statement, responding 'neither agree nor disagree', 'disagree' or 'strongly disagree'. It is possible that the looseness of the dissenting group might have accentuated some of the moral and social differences recorded.

BSA and NISA 1991 allow for a more even distinction. Respondents in both surveys were asked: 'Which of these statements comes closest to describing your feelings about the Bible?' They were then instructed to tick one of the following: 'The Bible is the actual word of God and it is to be taken literally, word for word'; 'The Bible is the inspired word of God but not everything should be taken literally, word for word'; 'The Bible is an ancient book of fables, legends, history and moral teachings recorded by man.' Not surprisingly, most weekly churchgoers chose the first or second option – even in Britain less than one in fourteen chose the third. As can be seen from table 10 more weekly churchgoers opted for the first in Northern Ireland than in Britain. Nevertheless in both surveys a majority chose the second. The very fact that most positively

Table 12 *Faith in two groups of weekly churchgoers* (Britain and Northern Ireland 1991 combined)

	Biblical literalists (n = 190)	Biblical non-literalists (n = 284)	Whole sample (n = 2069)
Definitely believe in . . .			
Heaven	92	75	40
Hell	68	50	30
Devil	61	50	25
Religious miracles	73	57	27
Life after death	71	70	35
Strongly agree . . .			
There is a God who concerns Himself with every human being personally	73	50	25
To me life is meaningful only because God exists	46	32	14
'I know God really exists and I have no doubts about it'	91	73	42
'I believe in God now, and I always have'	94	88	62
Had a turning point in life when you made a new and personal commitment to religion	52	50	22
Been 'born again' or had a 'born again' experience – a turning point in your life when you committed yourself to Christ (Northern Ireland only)	33	24	18
Attended church nearly every week as a child aged 11 or 12	95	91	69
Describe yourself as extremely/very religious	41	21	10
Definitely think there should be daily prayers in all state schools	84	64	43

In percentages.
Sources: BSA 1991 and NISA 1991 weighted equally.

chose the first or the second makes a distinction based upon these two options highly desirable. It is precisely this that is reported in table 12.

Of course the great merit of the BHPS survey is its size. On its own, BSA 1991 makes a division amongst the relatively small group of weekly churchgoers more risky. However, given the fact that on most issues weekly churchgoers in Britain and Northern Ireland appear so similar, it is tempting to combine them. The BSA and NISA groups, both responding to the same questions in 1991, can together make a reasonable sample which is capable of further division. Of course they have been weighted equally, since otherwise the larger NISA sample of weekly churchgoers would have swamped the BSA data.

The most striking finding in table 12 is that on almost every item of Christian belief the biblical literalists express greater levels of certainty and definiteness than non-literalists. Only the strongest expressions of belief are recorded here, since, if 'agree' responses are added to 'strongly agree' and 'probably believe' to 'definitely believe', the distinction between the two groups tends to disappear. It is not that the non-literalists lack faith. Even on this measure, the levels of belief that they record are clearly distinct from the sample as a whole. Rather what they seem to lack is the certainty of the literalists. So, to take a single example, almost all of the literalists opt for 'I know that God really exists and I have no doubts about it' rather than 'While I have doubts, I feel that I do believe in God.' Nevertheless, so do almost three-quarters of the non-literalists, compared with considerably less than half of the sample as whole.

Of course literalists themselves are likely to interpret table 12 rather differently. They might regard it as supplying clear evidence that non-literalists lack faith. The latter have become partly secularised and assimilated to the lack of faith of the rest of the world. Secularisation theorists, too, may be tempted to go down this path. Table 13 might, though, make them pause for a moment. It suggests that both groups are distinctive from society at large – albeit rather differently distinctive. That, however, must be for chapters six and seven.

What is worth noting now is that 'certainty' has too often

been conflated with 'religiosity' in previous sociological analyses in this area. The report *Religion in Britain and Northern Ireland* on the 1968 ITA survey[11] provides a clear example of this. The authors of this report constructed a 'religiosity scale' based upon responses to nine questions about religious attitudes and beliefs. In four of these, respondents had to give a 'certain' reply to be counted on the scale – certain that 'to lead a good life it is necessary to have some religious belief', that 'without belief in God life is meaningless', that 'religion helps to maintain the standards and morals of society', and that 'there is a God'. In addition, they had to agree that 'God watches each person' and that 'they are very likely to think of God when they are worried'. Only on three questions were they allowed to give less than certain or definite responses in order to qualify for the scale – namely, that they were 'very religious or fairly religious', 'very likely or fairly likely to think of God when they are happy', and that 'their everyday lives are affected a great deal or quite a lot by their religious beliefs'. Curiously there was no test of belonging in this much discussed religiosity scale. As a result many of the weekly churchgoers in the biblical non-literalist group might have recorded a negative score on the scale (five or more positive responses were required for a positive score).

Although they offer no religiosity scale, there is sometimes a lack of theological nuance in the otherwise excellent work of Leslie Francis and William Kay. It was noted earlier that they sensibly included both literalist and non-literalist questions on Christian beliefs in their survey of teenagers. However, their interpretation of the results is not always careful to make distinctions. For example, they write:

> Churchgoing teenagers, though they believe in the traditional teaching of the church much more frequently than non-attending contemporaries are, however, less than fully convinced of the great doctrines of scripture and the creeds. For example . . . 16% of weekly churchgoers cannot say they believe in God and 25% are unable to affirm the literal resurrection of Christ. As many as 40% of weekly churchgoers cannot declare they are certain about an afterlife and

[11] Independent Television Authority, *Religion in Britain and Northern Ireland: A Survey of Popular Attitudes*, ITA, London, 1970.

nearly two-thirds (64%) are not sure that Christianity is the only true religion. There is room here for a thorough exposition of Christianity to young churchgoers.[12]

For many non-literalists the problem here might be that Francis and Kay have jumbled together beliefs that would be endorsed by most Christians (such as the existence of God) with other beliefs that are more contentious (such as that Christianity is the only true religion). Of course a literalist position might insist that all of these doctrines *are* essential for 'orthodox' Christian belief. From this perspective it must be deeply disturbing that more than a quarter of weekly churchgoing biblical literalists in table 12 gave a less than certain response to a question about life after death. Again, in the 1984 and 1996 Gallup surveys sponsored by the Protestant Reformation Society,[13] which were cited in chapter three, there is evident an ambivalence amongst some of the Anglican clergy and bishops and many of the laity about a literalist understanding of the resurrection. The question asked there was distinctly more nuanced than the Francis–Kay statement, 'I believe that Jesus Christ really rose from the dead.' Gallup asked instead:

> Some people have believed and still believe that Jesus was raised bodily from the dead, three days after his crucifixion. Others have suggested that after the crucifixion Jesus was not raised bodily from the dead, but made his personality and presence known to his disciples in a spiritual but not bodily way. Which, if either, of these two views comes closest to your own?

Most bishops and four out of five clergy in 1984 and 1996 chose the first option. Anglican bishops have become wary over the last decade about questionnaire surveys, so whereas 43 responded the first time only 25 did the second. However, seven of them in the first survey and one in the second did not give this first response – nor, of course, did one out of five clergy. Amongst Anglican laity, who attended church in the last month, only half in both surveys chose the first option. Given their

[12] Leslie J. Francis and William K. Kay, *Teenage Religion and Values*, Gracewing, Fowler Wright Books, Herefordshire, 1995, p. 149.

[13] The two Gallup Polls of Church of England Laity and Clergy (1984 and 1996) sponsored by the Protestant Reformation Society are reproduced with permission.

conservative theological position, the sponsors suggest, not surprisingly, 'the conclusion [that] may be drawn from the findings of this survey is that the English Church and Nation is far from authentic Biblical Christianity'. However, weekly churchgoing non-literalists might be more hesitant about reaching such a conclusion. Whether or not one agrees with their position, it might at least be recognised by researchers that the latter does represent the beliefs of a large number of regular churchgoers. Evidence in chapters six and seven will suggest that it is a caricature to regard this group merely as secularised Christians – on some moral issues they differ more sharply from the general population than do the biblical literalists.

Perhaps the most surprising feature of table 12 is that it gives so little support for a once-born/twice-born thesis. Only the NISA question about being 'born again' or having a born again experience appears to give it some support. It might have been predicted that many more literalists would have reported a conversion experience, a turning point, and the non-literalists a contrasting pattern of continuous believing and belonging. In reality the two groups are very similar. It appears that half of the members of *both* groups report that they had 'a turning point in life' of new and personal religious commitment. Yet, unlike the rest of the sample, almost all of them attended church nearly every week when they were young. Most of them also respond that 'I believe in God now, and I always have.' There is even a slight tendency for more of the literalists to respond in this way than the non-literalists, but it is a very marginal difference. As noted earlier, it appears that most of those who start going to church as adults are renewing a practice of churchgoing rather than starting *de novo*.[14]

The distinction between biblical literalists and non-literalists is not the only way that weekly churchgoers can be differentiated. The NISA 'born again' question acts as an important indicator of theological differences. Unfortunately it was not asked in the corresponding BSA sample. And, even in the form

[14] See Mass-Observation, 'Why Do People Come to Church?', *British Weekly*, 13 January 1949, and John Finney, *Finding Faith Today*, British and Foreign Bible Society, Swindon, 1992.

in which it appears in NISA, it suffers from the same problem as the BHPS question on attitudes towards the Bible – namely, the group which responds negatively may be more diffuse than the group which responds positively. It remains the clinching advantage of the BSA/NISA question on attitudes towards the Bible that it is based upon two groups that answered positively.

Attitudes towards the Bible have long divided Christians. There is plenty of evidence in this chapter that these divisions remain on issues of Christian belief. In the next chapter it will be seen that these divisions extend more widely into many moral and social areas as well. A scholarly account of the significance of churchgoing for Christian ethics must take full account of these differences. Having argued up to this point that the significance of churchgoing has been underestimated by many other sociologists and theologians, a new note of caution is now necessary. Within a broad and distinctive pattern of altruism and teleology, the different types of churchgoing noted in BHPS data are also evident in BSA and NISA data. These differences and the sharp moral disagreements they generate are important for Christian ethics and must be considered carefully in the final chapter.

CHAPTER 6

Moral order in British Social Attitudes surveys

Real progress has now been made. The great fund of new data contained in British Social Attitudes establishes an unambiguous connection between churchgoing and Christian beliefs. An increase in churchgoing is significantly correlated with an increase in these beliefs. Patterns of believing amongst nonchurchgoers also depend upon whether or not people went to church as children and the prevailing levels of belief in their surrounding culture. A cultural theory of churchgoing has been identified as fitting this evidence much better than a persistence, separation or even secularisation theory. It is unnecessary to spend any more time on this particular debate. Perhaps it has occupied the attention of recent sociologists of religion for too long. A cultural theory of churchgoing makes some sharper insights possible, especially on moral issues, and raises again the question which preoccupied the pioneers of sociology – does religious belonging shape moral vision? The reverse of this question is just as interesting – can moral vision survive a collapse of religious belonging?

British Social Attitudes again provides a wealth of, largely unexplored, evidence which is directly relevant to these questions. Using this evidence, alongside that from the British Household Panel Survey, it becomes possible for the first time to measure and compare the attitudes, and sometimes behaviour, of churchgoers and nonchurchgoers accurately over a wide range of moral concerns. It is even possible to detect changes over time and, again, to discern different types of both churchgoers and nonchurchgoers. Most fascinating of all, it suggests important points of contact with some of the recent research done by New Testament scholars on early Christian morality. Using this research, continuities can be seen between the patterns and tensions on moral issues amongst the earliest Christian communities and those amongst churchgoers today.

The work of Wayne Meeks, especially, has helped to direct attention to the early Christian communities that shaped the New Testament. Within Christian ethics a standard temptation has been to treat the New Testament as a repository of moral injunctions and biblical principles. Meeks is aware that these are theologically important, but argues nonetheless that 'a description of early Christian morality cannot be limited to an account of the "Christian" theological ideas that bear on ethics, or of their moral rules, or of the structures of their moral arguments'.[1] By focusing instead upon the various communities lying behind the biblical texts, Meeks presents an unusually dynamic account of early Christian morality. For him there are sharp tensions and differences evident amongst early Christian communities, there are more than a few obvious continuities with surrounding pagan communities, and there are some discernible changes within emerging Christian communities. Over time these communities squabble, change and relate very differently to the outside world. Yet there are also patterns of believing and belonging which early Christian communities have in common. The distinctiveness of these communities does not disappear in Meeks' analysis, but it is more fluid than is sometimes allowed. A strong sense of moral order, particularly on matters of personal morality, is shared with many pagan communities, but the cruciform understanding of suffering and obligation is distinctively Christian. As in many other moral communities, heroes and heroic examples are important within early Christian communities. However, for the latter, it is Jesus Christ who is central. Christian and pagan communities in the first and second century were both concerned about decency and moral rectitude and used a variety of means to foster morality – lists of vices and virtues, moral injunctions and interdictions, hortatory aphorisms and proverbs, supplications

[1] Wayne A. Meeks, *The Origins of Christian Morality: The First Two Centuries*, Yale University Press, New Haven and London, 1993, p. 11.

and encouragements, powerful stories and angry moral rebukes. Meeks is adept at demonstrating these similarities and then allowing readers to see more clearly just how early Christian communities differed from their pagan rivals, not least in their christocentrism.

This mixture of moral enforcers, albeit set in a christocentric theology, is apparent in many of Paul's letters. It is clearly evident in the thirteenth chapter of Romans, which has proved so important and troublesome in the history of Christian ethics:[2]

> Everyone must *submit himself to the governing authorities*, for there is no authority except that which God has established. The authorities that exist have been established by God. Consequently, he who rebels against their authority is rebelling against what God has instituted, and those who do so will bring judgement on themselves . . . This is also why you *pay taxes*, for the authorities are God's servants, who give their full time to governing. Give everyone what you owe him: If you owe taxes, pay taxes; if revenue, then revenue; if respect, then respect; if honour, then honour. *Let no debt remain outstanding*, except the continuing debt to love one another, for he who loves his fellow man has fulfilled the law. The commandments, 'Do not commit adultery', 'Do not murder', 'Do not steal', 'Do not covet', and whatever other commandments there may be, are summed up in this one rule: 'Love your neighbour as yourself' . . . *Let us behave decently* . . . not in orgies and drunkenness, not in sexual immorality and debauchery, not in dissension and jealousy. Rather clothe yourselves with the Lord Jesus Christ, and do not think about how to gratify the desires of the sinful nature.[3]

The three features – Christian belief, teleology and altruism, that is, Faith, Hope and Love – are all present once again in this passage. The argument is christocentric and the summation is identified as love. However, the words in italics pick out the elements which are concerned with moral order. The point that Meeks repeatedly makes is that this underlying sense of moral order, and even the repeated and contrasting pairs of words that Paul uses here to emphasise it, would have been shared by early Christians and earnest pagans alike.

[2] See section two of my *A Textbook of Christian Ethics*, T. & T. Clark, Edinburgh, 2nd edn, 1995.

[3] Rmns 13.1–14 (IV; emphasis added).

This is also a pattern which characterises most regular churchgoers today. It is not an exclusively Christian pattern – it is still shared by many who respond that they 'never' go to church or that they have 'no religion' – and it is not a pattern that fits everyone who goes regularly to church. Yet it is a pattern that characterises churchgoers as a whole significantly more than nonchurchgoers. The more people go to church the more likely they are to correspond to the pattern of moral order depicted so vividly in this quotation from Romans. It provides a remarkably accurate summary of the BSA data on churchgoing and moral attitudes.

Everyone must submit himself to the governing authorities

These words have, of course, caused much anxiety to theologians over the centuries confronted by hostile political regimes. Luther, for example, famously concluded at a particularly difficult time in 1526:

> Suppose that a people would rise up today or tomorrow and depose their lord or kill him. That certainly could happen if God decrees that it should, and the lords must expect it. But that does not mean that it is right and just for the people to do it . . . On the contrary, we ought to suffer wrong, and if a prince or lord will not tolerate the gospel, then we ought to go into another realm where the gospel is preached.[4]

He immediately added, though, that it 'is only right that if a prince, king, or lord becomes insane, he should be deposed and put under restraint, for he is not to be considered a man since his reason has gone'. Only in this extreme situation – a situation which the devout Lutheran and pacifist Dietrich Bonhoeffer probably faced in the 1940s when he joined the bomb plot against Hitler – were Christians excused from submission to the governing authorities. Normally the gospel required them to be obedient.

Two questions asked several times in BSA between 1983 and 1994 show that churchgoers today remain obedient to the governing authorities. In the first of these respondents were

[4] From *Whether Soldiers, Too, Can be Saved*, in *Luther's Works*, vol. XLVI, Fortress Press, Philadelphia, 1967, p. 104.

asked: 'In general would you say that people should obey the law without exception, or are there exceptional occasions on which people should follow their consciences even if it means breaking the law.' They were then given three options: obey the law without exception, follow conscience on occasions, or don't know. Now it might be thought that churchgoers would choose the second option, that is, the principled option which specifically mentions conscience. In fact their commitment to moral order eclipsed this choice. In 1983–4 (in this chapter this will indicate that the results of two surveys – in this instance 1983 and 1984 – have been combined in order to make a larger sample) 57% of weekly churchgoers chose the first option in contrast to 44% of the no-religion group. In 1994 an even wider gap was evident (51% and 31%) with signs of directionality across the four levels of churchgoing–nonchurchgoing (51%, 44%, 48%, 44%). In the 18–34 age-group in 1994 this directionality was particularly striking (51%, 23%, 41%, 15%).

In the second question respondents were asked more simply, 'Are there any circumstances in which you might break a law to which you were strongly opposed?' Again, the most striking difference was between weekly churchgoers and the no-religion group. In 1983–4 only 22% of the first group but 40% of the second responded 'yes'; in 1994 the difference was a similar 17% and 40% with evidence again of directionality amongst churchgoers–nonchurchgoers (17%, 19%, 26%, 34%).

Now it might be concluded from this that churchgoers are relatively apolitical, especially when compared with the no-religion group. On this understanding, adult churchgoers, like the teenage churchgoers in the Francis–Kay survey[5] cited in chapter three, are simply more respectful of those in positions of authority (for example, a majority of teenage churchgoers thought that both teachers and the police 'do a good job').

This conclusion, however, would be an over simplification. A rather complicated question asked respondents: 'Suppose a law was being considered by Parliament which you thought was really unjust and harmful. Which, if any, of the things on this

[5] Leslie J. Francis and William K. Kay, *Teenage Religion and Values*, Gracewing, Fowler Wright Books, Herefordshire, 1995.

card do you think that you would do?: Contact my MP; Speak to an influential person; Contact a government department; Contact radio, TV or newspaper; Sign a petition; Raise the issue in an organisation I already belong to; Go on a protest or demonstration; Form a group of like-minded people; No, none of these.' Using the same options, they were then asked: 'And have you ever done any of the things on this card about a government action which you thought was unjust and harmful?' So the interesting feature of this double-barrelled question is that it tests both stated attitudes and behaviour.

Using the 1994 results, weekly churchgoers appeared to be distinctive on both of these counts. Those who would contact their MP (68%) were more numerous than the no-religion group (54%) and there was evidence of directionality, especially in the 35–59 age-group (80%, 71%, 64%, 67%). These differences remained amongst those saying that they had actually done this. In 1989 and 1991 twice as many weekly churchgoers (32%) as the no-religion group (15%) said that they had and directionality in the 34–59 age-group in 1994 was particularly striking (39%, 21%, 16%, 16%). In all three surveys regular churchgoers appeared to be more inclined to act in this way than other people. Significant directionality can also been seen in those responding in 1994 that they had contacted a government department, especially in the middle-aged group (18%, 3%, 5%, 2%). This is surely the group which is best placed to act in this way and, significantly, only a quarter of these middle-aged weekly churchgoers responded that they had 'done no such thing' – about half the proportion of other groups. It is only on the option 'Go on a protest or demonstration' that differences between regular churchgoers and others tend to disappear. But perhaps taking an active part in protests and demonstrations begins to look like breaking the law.

A recent study of congregations in the Church of Wales suggests that theological differences may be important on such issues. The authors conclude that 'those with "catholic" views seemed more oriented in their secular judgments to rule breaking or a challenge to authority, while "evangelicals" reacted more strongly to that which could be viewed as unconscionable behaviour (thereby sometimes arriving at the same conclusion by different routes)'.[6] The parenthesis here is a timely reminder that such differences may still be compatible with an overall shared moral framework.

Again, in their fascinating, but polemical, book *Religion, Deviance and Social Control*, Rodney Stark and William Sims Bainbridge argue that there are extensive, but largely ignored, American data which connect high levels of churchgoing with low levels of crime. For example, from a data base drawn from the *General Social Survey* of some nine thousand cases in the 1970s and 1980s, they show that only 5% of weekly churchgoers report that they 'have been picked up by the police', in contrast to 21% of those who never go to church. Using the same churchgoing–nonchurchgoing categories as those for the BSA data, a clear pattern of directionality can be seen here (5%, 9%, 15%, 21%). Stark and Bainbridge conclude from this and related data about those actually convicted:

> The data we have examined here suggest that religion plays a central role in sustaining the moral order. Cities with higher proportions of church members have lower rates of crime than do more secular cities. Indeed, low church membership rates help explain a very marked regional difference in crime rates: although the fact has received remarkably little public notice, the Pacific region has a substantially higher crime rate than do other parts of the nation. And the Pacific region has by far the lowest church membership rates.[7]

Unfortunately BSA data do not allow such connections to be tested in Britain. They do, however, suggest that churchgoers are significantly more opposed than nonchurchgoers to the portrayal of violence in the media. Using multivariate analyses on data from BSA 1996, Steven Barnett and Katarina Thomson[8] find that different rates of attendance at religious

[6] Richard Startup and Christopher C. Harris, 'Elements of Religious Belief and Social Values Among the Laity of the Church of Wales', *Journal of Contemporary Religion*, 12:2, 1997, p. 225.

[7] Rodney Stark and William Sims Bainbridge, *Religion, Deviance and Social Control*, Routledge, New York and London, 1996.

[8] Steven Barnett and Katarina Thomson, 'How We View Violence', in Roger Jowell, John Curtice, Alison Park, Lindsay Brook, Katarina Thomson and Caroline Bryson (eds.), *British Social Attitudes the 14th Report*, Social and Community Planning Research, Ashgate, Aldershot, 1997, p. 183.

worship are 'a strong predictor of attitudes' to such portrayal. This remains the case even after allowing for the important fact that congregations tend to be more elderly than the population at large.

Given all of this evidence it would be difficult to claim that churchgoers are apolitical or unconcerned about issues of justice. The BHPS data reviewed in chapter four suggests, on the contrary, that churchgoers are disproportionately represented in the membership of political parties. They do not appear to be apolitical, but rather to be more concerned than others to submit to the governing authorities and to be law-abiding. Churchgoers, it seems, have a particular concern for civic order both in theory and in practice.

Pay taxes . . . and let no debt remain outstanding

In a number of BSA surveys going back to 1983 respondents have been asked: 'It is said that many people manage to avoid paying their full income tax. Do you think that they should not be allowed to get away with it – or do you think good luck to them if they can get away with it?' The 1983 survey showed clear directionality in those believing that people should not be allowed to get away with this (86%, 79%, 77%, 75%) and a lower level again in the no-religion group (64%). In 1991 respondents were asked whether under-reporting of tax is wrong – again showing a directional pattern amongst churchgoers–nonchurchgoers believing that it is wrong (82%, 87%, 74%, 68% and no-religion 67%). Now, of course, this demonstrates that most people, whether churchgoers or not, believe that taxes ought to be paid and that it is wrong not to do so. Similarly, when given a variety of situations involving not paying VAT, most people think that it is wrong. Yet the level of moral seriousness is clearly related to churchgoing. For example, when asked in 1991 whether it was 'seriously wrong or wrong' to pay a plumber cash to avoid VAT, those respondents who thought this again showed clear directionality (56%, 44%, 49%, 44% and no-religion at 38%). Nevertheless these are relative differences. Regular churchgoers are clearly not alone in believing that taxes and debts to society should be paid, even though they appear to be somewhat more scrupulous than others.

Questions on personal honesty are one of the very few areas where the annual British Social Attitudes Reports tend to notice that churchgoing is a significant variable.[9] In chapter seven it will be seen that this does supply a certain amount of information both on attitudes to honesty and on stated behaviour amongst churchgoers. Unfortunately, some of the examples given are rather trivial. Perhaps this in itself is indicative: the authors of the reports tend to notice the significance of churchgoing on matters of petty honesty but seldom on issues of deeper moral concern. Whatever the reason behind this, there is general agreement that churchgoers do expect to pay their direct and indirect taxes.

Let us behave decently . . . not in sexual immorality and debauchery

Questions about sexuality abound in the BSA surveys. Questions about drinking and drug abuse also occur at regular intervals. Both provide abundant evidence of differences between churchgoers and nonchurchgoers in their attitudes and, indeed, in their behaviour. Perhaps it would be surprising if it were otherwise. Because these questions are so frequent, they offer an invaluable opportunity to test differences between regular churchgoers in different denominations and holding different views on biblical literalism. They also offer an opportunity to test changes in attitudes toward sexuality in the context of a society that is itself changing fast. The overall pattern that emerges undoubtedly resonates with Romans 13. Regular churchgoers do tend to show a considerable concern to 'behave decently' in these areas of personal morality. Yet their concept of 'decent behaviour' is also changing – and changing quite fast. This can be illustrated best by using other surveys alongside the BSA data.

[9] E.g. see Michael Johnston, 'The Price of Honesty', in Roger Jowell, Sharon Witherspoon and Lindsay Brook (eds.), *British Social Attitudes the 5th Report*, Social and Community Planning Research, Gower, Aldershot, 1988, p. 15.

For example, the issue of whether or not divorcees should be allowed to marry in church has been measured for half a century in Britain by Gallup Polls.[10] In 1947 it appeared that a third of the general public (34%) thought that divorcees should not be allowed to do so and well over half (58%) that they should. By 1955 the negative group had declined somewhat (to 28%) whilst the positive group had changed little (59%) and by 1984 the negative group had declined again to less than a quarter (24%) where it remained in 1996 (by now the positive group is 55%). In other words throughout this period of time a clear majority of the general population thought that divorce should not be a barrier to a church wedding. In contrast, 'communicant churchgoers' (as Gallup termed them, but without any further information) in 1955 were distinctly more opposed. A majority of this group (55%) opposed the marriage of divorcees in church and little more than a third (37%) supported it. Yet by 1984 this difference had largely disappeared. Now a majority (55%) of Anglicans who had attended church in the last month thought that divorcees should be allowed and less than a third (29%) thought they should not. Exactly half of Roman Catholic churchgoers remained opposed and so did a sizeable group of Anglican clergy (44%), with less than a quarter of the latter (21%) positively supporting. Yet by the 1990s opposition by the clergy was clearly waning. Ted Harrison's Poll[11] in 1994 showed less than a third (32%) still opposing church weddings for divorcees and a Gallup Poll in 1996 showed even less (28%).

What had happened in this time? It is not too difficult to guess. Divorce has considerably increased during these five decades throughout the Western world and has begun to affect congregations directly. This is illustrated vividly by responses from churchgoers to the 1991 Australian National Church Life

[10] For Gallup Poll data, see George H. Gallup (ed.), *The Gallup International Public Opinion Polls: Great Britain 1937–1975*, Random House, New York, 1976; Gordon Heald and Robert J. Wybrow (eds.), *The Gallup Survey of Britain*, Croom Helm, London, 1986; *The International Gallup Polls* (1978); and *Gallup Political and Economic Index* (annual).

[11] Ted Harrison, *Members Only?*, Triangle, SPCK, London, 1994.

Survey.[12] Asked 'Should people who have been divorced be allowed to remarry in a church?', 87% responded either 'Yes, definitely' or 'Yes, in certain circumstances' and only 8% 'No, marriage is for life and should not be dissolved.' Baptists were least enthusiastic, but even amongst them 79% answered positively and only 14% negatively, and amongst those identified as biblical literalists negative responses increased only to 15%. In Britain, not only will parish priests and ministers have requests from nonchurchgoing divorcees for church marriages, but increasingly they are likely to have such requests from regular churchgoers as well. Despite the fact that the issue has been debated in the General Synod of the Church of England several times, there has as yet been no agreement to change at an official level. Yet unofficially change has already taken place in an increasing number of Anglican parishes and pressure to change can be found in most parishes. Faced with a strong claim from parishioners, many clergy, despite their generally more conservative views, find themselves following this unofficial path.

Yet a comparison of the 1954 BBC Poll[13] with more recent BSA surveys shows that unease about divorce remains amongst British churchgoers (a similar unease amongst Australian churchgoers[14] was noted in chapter two). The BBC Poll showed a sharp difference of attitude on divorce between churchgoers and the general public: a majority (53%) of those who reported that they went to church 'most Sundays' thought that the divorce laws then should be made more difficult, whereas less than a third (30%) of the total sample held this view. Decades later BSA showed clear directionality amongst churchgoers–nonchurchgoers who thought that divorce in Britain should be more difficult, in 1983–4 (54%, 38%, 31%, 28%) and then again in 1994 (61%, 41%, 38%, 27%). This directionality is apparent in all age-groups: in 1994 in the 18–34 age-group (55%, 42%,

[12] Peter Kaldor and Ruth Powell, *Views From the Pews: Australian Church Attenders Speak Out*, Openbook Publishers, Sydney, 1995.

[13] British Broadcasting Corporation, *Religious Broadcasts and the Public*, Audience Research Department, BBC, 1955.

[14] See Gary D. Bouma and Beverly R. Dixon, *The Religious Factor in Australian Life*, MARC Australia, World Vision and the Zadok Centre, 1986.

40%, 30%), in the 35–59 age-group (62%, 32%, 34%, 27%) and in the 60+ age-group (59%, 54%, 51%, 43%). In contrast, less than one in five of those under 60 years in the no-religion group agreed.

If the data from three BSA surveys in the 1980s are combined, it is possible to make comparisons across denominations on this question. Directionality amongst churchgoers–nonchurchgoers is at least as evident amongst Anglicans (64%, 41%, 34%, 31%) as it is amongst Roman Catholics (57%, 41%, 32%, 25%) and the Free Churches (54%, 41%, 26%, 34%). The only mainline denomination in which less than a majority of weekly churchgoers believe that divorce should be more difficult is the Presbyterian Church (27%) – a denomination which has allowed divorcees to marry in church for many years.

Taken together this evidence about attitudes towards divorce and to church marriages of divorcees shows that churchgoers remain more cautious than nonchurchgoers. Many have come to accept that it is right for divorcees to marry in church, but they remain convinced across most denominations that divorce should be more difficult to obtain than it is. They are also less inclined themselves to divorce. If all the BSA surveys for the 1980s and the 1990s are compared, then there are clear differences between churchgoers and nonchurchgoers in the proportions of those listed as divorced or separated. Yet there are also changes in the churchgoing–nonchurchgoing patterns of the 1980s (3.1.%, 3.1%, 4.6%, 5.4%) and of the 1990s (5.5%, 5.6%, 5.4%, 7.2%): the level of divorce has increased considerably in every group, including regular churchgoers. Obviously the marriages of some churchgoers do break down and, increasingly, this is also happening amongst non-Roman Catholic clergy. Nevertheless divorce is still more common amongst nonchurchgoers: a difference, but not an absolute difference, remains.

Another area which shows a similarly confusing pattern – of both change and persisting differences – is data on attitudes and behaviour on sex before marriage and cohabitation. Asked in a Gallup Poll in 1964 whether they approved of sex before marriage, almost two-thirds (64%) of the sample of the general public replied 'no', a tenth 'yes', and just over a quarter (26%)

were 'not worried'. Anglican churchgoers were even more opposed (79%). By 1978 Gallup suggested that attitudes in the general population had changed radically: just over a quarter (26%) now replied 'no', 17% 'yes', and a majority reported that they were 'not worried' (55%). BSA surveys also suggest a shift in public perceptions: in 1983 less than half (42%) responded that sex before marriage was simply 'not wrong' and not quite a third (28%) that it was 'always or mostly wrong', whereas in 1993 a majority (54%) held the first position and less than a fifth (18%) the second. Asking a similar question, but this time whether it is right for a couple to live together without intending to get married, BSA in 1993 found that almost two-thirds of the general population (64%) thought that it was. A Gallup Poll in 1996 found a very similar proportion (68%), and it also found that a majority (56%) of adult churchgoing Anglicans also believed this. Once again it was the clergy who were distinctly more conservative: little more than a third of them (36%) agreed: most (52%) disagreed.

Amalgamating BSA surveys, it is again possible to detect finer and highly significant distinctions and changes amongst churchgoers and between denominations. A decline in every group can be seen in those believing that it is 'always or mostly wrong . . . if a man and a woman have sexual relations before marriage', comparing the churchgoing–nonchurchgoing patterns of 1983–4 (64%, 35%, 28%, 26%) with 1993–4 (53%, 25%, 15%, 13%). In the no-religion group it is now only one in twenty who hold this view. Although significant directionality can be found in every age-group, levels are much higher amongst older people. So in the surveys 1983–7 the following patterns can be seen: 18–34 age group (40%, 6%, 3%, 5%); 35–59 age-group (58%, 30%, 25%, 17%); 60+ age-group (75%, 56%, 50%, 46%). In addition, changes seem to be taking place across denominations. In the 1983–7 surveys, amongst weekly churchgoers, a majority of Anglican (59%), Roman Catholic (51%) and Free Church (72%) weekly churchgoers believed pre-marital sex to be wrong. Yet by 1993–4 a minority of Anglican (46%) and Roman Catholic (47%) and a declining majority of Free Church (64%) weekly churchgoers believed this. Whilst clear differences remain, moral attitudes towards pre-marital sex are changing both within society at large and amongst regular churchgoers.

It is not just moral beliefs which are changing amongst churchgoers in this area but also the relative strength of these beliefs. In 1989 and 1994 BSA asked respondents if they 'strongly agreed or agreed' that people who want children ought to get married. Directionality was highly significant in both surveys, suggesting that support had declined in every churchgoing–nonchurchgoing group except weekly churchgoers between 1989 (86%, 78%, 77%, 74% and no-religion 56%) and 1994 (87%, 63%, 61%, 64% and no-religion 40%). However, if 'strongly agree' responses are analysed alone, support even amongst weekly churchgoers declined from 44% to 32% (and in every other group as well). Many people – churchgoers and nonchurchgoers alike – do seem to be less confident about this moral issue than they were in the past. Asked in a different way, it does appear that weekly churchgoers are much more likely than others to believe that it is 'always wrong' if the unmarried decide to have a baby, as the 1994 pattern shows (55%, 30%, 30%, 27% and no-religion 14%). Yet even here they are by no means as decisive as once they might have been.

A very similar pattern of change on sexual issues, even amongst regular churchgoers, can be detected elsewhere in Europe. Reviewing comparative data from the two European Value Systems Study Group surveys in the early 1980s and 1990s, Loek Halman and Thorleif Pettersson conclude:

> It can generally be concluded that in many cases, the frequent church attenders seemed to follow the same general direction of value change occurring in the various countries. In this sense, the religious sector appears to be affected by the same cultural changes as the non-religious sectors. From such findings, it can be argued that the churches do not seem to lead the cultural changes, but rather to follow them. Only occasionally do the views of the core members develop differently than the views of the general public. In this regard, the findings are similar both in secularized Sweden and less secularized Spain.[15]

15 Loek Halman and Thorleif Pettersson, 'Morality and Religion: A Weakened Relationship', *Journal of Empirical Theology*, 9:2, 1996, p. 44.

All of this fits the findings of the Francis–Kay survey of British teenagers. As noted earlier, less than a quarter of Roman Catholic teenagers who go regularly to church believe premarital sex to be wrong, and less than a third believe that sex is wrong even under the legal age of sixteen. Those in the youngest group of churchgoers in BSA are more conservative compared with these teenagers (none in 1994 agreed with under-sixteens having sex), yet they too increasingly condone sex between unmarried, adult men and women. Soon it may only be elderly churchgoers, especially in the Free Churches, who in any great numbers believe otherwise.

It is not simply moral beliefs, or the strength of these beliefs, which are changing amongst churchgoers, behaviour is also changing. Asked in BSA 1989 'Did you cohabit before marriage?' none of the churchgoers, regular or irregular, in the oldest age-group admitted to this. However, 9% of weekly churchgoers in the 35–59 age-group did and 13% of those in the 18–34 age-group. The youngest group still showed directionality (13%, 18%, 14%, 24%), but they were clearly different from their elders. These changes in behaviour can also be seen in the different patterns of those listed as 'living as married', comparing 1983/85 (0.2%, 0.8%, 1.2%, 1.7% and no-religion 4.0%) with 1993–4 (1.6%, 4.0%, 4.8%, 5.6% and no-religion 10.4%). Gary Bouma and Beverly Dixon's conclusion about Australians applies equally to the British: 'The more religious persons are, the more likely are they to be married only once, and the less likely to have lived in a de facto relationship.'[16] Yet in both countries there is growing evidence of re-marriage after divorce and cohabitation even amongst regular churchgoers.

The overall shape of this evidence suggests that the general population changes first, then churchgoers change, and finally the clergy change. Yet supposing this perspective is reversed and change is seen as something that is allowed or disallowed by the clergy. According to this perspective it is a duty of clerical leadership to maintain right beliefs and practices amongst the faithful – orthodoxy and orthopraxis – whatever changes take

[16] Bouma and Dixon, *The Religious Factor*, p. 100.

place in secular society and however much these changes might at times mislead their congregations. A strong clerical leadership on sexual issues is considered vital to maintain the distinctiveness of Christian morality amongst churchgoers.

There is one area which provides evidence about the effectiveness or non-effectiveness of clerical leadership on sexual issues, albeit in the Roman Catholic, not the Anglican, Church. Gallup Poll data suggest that in 1964 a considerable majority of both the general population and non-Roman Catholic churchgoers approved of contraception within marriage. One survey in that year set general approval at 79% and another at 81%: only about one in ten people disapproved. Amongst Anglican churchgoers this approval rose to 85% and amongst Free Church churchgoers it was 75%. Perhaps not surprisingly, it was only amongst Roman Catholic churchgoers that a majority (59%) disapproved of contraception within marriage, although even within this group almost a third (32%) approved. In 1965, before the publication of Pope Paul VI's encyclical *Humanae Vitae*, a sample of the general population was asked if it would approve if the Roman Catholic Church were to change its teaching on contraception. Over two-thirds (69%) responded 'yes' and only 4% 'no'. Conversely, in 1968 after publication, most people (59%) did not approve of the Pope's recent teaching on contraception. Apparently it was only Roman Catholic churchgoers who approved of the firm teaching of their church leaders on contraception in any significant numbers.

Yet it soon became apparent that, despite the firm teaching of both Pope Paul VI and Pope John-Paul II, sexually active Roman Catholics in many parts of the Western world did resort to contraception (and abortion) in proportionate numbers to their non-Roman Catholic counterparts. Perhaps they felt more guilty than others about using proscribed forms of contraception, but the obvious burden of not using barrier and hormonal forms of contraceptive soon persuaded them to act otherwise. As was seen earlier, the Francis–Key research amongst teenagers suggests that this generation may not even feel guilty. The attitudes of Anglican and Roman Catholic churchgoing youngsters appear indistinguishable: almost three-quarters of both groups (72%) disagreed with the proposition that contraception is wrong: only one in twenty now believed it to be wrong. Chapter seven will look at related BSA evidence about abortion and fertility treatment, comparing the views of churchgoing Anglicans and Roman Catholics. Here too it will be seen that, provided the situation is defined carefully, a majority of adult weekly churchgoers in both denominations believe that IVF and abortion (especially after rape or when the woman's health is endangered) should be allowed.

This evidence is highly significant. In the second half of the twentieth century the hierarchy of the Roman Catholic Church has taken a determined, and for some courageous, stand against public opinion on a matter of sexual ethics which affects most sexually active people. Almost alone in any major Christian denomination, this hierarchy has decided to take a stand against prevailing mores and uphold a traditional sexual standard. It may even have done this despite the alienation of many of its own sexually active churchgoers. Yet the evidence suggests that this stand has not substantially altered either the practice of Catholic laity or even the attitudes of young Catholics. Despite one of the most systematic attempts at ecclesiastical teaching and control during this period, Roman Catholic churchgoers now appear little different from the general population in attitudes towards, or practice of, proscribed forms of contraception. Chapter nine will return to the important issues of conflict and power involved in this crucial and highly instructive example.

Another area that provides an abundance of opinion poll data is that of attitudes towards homosexuality. Here the evidence suggests considerable ambiguity both amongst the general population and amongst churchgoers. Once again clergy appear to be more conservative than other groups. In a Gallup Poll in 1957 little more than a third of the population (38%) thought that homosexuality should be de-criminalised for adults. As with the slightly later abolition of capital punishment, British government reform on this issue probably did not have popular support at the time of its introduction. In 1964 again little more than a third of both the general population (36%)

and churchgoers thought that society should be tolerant of homosexuals. BSA surveys in 1983 and 1993 also suggest continuing antagonism towards homosexuality: in both exactly half of the general population thought that homosexual relations between adults were 'always wrong' and a further fifth that they were 'mostly or sometimes wrong'. Amongst churchgoers–nonchurchgoers there is clear and statistically significant evidence of directionality in those believing homosexuality to be 'always or mostly wrong', but little sign of change between 1983–4 (79%, 66%, 68%, 66% and no-religion 56%) and 1993 (80%, 68%, 69%, 69% and no-religion 52%). Amalgamating data for 1983–7, a large majority of weekly churchgoers in Britain (as in Australia[17]) in all mainline denominations hold this belief, as do churchgoers in all age-groups.

Perhaps this evidence is not altogether surprising. In a predominantly heterosexual population, homosexuality is by definition a minority issue. Unlike contraception or sex before or outside marriage, it is an existential issue for the few not for the many. Nonetheless, there is some evidence of change even here. In 1977 a Gallup Poll suggested that two-thirds of the population believed that a homosexual could be 'a good Christian/Jew etc.'; by 1981 this had increased to 77%. And some two-fifths of the population in both surveys thought that homosexuals could 'be hired as clergy'. Asked in a different form, in 1984 just less than half of the population (45%) thought that the 'Church can never approve homosexual acts'. Anglican churchgoers were slightly more conservative (52%) and Anglican clergy even more so (61%). The divide between Anglican laity and clergy was again suggested by a *Guardian* survey[18] of newly elected General Synod members in 1996 which found that 45% of laity and 70% of clergy agreed that the Church could not approve homosexual acts. (This difference is particularly important, as will be seen again in chapter nine, for understanding the 1998 Lambeth Conference debate on homosexuality.) A Gallup Poll in 1996 found a rather narrower gap of 53% of Anglican churchgoers and 59% of the clergy. And BSA re-

[17] See Bouma and Dixon, *The Religious Factor.* [18] *Guardian* 8 July 1996.

sponses to the suggestion that gays should not be allowed to teach in school does seem to command less support from 1983 (61%, 53%, 54%, 60% and no-religion 45%) to 1993 (42%, 36%, 42%, 44% and no-religion 30%).

However, it is again the Francis–Kay survey which supplies the most striking evidence of changing attitudes: less than a third (30%) of Anglican teenagers who went regularly to church thought that homosexuality was wrong. Consonant with this, the analysis of Ronald Inglehart[19] of data from the *World Values Survey* of the early 1980s shows significant differences in fourteen out of sixteen countries between the youngest and oldest age groups on the issue of homosexuality. It provides persuasive evidence of what he terms 'cultural shift'. Analysing the responses of those who answered that homosexuality can 'never' be justified, he found that across nations less than two-fifths (39%) of those aged 18–24 responded in this way, whereas almost three-quarters (73%) of those aged 65 or over did. The British figures (31% and 72% respectively) were very close to this international mean. Significantly this is a progressive mean: in every age band the international mean rises, reaching 50% in those aged 35–44.

Age, though, is by no means the only factor at work here. Table 13 suggests that there are important differences between biblical literalists and non-literalists in the amalgamated data from BSA 1991 and NISA 1991. Similar differences can be found in the 1991 Australian National Church Life Survey:[20] 88% of biblical literalists responded negatively to the question 'Do you agree with sex outside marriage?' as distinct from 67% of churchgoers holding the most liberal views on the Bible. The two groups in Britain and Northern Ireland also seem to have distinctive moral beliefs about what it is to *behave decently*. If the strongest form of response is taken – that it is 'always wrong' – then the beliefs of the biblical literalists are decidedly more definite about pre-marital sex, homosexuality and, indeed, adultery. If 'mostly wrong' responses are added, then adultery is

[19] Ronald Inglehart, *Culture Shift in Advanced Industrial Society*, Princeton University Press, New Jersey, 1990.

[20] See Kaldor and Powell, *Views From the Pews*.

Table 13 *Morality in two groups of weekly churchgoers* (Britain and Northern Ireland 1991 combined)

	Biblical literalists (n = 190)	Biblical non-literalists (n = 284)	Whole sample (n = 2069)
Think it is always wrong . . .			
Sex before marriage	55	39	21
Homosexuality	86	72	62
Adultery	95	79	67
Strongly agree/agree that . . .			
A husband's job is to earn the money, a wife's job is to look after the home/family	57	35	34
Women shouldn't try to combine a career and children	35	26	25
Politicians who do not believe in God are unfit for public office	44	19	17
Books/films that attack religions should be prohibited by law	63	46	37
Censorship of films/magazines is necessary to uphold moral standards	76	81	61
People should look after themselves and not rely on charities	43	25	32
We should support more charities which benefit people in Britain, rather than people overseas	51	31	51
I can't refuse when someone comes to the door with a collecting tin	64	61	57
People convicted of murder should be subject to the death penalty	44	31	49

Table 13 (*cont.*)

	Biblical literalists (n = 190)	Biblical non-literalists (n = 284)	Whole sample (n = 2069)
For some crimes, the death penalty is the most appropriate sentence	49	35	54

In percentages.
Biblical literalists = weekly churchgoers choosing 'The Bible is the actual word of God and it is to be taken literally, word for word' (BSA n = 30; NISA n = 160). Non-literalists = weekly churchgoers choosing 'The Bible is the inspired word of God but not everything should be taken literally, word for word' (BSA n = 84; NISA n = 200).
Sources: BSA 1991 and NISA 1991 weighted equally.

thought to be wrong by most churchgoers and nonchurchgoers, as can be seen in the 1993 responses (80%, 68%, 69%, 69% and no-religion 52%). Removing 'mostly' reveals this difference amongst these two groups of churchgoers – a difference very similar to that on Christian beliefs discussed in the previous chapter. It also shows that condemnation of pre-marital sex and homosexuality is markedly more muted amongst the non-literalists, as it was in the BHPS data on cohabitation.

Other important differences can be seen between these two groups of regular churchgoers, especially on gender roles. Just as table 9 shows that, using BHPS data, a majority of biblical literalists believe that a 'man should be head of the household', so here in table 13 they believe that 'a husband's job is to earn the money and a woman's job is to look after the home and family'. In contrast, a majority of non-literalists dissent from this claim and are happier about a woman combining a career and children. Traditional gender roles evidently are an important part of the moral order for biblical literalists in a way that they are no longer for non-literalists or for the population at large. Similarly, biblical literalists are more than twice as likely as non-literalists or the general population to believe that 'politicians who do not believe in God are unfit for public office'.

Questions about censorship, reported in table 13, sometimes divide regular churchgoers and at other times sharply differentiate them from nonchurchgoers. So, censorship of books and films that are considered blasphemous is much more likely to be supported by biblical literalists, whereas censorship to uphold moral standards is strongly supported by most weekly churchgoers. This is an instructive distinction. In BSA 1994 weekly churchgoers across every age-group overwhelmingly agreed that 'the right to show nudity and sex in films and magazines has gone too far': in the 18–34 age-group (100%, 50%, 60%, 38%), in the 35–59 age-group (85%, 82%, 69%, 53%) and in the 60+ age-group (89%, 89%, 88%, 86%). Directionality is highly significant in the first two age-groups – it is only in the oldest group that churchgoers and nonchurchgoers think alike. Support clearly increases with age amongst all groups except amongst weekly churchgoers. For once the latter are almost completely united. However, this unity soon disappears if the question is made more forceful. So in BSA 1983 and 1987 it was suggested that 'pornography should be banned altogether'. Directionality is still clear across age-groups, but the young are very much less enthusiastic than the old: the 18–34 age group (39%, 8%, 9%, 12%), the 35–59 age-group (58%, 41%, 31%, 30%), and the 60+ age-group (78%, 77%, 63%, 63%). Surprisingly, amongst weekly churchgoers support is lower amongst Roman Catholics (57%) than amongst Anglicans or the Free Churches (66% each).

Table 13 also shows that there are important differences between biblical literalists and non-literalists on questions about both charity and the death penalty. Chapter seven will return to these since they raise important distinctions about perceptions of altruism. Nevertheless, it will already be clear that churchgoers are united only on certain moral issues – on others they are divided and caught between changing or not changing. Perhaps there is nothing particularly new about this. Paul in Romans continues:

> Accept him whose faith is weak, without passing judgment on disputable matters. One man's faith allows him to eat everything, but another man, whose faith is weak, eats only vegetables. The man who

eats everything must not look down on him who does not, and the man who does not eat everything must not condemn the man who does, for God has accepted him . . . One man considers one day more sacred than another; another man considers every day alike . . .[21]

Behind these words it is not too difficult to spot unresolved differences of moral belief amongst early Christians. United by a common belief in moral order and 'decency', they were nonetheless divided about how decency should be particularised. Even the celebrated Council at Jerusalem in Acts 15, called to resolve the disputes between Paul and Barnabas (acting together), and other Christians, concluded with Paul and Barnabas having 'such a sharp disagreement that they parted company'.[22]

Let us behave decently . . . not in drunkenness

One final area of moral order, which again both unites and divides churchgoers, needs to be mentioned. BSA provides a wealth of data on attitudes towards illegal drugs, alcohol and smoking, all of which are correlated to some degree with churchgoing. Attitudes towards, and use of, illegal drugs show a strong statistical relationship with churchgoing. Aspects of this relationship were noted in chapter two for Australia.[23] However, BSA allows a ten-year comparison of those who agree that cannabis should be legalised, comparing those in 1983 (7%, 8%, 11%, 10% and no-religion 18%) with those in 1993 (7%, 15%, 11%, 19% and no-religion 29%). A minority, but a growing minority amongst nonchurchgoers and the no-religion group, appears to believe that cannabis should be legalised in Britain. A small group of weekly churchgoers also agrees. Another question in 1993 shows that about the same number of the 18–34 age-group of weekly churchgoers admits to taking cannabis 'often or occasionally' (8%, 11%, 8%, 14% and no-religion 22%). Now, of course, all of this shows that most people, whether churchgoers or not, neither agree with legalising cannabis nor admit to taking it even occasionally. Indeed, a

[21] Rmns 14.1–5 (IV). [22] Acts 15.39 (IV).
[23] See Bouma and Dixon, *The Religious Factor.*

1993 question about legalising heroin shows overwhelming opposition in every group. Yet amongst a minority a familiar pattern can be seen in relation to cannabis – regular churchgoers remain distinctive but are showing signs of change, especially amongst the young. In turn, this again fits closely the findings of the Francis–Kay survey of teenagers.

In America, too, there is beginning to be a new interest in the relationship between religious belonging and substance abuse. In a judicious review of research in this area, William Miller concludes:

> There is strong evidence that spiritual/religious involvement is generally associated with decreased risk of alcohol/drug use, problems and dependence. Data pertinent to this question have often been gathered incidentally as a part of larger survey research. Reviews of this literature have concluded that religiously involved individuals are consistently less likely to use alcohol and other drugs, and when they do so are less likely to engage in heavy use and suffer its adverse consequences.[24]

Miller regrets that this issue seldom attracts dedicated research funding and sees in this an interesting example of secular bias. Given such funding, he believes that it would, for example, be interesting to test how effective or not religious belonging might be in recovery from alcohol/drug problems. Stark and Bainbridge also trace correlations here, yet they argue that the connection between religion and alcohol is distinctly more ambiguous than that between religion and other drugs. So, across denominations, high school churchgoers appear less inclined to use marijuna than nonchurchgoers, whereas 'the effects of religion on alcohol display substantial denominational variations at both the aggregate and individual level of analysis'.[25] They argue that nineteenth-century statistics on death rates from 'delirium tremens and intemperance', and early-twentieth-century statistics on cirrhosis deaths and prohibition violations, all feature a disproportionate number of

[24] William R. Miller, 'Researching the Spiritual Dimensions of Alcohol and Other Drug Problems', *Addiction*, 93:7, 1998, pp. 981–2. See also Peter L. Benson, 'Religion and Substance Use', in John F. Shumaker (ed.), *Religion and Mental Health*, Oxford University Press, New York, 1992.

[25] Stark and Bainbridge, *Religion, Deviance and Social Control*, pp. 81–2.

Catholics. It is Protestants, especially conservative Protestants, who are significantly less likely than others to be involved in alcohol abuse.

The BSA evidence, too, about alcohol use is somewhat ambiguous, perhaps also because of long-standing differences between Roman Catholics (and many Anglicans) and the Free Church members. In 1991 those who say that they 'never drink' are disproportionately female but are only marginally more inclined to go regularly to church. So 22% of weekly churchgoers respond 'never' and only 11% of the no-religion group, but then 20% of those 'never' going to church also do. Within theologically conservative churches in Australia the proportion of 'abstainers' rises very considerably: 54% of Baptist churchgoers, 56% of the Assembly of God and 88% of the Salvation Army.[26] Weekly churchgoers in Britain, taken as a whole, are more inclined to say that they are 'light drinkers' (79%) than either nonchurchgoers (70%) or the no-religion group (65%). However, the proportions who say that either they drink more now than they did two or three years ago (about one in ten) or that they intend to drink less (about one in five) differ little between these groups. At most, differences between churchgoers and others revealed here are very slight. Which surely is surprising. Given the amount of attention that has been given to alcohol, especially amongst Reformed Christians, it might be predicted that questions in this area would be strongly directional. Yet they are not. Instead, they are dwarfed by the data on smoking.

The strong connection between non-smoking and churchgoing has already been demonstrated at length using BHPS data. Although it is confirmed many times over by the BSA data, it would tedious to report all of this here.[27] A small sample will be sufficient. The 1990 BSA questions all show a clear and significant directionality: amongst all those who respond that they 'smoke cigarettes nowadays' (15%, 20%, 25%, 37%),

[26] See Kaldor and Powell, *Views From the Pews*.

[27] For a much fuller account see Christopher C. H. Cook and Robin Gill, 'Drinking, Smoking and Drug Use in the British Social Attitudes Surveys: The Influence of Church Attendance', forthcoming.

amongst women who do (12%, 18%, 30%, 37%), amongst those who have 'never smoked regularly' (53%, 57%, 50%, 36%), amongst those who agree that all cigarette advertising should be banned (80%, 63%, 65%, 57%) and amongst those who believe that employers should ban smoking altogether (78%, 68%, 65%, 52%). Evidently regular churchgoers smoke significantly less, now and in the past, than other people and have stronger views about banning smoking at work and about cigarette advertisements. Their attitudes and behaviour in this area are far more distinctive than they are on questions about alcohol. As the earlier chapter on BHPS data found, churchgoers are strikingly smokeless. This does seem to be a distinctive feature of the churchgoing culture.

Whether or not non-smoking relates to a churchgoing culture's strong sense of moral order is debatable. However, BSA, as has been seen, supplies a rich vein of data from several other areas which acts as much better evidence. Despite all of the moral differences that have been seen amongst churchgoers in this chapter, a strong sense of teleology remains. Moral order does seem to characterise the measurable beliefs and the behaviour of churchgoers.

CHAPTER 7

Love in British Social Attitudes surveys

Love is patient; love is kind and envies no one. Love is never boastful, nor conceited, nor rude; never selfish, not quick to take offence. Love keeps no score of wrongs; does not gloat over other men's sins, but delights in the truth. There is nothing love cannot face; there is no limit to its faith, its hope, and its endurance. Love will never come to an end . . . In a word, there are three things that last for ever: Faith, Hope and Love; but the greatest of them all is Love.[1]

There is no possibility whatsoever of capturing this heavenly depiction of the Christian life in the crude nets of attitude surveys. Their function is to trawl through and test the relative strength of complex variables, but not to penetrate the deepest layers of moral character. Yet this very act of trawling should be able to detect the traces of love, but not of course the quality or depths of love, amongst the shoals of churchgoers.

It should be possible at least to see whether or not church-goers intend to put others first as they are instructed to in the Dominical Commands. The New Testament, Christian prayers and Christian liturgies are saturated with the theologic articulated so concisely in the Johannine Epistles, 'Dear friends, since God so loved us, we also ought to love one another',[2] and so dynamically in the eschatological parable of the sheep and the goats:

When the Son of Man comes in his glory, and all the angels with him, he will sit on his throne in heavenly glory. All the nations will be gathered before him, and he will separate the people one from another as a shepherd separates the sheep from the goats. He will put the sheep on his right and the goats on his left. Then the King will say

[1] 1 Cor. 13.4–8, 13 (NEB). [2] 1 John 4.11 (NIV).

to those on his right, 'Come, you who are blessed by my Father, take your inheritance, the kingdom prepared for you since the creation of the world. For I was hungry and you gave me something to eat, I was thirsty and you gave me something to drink, I was a stranger and you invited me in, I needed clothes and you clothed me, I was sick and you looked after me, I was in prison and you came to visit me.' Then the righteous will answer him, 'Lord, when did we see you hungry and feed you, or thirsty and give you something to drink? When did we see you a stranger and invite you in, or needing clothes and clothe you? When did we see you sick or in prison and go to visit you?' The King will reply, 'I tell you the truth, whatever you did for one of the least of these brothers of mine, you did for me.'[3]

The praxis indicated in this parable should leave visible traces and it should, in turn, be possible to see whether or not those who take part regularly in Christian worship think and sometimes act in such altruistic ways.

The BSA data makes three distinct tests of altruism possible. The first is the most visible and perhaps the most important. Are churchgoers more involved than others in voluntary service in the community? The second is about attitudes and motivation. When churchgoers articulate their moral concerns, are they especially concerned about the vulnerable and needy? And the third test of altruism contains a mixture of attitudes and behaviour. Is there evidence that the charitable giving and sensitivities of churchgoers differ from those of other people?

Test 1

Two sources have already been trawled to test a possible relationship between churchgoing and voluntary service in the community and they have both been found to be significant. The first of these was the two sets of surveys of the European Value Systems Study Group in the early 1980s and 1990s. It was noted that churchgoers in Britain, and more widely in Europe, were two or three times more likely than other people to be involved in some form of voluntary service. EVSSG used a

[3] Mtt. 25.31–40 (NIV).

rather wide concept of 'voluntary service' and found that half of regular churchgoers were involved in one way or another. Even when specifically church related voluntary service was taken out of the analysis, it still appeared that churchgoing was a highly significant variable. In other words, churchgoers were disproportionately involved in secular forms of voluntary service in the community. Comparing a churchgoer with a nonchurchgoer who had no belief in God, the former was some three times more likely to be involved in voluntary service than the latter.

The second source was, of course, the British Household Panel Survey data. These rich data allowed a series of detailed comparisons to be made between the active membership of religious groups and other caring groups. It was seen that the churchgoing rates of members of voluntary service groups were more than double those of the population at large. Members of religious groups were more than three times as likely as non-members to be involved in voluntary service. They were also disproportionately involved in all of the other caring groups – such as community groups, environmental groups, Scouts and Guides – as well as in self-help groups – such as tenants groups, parents associations, pensioners groups and political parties.

It was seen in chapter four that there is a suggestion, both from BHPS data and from American data,[4] that different theological positions may influence churchgoers' involvement in voluntary service in the community. The Australian National Church Life Survey of 1991 provides additional evidence here. Since this was a survey of churchgoers alone, the results cannot be compared readily with levels of voluntary service in the rest of society (although, as noted earlier, there is other Australian evidence which can be[5]). Instead it provides an important comparison of different levels of involvement within Anglican and Free Churches. Overall 27% of churchgoers in the survey were 'involved in wider community care/welfare/social action'.

[4] See John Wilson and Thomas Janoski, 'The Contribution of Religion to Volunteer Work', *Sociology of Religion*, 56:2, 1995.

[5] See Peter Bentley and Philip J. Hughes, *Australian Life and the Christian Faith: Facts and Figures*, Christian Research Association, Kew, Victoria, Australia, 1998, p. 66.

However, it was churchgoers within the more theologically liberal denominations who were most involved. Within the Uniting Church the level of involvement rose to 36% and within the Anglican Church it was 32%. In contrast, it was just 12% in the highly conservative Westminster Presbyterian Church, 13% in the Foursquare Gospel Church, and 15% in the Assemblies of God, the Christian Revival Crusade and the Church of the Nazarene. One factor involved in these differences was the age profile of churches, since older churchgoers were typically more involved than younger churchgoers. Yet this was not the only factor. A strong association was also found between engagement in voluntary service and involvement in a small group within a church.[6] As the authors of the NCLS point out: 'this challenges the notion that involvement in church life isolates people from wider community affairs'.[7]

British Social Attitudes data add further evidence to this profile of churchgoers. Respondents in 1994 were shown a card listing nine different options and were asked, 'Are you currently a member of any of these?: Tenants'/residents' association; Parent–teachers association; Board of school governors/school board; A political party; Parish or town council; Neighbourhood council/forum; Neighbourhood watch scheme; Local conservation or environmental group; Other local community or voluntary group.' A strongly significant directional pattern emerges in the four levels of churchgoing–nonchurchgoing amongst those who responded that they were a member of a community/voluntary group (15%, 17%, 8%, 3%). If those aged 35–59 are isolated, an even clearer directional pattern is apparent (20%, 19%, 11%, 5%). In both instances only 3% of those who gave a no-religion response were members of such a group. So, to express this difference at its sharpest, a middle-aged weekly churchgoer here was four times more likely to be a member of a community or voluntary group than a middle-

6 Cf. Robert Wuthnow, *Sharing the Journey: Support Groups and America's New Quest for Community*, The Free Press, New York, 1994.

7 Peter Kaldor, John Bellamy and Ruth Powell, *Shaping a Future: Characteristics of Vital Congregations*, Openbook Publishers, Sydney, 1996, p. 47.

aged nonchurchgoer and almost seven times more likely than someone in the no-religion category.

The groups mentioned in this BSA question are different from those in BHPS (for example, the latter includes sports and social groups). Nevertheless there is a similar pattern, suggesting that churchgoing is strongly related to voluntary service. In BSA, as in BHPS, members of the voluntary groups are twice as likely to go regularly to church as the population at large. In both BSA and BHPS 27% of these members are weekly churchgoers, and 46% in the first and 42% in the second go at least once a month. Membership of the other groups taken together also shows that churchgoers are more heavily involved than other people. Amongst those in BSA who report that they are members of *none* of the nine groups listed, there is a significant pattern of churchgoing–nonchurchgoing directionality (70%, 76%, 83%, 86%). Again, as was noted in BHPS data, the involvement of churchgoers in environmental groups is higher than is sometimes portrayed. In this instance membership can be tested across two BSA surveys. Amalgamating data from BSA 1993 and 1994, churchgoers appear to be at least as likely to be members of an environmental group as nonchurchgoers (8%, 9%, 7%, 5% and no-religion 7%).

It is important once again not to exaggerate differences between churchgoers and other people. Most of those involved in voluntary service in these samples do not go to church regularly and most regular churchgoers are not involved in nonchurch voluntary service. Furthermore, although regular churchgoers in BSA 1993 were more inclined to agree that 'everyone has a duty to volunteer', a proportion of nonchurchgoers did too (46%, 27%, 39%, 31% and no-religion 27%). Nonetheless, a surprisingly high proportion of voluntary workers do go to church and churchgoers themselves are far more likely than other people to become voluntary workers. Linear regression analysis indicates that frequency of churchgoing in BSA 1994 is a highly significant variable in predicting voluntary service (as it is in EVSSG and BHPS) – it is as significant as age and tertiary qualifications and more significant than gender, income or schooling.

There is probably no need to test this particular relationship any further. These three sources of data really do establish beyond reasonable doubt a significant link between churchgoing and voluntary service. Instead, what is needed is detailed qualitative research in this area. For example, it would be very instructive if a map could be drawn in one locality of all the interactions between those involved in voluntary service. A number of historians have begun to do this,[8] but by focusing so much on the decline of religious and voluntary organisations they may, in the process, have underestimated the present-day involvement of churchgoers and, perhaps, former churchgoers. Because it no longer tends to be administered by churches themselves, in contrast to Victorian times when typically it was, voluntary service in Britain today can too easily be regarded as largely secularised. The continuing high involvement of churchgoers, however, suggests otherwise. Again it would be helpful for qualitative research in this area to uncover some of the motivations of these churchgoers. How far do *they* see their voluntary service as a part of their Christian commitment? Early qualitative research in this area by Tom Frame[9] suggests that churchgoers do not always make overt connections until prompted to do so: voluntary service appears typically to be an unspoken part of churchgoing culture.

Another area which could usefully be investigated is the influence, if any, of past churchgoing upon voluntary service. It will be seen again, in a moment, that there is a certain amount of evidence that those brought up going to church retain some of the same values as churchgoers despite not going to church now. The evidence is tentative, but it does suggest a fruitful line of future research. A focus solely upon current churchgoing is likely to be limited, especially since it has long been known that few individuals maintain a pattern of unbroken churchgoing

[8] Eg. Stephen Yeo, *Religious and Voluntary Organizations in Crisis*, Croom Helm, London, 1976, and Jeffrey Cox, *The English Churches in a Secular Society: Lambeth, 1870–1930*, Oxford University Press, Oxford, 1982. For a critique of Cox see my *The Myth of the Empty Church*, SPCK, London, 1993.

[9] In an unpublished study for the MA in Applied Theology at the University of Kent, Canterbury, 1997.

throughout their lives.[10] Unfortunately, BSA data do not allow this possible link to be explored in relation to voluntary service.

For all those interested in the relationship between churchgoing and Christian ethics, involvement in voluntary service is particularly important. It illustrates both the fragility of the Christian life and its distinctiveness. Voluntary service in the community always offers an impossible challenge for churchgoers and lays them open to the damaging criticism of hypocrisy. There is no limit to the voluntary service that could be given since human need is so unbounded. As the plight of the urban destitute increases even in the affluent North, so opportunities for voluntary service become ever more pressing for those with eyes to see and ears to hear. And as the population of the South continues to rise, so do the cries of the world's poor and hungry become more and more desperate. The parable of the sheep and the goats becomes an ever sharper critique of the actual lives of Christians in both North and South. It can hardly be surprising that Christians are so often accused of hypocrisy – the demands of faith are so high and the capacity of the faithful so limited. At the same time churchgoers do seem to be more likely to serve than other people.

This ambivalence is aptly expressed in this Synoptic story:

> A dispute arose among the apostles, which of them was to be regarded as the greatest. And Jesus said to them, 'The kings of the Gentiles exercise lordship over them; and those in authority over them are called benefactors. But not so with you; rather let the greatest among you become as the youngest, and the leader as one who serves. For which is the greater, one who sits at table, or one who serves? Is it not the one who sits at table? But I am among you as one who serves.[11]

Once again, the Christian life is finally set into a theological, christocentric context. It is in Jesus Christ that true service can be seen. Amongst his followers only traces of this service are to be found. Yet the evidence collected here shows that these traces can indeed still be found.

[10] Cf. Mass-Observation, 'Why Do People Come to Church?', *British Weekly*, 13 January 1949.

[11] Luke 22.24–7 (RSV).

Test 2

BSA provides a wealth of data about altruistic attitudes and motivation. Often these are strongly linked to age and gender. Nevertheless there is much evidence that churchgoing is also an important factor. Those who go regularly to church do appear to be more honest and altruistic in their attitudes than other people. They also have distinctive moral perspectives on such issues as medical ethics, euthanasia and capital punishment. There are, though, tensions and differences detectable as well amongst churchgoers on many of these issues and continuities with nonchurchgoers. Here, too, the distinctiveness of churchgoers is relative rather than absolute.

In the analysis of BHPS data two further areas of altruism were noted, namely advice to the young to 'help others' and to look after elderly parents. Both showed a significant directionality with churchgoing. BSA data provide two similar pieces of evidence. In BSA 1989 respondents were asked to identify the 'most important factor in choosing a new job', suggesting 'to help others' as one of the options. Respondents were given three separate choices altogether. Adding these together, there is a clear difference between churchgoers and nonchurchgoers amongst those choosing 'to help others' as an option (28%, 23%, 16%, 6%). Similarly in BSA 1983 clear differences are apparent between churchgoers and nonchurchgoers amongst those who agreed that 'children should look after aged parents' (55%, 42%, 42%, 39%). As was found in BHPS, it is those aged 18–34 who showed the strongest directionality on this issue (57%, 26%, 36%, 34%). The elderly themselves – perhaps for just as altruistic reasons – were more reluctant to agree to this.

Clearly there are continuities as well as discontinuities here between churchgoers and nonchurchgoers. Continuity is very evident, for example, in the proportions of adult churchgoers and nonchurchgoers who in BSA 1986 agreed that 'parents should teach children unselfishness' (78%, 71%, 77%, 79% and no-religion 75%). Again, in the same survey most people agreed that 'faithfulness is very important for marriage' (93%, 88%, 87%, 89% and no-religion 82%). Some values do seem to be shared widely across society on such personal issues, even though small differences between churchgoers and nonchurchgoers can still be detected.

This last point is a strong feature of BSA questions that have recurred over the years on personal honesty. At the end of reviewing BSA 1984 and 1987 data, Michael Johnston concluded:

> 'Moral traditionalism' remains a firm feature of British life. And while sections of the population differ, sometimes to a marked degree, in how they feel they would act in ethically challenging situations, they still seem to agree upon the *relative* seriousness of a range of 'rule-breaking' behaviours. Moreover, there is even less variation between subgroups in the ways they respond to the actions of others – judgements which contribute to the 'civic' aspects of the culture. Taken together, the evidence hardly portrays a breakdown in British social ethics.[12]

Johnston's tables do suggest that frequency at religious worship (he did not separate churchgoers from those attending services in other faiths) is a relevant factor in all of the nine ethical situations reviewed. It is mostly matched by differences of age (the younger respondents being both less honest and less inclined to attend religious worship than the older respondents), but as he noted three years earlier, 'religious observance had an independent relationship to people's views . . . religion appeared to have more influence on evaluations of everyday personal transactions than it did on judgements of more distant relationships in business and government'.[13] These personal situations were, for example, employees fiddling expenses to make an extra £50, a milkman overcharging customers by £200, an antique dealer concealing woodworm in furniture to make £50, and a householder over-claiming on insurance by £500. The greater the dishonesty on such issues, the more most groups believed it to be wrong, whether they currently attended

[12] Michael Johnston, 'The Price of Honesty', in Roger Jowell, Sharon Witherspoon and Lindsay Brook (eds.), *British Social Attitudes the 5th Report*, Social and Community Planning Research, Gower, Aldershot, 1988, pp. 12–13.

[13] Michael Johnston and Douglas Wood, 'Right and Wrong in Public and Private Life', in Roger Jowell and Sharon Witherspoon (eds.), *British Social Attitudes the 2nd Report*, Social and Community Planning Research, Gower, Aldershot, 1985, p. 131.

religious worship or not. In contrast, issues such as expensive entertainment for business managers or council officials, showed little or no influence by religious observance.

Rather more interesting questions were asked in BSA 1991, involving not just ethical judgments about situations but also the additional question, 'Might you do this if the situation came up?' Asked in this form, rather sharper differences appeared between churchgoers and nonchurchgoers, as well between those who had been brought up regularly going to church and those who had not. Particularly striking were the responses to this situation:

A man gives a £5 note for goods he is buying in a big store. By mistake, he is given change for a £10 note. He notices but keeps the change. Please say which comes closest to what you think ... Nothing wrong; Bit Wrong; Wrong; Seriously Wrong; Very Seriously Wrong.

In the sample as a whole, three-quarters thought this to be wrong (i.e. 'wrong' through to 'very seriously wrong'), but only one quarter said they might do it themselves. A high level of moral consensus was obviously present here as well. Yet significantly different levels between churchgoers and nonchurchgoers were still evident both amongst those believing this to be wrong (94%, 83%, 79%, 76% and no-religion 67%) and amongst those saying that they might do it themselves (6%, 15%, 18%, 25% and no-religion 37%). Although both of these patterns are statistically significant using directional analysis, age and gender appear to be more significant factors here than churchgoing. So older respondents and women are considerably less likely to say they might keep the extra £5 than the younger male respondents. Nevertheless, the churchgoing–nonchurchgoing patterns of those saying they might do this amongst the 18–34 age-group (6%, 35%, 39%, 44% and no-religion 54%) and amongst men (4%, 25%, 27%, 33% and no-religion 39%), both show that regular churchgoers are distinctive. There is also a sharp difference between two groups of nonchurchgoers (including no-religion respondents here): amongst those who had never been to church as children 51% said that they might do this, whereas only 21% did of those who had been regularly as children. Some caution is needed here, since this second group is more elderly and female that the first. However this is a large difference.

Two other questions were asked in this double form in BSA 1991. Both show differences, although not quite such sharp differences, in these various groups. One of these suggested that, 'In making an insurance claim, a man whose home has been burgled exaggerates the value of what was stolen by £150.' Differences were evident amongst churchgoers–nonchurchgoers both in those believing this to be wrong (87%, 83%, 73%, 71% and no-religion 66%) and those saying they might do it themselves (10%, 17%, 19%, 28% and no-religion 31%). A very similar question in BSA 1987 found the same pattern. BSA 1991 also found sharp differences between the two groups of nonchurchgoers saying they might do it (41% and 23% respectively). The final situation in BSA 1991 suggested, 'A householder is having a repair job done by a local plumber. He is told that if he pays cash he will not be charged VAT. So he pays cash.' Rather narrower differences were found amongst those believing this to be wrong (55%, 44%, 49%, 44% and no-religion 38%) and those saying they might do it themselves amongst both churchgoers–nonchurchgoers (58%, 64%, 70%, 73% and no-religion 78%) and the two groups of nonchurchgoers (87% and 75%).

All of this fits the Australian evidence,[14] reviewed in chapter two, about the distinctive levels of honesty found amongst churchgoers. It also fits Michael Johnston's conclusion that, even in a broad setting of moral consensus, religious observance does have an influence upon matters of personal ethics over and above the influence of age. In addition, it suggests the fascinating possibility that churchgoing as a child may have some influence upon individual attitudes and behaviour even in the absence of adult churchgoing. Much remains to be tested here, but this does seem to be a possibility.

Yet what of Johnston's other conclusion that attitudes on less personal moral issues appear unaffected by religious observance? BSA provides some interesting examples which suggest

[14] Gary D. Bouma and Beverly R. Dixon, *The Religious Factor in Australian Life*, MARC Australia, World Vision and the Zadok Centre, 1986.

otherwise, especially in those socio-political areas which cluster around the belief of churchgoers that life is God-given. Attitudes to abortion, euthanasia and capital punishment all supply this contrary evidence. At the same time each of these highlights differences and changes amongst churchgoers themselves.

One of the factors which prompted the legalisation of abortion in Britain in 1968 was a change in public opinion. Doubtless this was, in turn, shaped by such factors as evidence about the prevalence of illegal and particularly septic abortions. Whatever the reasons for the change, by the mid-1980s there was widespread support for abortion, especially in those cases where the woman's health was endangered, where the woman had been raped, or where there was a defect in the embryo. What is more, regular churchgoers also tended to support abortion in such cases. Sharp differences between churchgoers and non-churchgoers emerged only in cases of abortion where the couple reported that they could not afford to have a baby or where the woman simply said that she did not wish to have child. Even then, there was a minority of regular churchgoers, even amongst Roman Catholics, who supported abortion on financial or pro-choice grounds.

MORI polls[15] for the 1980s and 1990s show how public opinion has changed in this area. Asked in 1983 'Do you think that unmarried women having abortions is morally wrong or not?', 38% replied yes and 47% no: by 1996 those responding yes had decreased to 21% and no had increased to 65%. MORI also asked people 'Do you think Britain's abortion law should be changed to make it more difficult for women to obtain an abortion, changed to make it easier for women to obtain an abortion, or should it be left as it is?' Those stating that it should be left as it is increased from 37% in 1980 to 55% in 1996. Abortion does seem to have become morally acceptable to most people.

BSA data 1983–7 combined show how these changing attitudes have also affected regular churchgoers. Asked whether or not abortion should be allowed on the grounds of the woman's

[15] Reported in *British Public Opinion*, August/September 1996.

health being endangered, 92% of Anglican weekly churchgoers thought that it should, as did 65% of Roman Catholic weekly churchgoers. 88% of Anglican and 63% of Roman Catholic weekly churchgoers thought that abortion should be allowed on grounds of rape. Amongst Roman Catholic monthly churchgoers this rose to 81%. In chapter two it was noted that, in the Francis–Kay survey of churchgoing teenagers, most Roman Catholics did not follow official teaching on contraception, although they did on abortion. BSA data show that adult Roman Catholics are also selective about official teaching in a number of related areas. For example, in the 1985 and 1987 surveys combined, 73% of their weekly churchgoers supported artificial insemination by the husband and 66% support *in vitro* fertilisation, both of which are condemned by the Vatican. Amongst Anglicans, the Church of England's Board of Social Responsibility 1965 report, *Abortion: An Ethical Discussion*, argued against defective embryos being allowed as a legal ground for abortion, since this would further disadvantage the disabled and give credence to a less than Christian understanding of what it is to be a person. However, in the BSA surveys two decades later, 82% of Anglican weekly churchgoers now supported abortion in such cases. Roman Catholic weekly churchgoers at 43% were distinctly less supportive, but amongst their monthly churchgoers support rose to 76%.

This is not to argue that churchgoers simply mirror the views of secular society in all of these areas. Clear and statistically significant differences emerged on financial and pro-choice grounds for abortion. Whereas 55% of nominal Anglicans who never went to church supported abortion on purely financial grounds and 45% on pro-choice grounds, amongst weekly churchgoers this reduced to 30% and 25% respectively. Amongst Roman Catholic weekly churchgoers support reduced still further to 15% and 12% respectively. So on these two grounds – financial and pro-choice – churchgoers on average were different from nonchurchgoers. Yet this was not an absolute difference. More than a fifth of weekly churchgoers across denominations and more than a third of monthly churchgoers supported abortion even on these two grounds. Conversely about a half of the nonchurchgoers withheld support for such abortions.

A very similar pattern amongst churchgoers and between churchgoers and nonchurchgoers now seems to be emerging on the issue of euthanasia. There is increasing evidence of popular support for legalising euthanasia in certain circumstances, even amongst regular churchgoers. BSA 1983–4 shows that most people, including many churchgoers, support changes in the law which would allow medically assisted suicide for the terminally ill. Conversely, few people support the legalisation of euthanasia for those who are simply tired of living but are not terminally ill. As was seen in chapter two using Australian data,[16] there are clear differences between churchgoers and nonchurchgoers in this area, yet they are by no means absolute differences.

Of the whole BSA sample in 1983–4 76% were in favour of euthanasia being allowed for the terminally ill and in 1994 this rose to 82%. Support amongst monthly churchgoers across denominations in these two decades differed little from the sample as a whole: it was only amongst weekly churchgoers that a statistically significant difference emerged. Thus, although highly significant directionality was evident both in 1983–4 (48%, 72%, 78%, 77%) and in 1994 (45%, 84%, 84%, 87%), support for euthanasia for the terminally ill increased in every group except weekly churchgoers taken as a whole. Amongst Anglican weekly churchgoers, however, in 1983–4 support was much higher at 66%. Clearest opposition to this form of euthanasia was amongst Roman Catholic weekly churchgoers (39%), although three-quarters of their monthly attenders supported it. Amongst the 1983–4 weekly churchgoers across denominations, age was not a strong predictor of attitudes: 47% of those aged 18–34 and 51% of those aged 60+ expressed support for euthanasia being allowed for the terminally ill.

In Australia in 1991 the National Church Life Survey asked churchgoers to respond to the statement that 'People should be able to choose to die to relieve suffering from an incurable

[16] Bouma and Dixon, *The Religious Factor.*

illness.'[17] More churchgoers responded positively (42%) than negatively (30%). Support was strongest in the more liberal denominations, the Uniting Church (57%) and the Anglican Church (51%), and weakest in the more conservative denominations, the Assemblies of God (24%) and the Baptists (34%). Opposition was strongest amongst those identified as biblical literalists (47%). Nevertheless, clear differences on this issue were evident within all of the denominations surveyed.

In 1994 BSA asked people whether they thought that the law should let close relatives assist the suicide of the terminally ill. Of the sample as a whole 54% agreed that it should. Again only 25% of weekly churchgoers agreed, yet amongst monthly churchgoers this rose to 52%. Directional statistical analysis on this and the previous question does suggest that the more individuals go to church the less likely they are to accept the legalisation of euthanasia or assisted suicide. Nonetheless, there is still a minority of weekly churchgoers who do accept such legislation and a minority of nonchurchgoers who do not. Even the 1983–4 question about allowing euthanasia for those who are simply tired of living showed that 6% of weekly churchgoers, as distinct from 12% of the sample as a whole, agreed to this.

The 1995 BSA survey[18] for the first time asked people to make judgments about eight different euthanasia scenarios, ranging from euthanasia for the permanently comatose to assisted suicide for those who are tired of living. Once again it suggests strong popular support for medically administered euthanasia for the terminally ill, together with a fairly nuanced understanding of differences between the scenarios. People do seem prepared to make distinctions and do not give undifferentiated support for euthanasia in any form. So there appears to be strong support for euthanasia/assisted suicide for those who are terminally ill, but little for those who are not but are

[17] Peter Kaldor and Ruth Powell, *Views from the Pews: Australian Church Attenders Speak Out*, Openbook Publishers, Sydney, 1995.

[18] For a discussion, see David Donnison and Caroline Bryson, 'Matters of Life and Death: Attitudes to Euthanasia', in Roger Jowell, John Curtice, Alison Park, Lindsay Brook and Katarina Thomson (eds.), *British Social Attitudes the 13th Report*, Social and Community Planning Research, Dartmouth, Hants, 1996, pp. 161–83.

simply tired of living. There is also strong support for withdrawing life support from the permanently comatose. In addition, attendance at worship (here again churchgoers are not differentiated from those attending services in other faiths) appears to be a highly significant variable in predicting attitudes towards euthanasia. Indeed, regular religious observance is a more significant variable here than age, gender or social class. Combining all the different scenarios, weekly worshippers have a rating of 3.95 on an 8 point scale (i.e. just less than half support the different forms of euthanasia) whereas nonworshippers have a rating of 5.08 and those in the no-religion group 5.53.

Questions about capital punishment also show distinctive patterns amongst and between churchgoers. Clear, statistically significant differences between churchgoers and nonchurchgoers are consistently shown in BSA data on this issue. Despite having been abolished in Britain thirty years ago, capital punishment remains a political issue and still has widespread public support. BSA have regularly tested this support, usually by giving people three different scenarios. In the first, respondents are asked if they 'favour capital punishment' for terrorist murder. The results show clear directionality in 1983–5 (61%, 76%, 81%, 80%) and in 1993–4 (61%, 69%, 77%, 78%) albeit with a slight overall decline in support. A very similar pattern is evident when respondents are asked if they favour capital punishment for police murder in 1983–5 (58%, 73%, 77%, 76%) and 1993–4 (63%, 65%, 74%, 76%), and when asked if they favour it for 'other murders' in 1983–5 (49%, 62%, 68%, 72%) and 1993–4 (49%, 56%, 67%, 67%). This is impressively consistent data. Age is a very significant factor in shaping attitudes on capital punishment, with the young less supportive than the old. However, churchgoing remains influential on this issue amongst the young who do go to church. To give a single example, there is clear directional support in the 1980s data about capital punishment for police murder in the 18–34 age-group (37%, 60%, 62%, 75%).

If data from all three scenarios is added together, then support for capital punishment in the sample as a whole drops slightly over the decade from 71% to 68%. The effect of this is to bring irregular churchgoers and nonchurchgoers closer to the position of weekly churchgoers, as a comparison of the pattern for 1983–5 (56%, 70%, 75%, 76% and no-religion 70%) with that for 1993–4 (57%, 63%, 73%, 74% and no-religion 66%) shows.

It appears, then, that many weekly churchgoers are hesitant about supporting capital punishment, just as they are more hesitant than others about supporting abortion on economic grounds or euthanasia. This does seem to be consistent with their distinctive belief, mapped earlier, that life is God-given. However, table 13 suggests that there is a difference between regular churchgoers who are biblical literalists and those who are non-literalists. On both of the BSA 1991 questions on capital punishment, the views of the literalists were much closer to those of the whole sample, supporting capital punishment, than were the views of the non-literalists. However, on questions about abortion these two groups of weekly churchgoers were much closer to each other, differing significantly from the sample as whole. It might be speculated here that it is once again moral order rather than the status of human life which most divides these two groups.

In their analysis of BSA 1995 data, David Donnison and Caroline Bryson found that in the sample as a whole those supporting euthanasia also tended to support abortion, suicide and capital punishment. In contrast, 'those attending religious services regularly are more likely to think of life as God-given, and so something that individuals have no right to end. Given the growing secularisation of Britain, these findings suggest that support for the legalisation of euthanasia will increase over time.'[19] It can now be seen that this analysis is not quite accurate: churchgoers are somewhat less predictable than this suggests. Both of the churchgoing groups do indeed accept that life is God-given, but the literalists appear more inclined than the non-literalists to believe that in the context of murder the demands of order may overrule the requirement not to take

[19] *Ibid.* p. 172.

human life. Furthermore, cautious acceptance of both abortion and euthanasia (and perhaps tolerance of suicide) does seem to be increasing even amongst churchgoers – albeit allied to a strong concern for the vulnerable.

If all of this suggests the presence of a variety of altruistic attitudes amongst churchgoers, there is one piece of evidence which is usually thought to count against. It has often been claimed that churchgoers tend to be more racist than other people.[20] Responses to a number of BSA questions asked over the years tend to suggest that the opposite is the case. One question that has been asked several times is, 'How would you describe yourself . . . as very prejudiced against people of other races . . . a little prejudiced . . . or, not prejudiced at all?' A significant directionality is once again evident. For example, in the 1983–7 surveys combined, this can be seen in the pattern of those responding 'not prejudiced at all' (76%, 65%, 63%, 58% and no-religion 60%). It is also evident, in 1994, amongst those responding 'very' or 'a little' prejudiced (28%, 32%, 36%, 42% and no-religion 37%). Age is an important factor here, yet the same pattern is present in the 18–34 age-group (13%, 29%, 35%, 40% and no-religion 37%). Similarly, the pattern of those agreeing in 1994 that 'attempts to give equal opportunities to black people and Asians in Britain have gone too far' (19%, 27%, 30%, 24% and no-religion 26%) suggests that churchgoers are, if anything, less prejudiced than other people. When asked whether they would mind if a black person or Asian were appointed as their boss or married a close relative, churchgoers do not appear to be any more prejudiced than other people. Frankly it is difficult to find any support in the BSA data for this long-standing belief about churchgoers. Even on the issue of specifically religious prejudice, evidence of greater prejudice amongst churchgoers is lacking. The combined 1989–91 data of those saying that they were 'not prejudiced at all . . . against other religions' (91%, 91%, 88, 88% and no-religion 89%) does not suggest such prejudice.

[20] For a discussion of this, see section five of my *A Textbook of Christian Ethics*.

Test 3

There is one area which consistently shows that regular churchgoers are different from other people, namely in their views and actions on charity. Here BSA provides some very important and nuanced evidence. The most striking feature of this evidence is that churchgoers have distinctive views about where charity should be directed. And even when they disagree amongst themselves about the relative importance of particular charities, that does not prevent them from giving more readily than other people.

In BSA 1993 respondents were given two choices to name the 'most important cause to raise money for in Britain' out of six options: medical supplies to Africa; homeless people in the UK; starving people in poor countries; protecting rare animals throughout the world; kidney machines in the UK; and preventing cruelty to animals in the UK. If the two overseas options involving people are combined – namely, medical supplies to Africa and starving people in poor countries – then a very distinctive churchgoing–nonchurchgoing pattern emerges (67%, 50%, 38%, 32% and no-religion 36%). If the two options involving animals are taken, then the pattern is reversed (6%, 8%, 9%, 15% and no-religion 15%), albeit at a much lower level of general support. The mean score for those opting for either homeless people or kidney machines in the UK shows a similar pattern (46%, 69%, 76%, 77% and no-religion 72%) but at a higher level. Weekly churchgoers evidently take the needs of the poor overseas more seriously than do other people.

Exactly the same point emerges from an analysis of BSA 1994 choices of what would be 'an excellent' or 'very good' way for national lottery money to be spent. In this instance respondents were not asked to choose between different options, but instead were allowed to consider each of the eleven options separately. This helps to adjust some of the distortion that may have resulted from the previous question. In that there was no way of telling whether or not someone, say, who opted for overseas aid was actually against animal or British-bound causes. In other words, it tested preferential options but not discrete sympathies. The lottery question provides a fuller picture of the latter.

The three lottery options which show a highly significant directionality amongst churchgoers–nonchurchgoers are: 'helping starving people in poor countries'; 'helping ex-prisoners to find homes and jobs'; and 'helping to prevent cruelty to animals in Britain'. Frequency of churchgoing has a positive influence on agreeing with the first two options, but a negative influence on agreeing with the third. Or to express this in English, regular churchgoers are far more likely than other people to support money going to help the starving and ex-prisoners (as the parable of the sheep and the goats requires), and far less likely to support it going to help animals. This is shown clearly in the patterns of those believing that it is *not* a good way to spend the money on the starving (22%, 42%, 48%, 54%), ex-prisoners (29%, 37%, 48%, 51%) and, quite oppositely, animals (35%, 23%, 26%, 14%).

It is worth exploring this relationship in a little more depth. Attitudes towards spending lottery money on the starving overseas are strongly influenced by both age and by churchgoing. Yet, amongst both young and old, weekly churchgoers differ from irregular and non-churchgoers. This is clear from the patterns of those believing that this is not a good way amongst respondents aged 18–34 (15%, 33%, 29%, 44% and no-religion 40%) and those aged 60+ (23%, 54%, 57%, 58% and no-religion 63%). It would be tedious to express all these patterns positively: the overall pattern of those agreeing that this 'an excellent' or 'very good' way to spend the money will suffice (48%, 35%, 23%, 19% and no-religion 22%). This finding also matches negative responses to the BSA statement, 'We should support more charities which benefit people in Britain, rather than people overseas', as the significant patterns for 1991 (37%, 44%, 61%, 74% and no-religion 54%) and 1993 (42%, 56%, 66%, 77% and no-religion 66%) both show.

The evidence here is clear. As was seen in chapter two looking at Australian churchgoers,[21] regular churchgoers in

[21] Bouma and Dixon, *The Religious Factor.*

Britain seem to be significantly more concerned than other people about charitable money going to the poor overseas. Why is this? A theological answer would point to such biblical passages as Matthew 25 (as I have just done). Churchgoers have this concern because a bias towards the poor and needy is present in so many parts of Jewish and Christian Scripture.[22] A cultural answer might differ somewhat. Churchgoers are part of a culture which presents the needs of the poor and suffering in many different ways . . . not just in biblical readings and sermons, but also in intercessions, in appeals to give to *Christian Aid* or to *Tear Fund*, in pictures and posters decorating churches, and even in the words of many modern hymns. In cultural terms, as will be seen in chapter eight, people gathering regularly for Christian worship today are sensitised from many different directions about the poor overseas. It would, perhaps, be surprising if they were not influenced by this.

All of this makes the finding about biblical literalists in table 13 particularly surprising. They seem to agree with the rest of the population (but not with other churchgoers) that, 'We should support more charities which benefit people in Britain, rather than people overseas'. Are they less charitable than other churchgoers? Table 13 does seem to suggest that they are more inclined than other people to believe that 'people should look after themselves and not rely upon charities'. However, their response to the statement, 'I can't refuse when someone comes to the door with a collecting tin' suggests otherwise. The combined 1991 and 1993 pattern of those agreeing with this statement (60%, 48%, 52%, 51% and no-religion 41%) shows a clear difference between churchgoers and nonchurchgoers. And not a single weekly churchgoer of any description responded that they 'never' gave to charity.

Very detailed data about American churchgoers[23] also makes it very unlikely that British literalist churchgoers are

22 See Garth L. Hallett, *Priorities and Christian Ethics*, Cambridge University Press, New York and Cambridge, 1998.

23 Dean R. Hoge, Charles Zech, Patrick McNamara and Michael J. Donahue, *Money Matters: Personal Giving in American Churches*, Westminster John Knox Press, Louisville, Kentucky, 1996.

uncharitable. Rather the reverse, they are highly likely to give a much greater proportion of their income away than non-literalists. Yet, if the American data apply to British churchgoers, literalists are likely to confine most of their giving to church-based causes. Again, the Australian National Church Life Survey[24] provides evidence missing from the British data. Churchgoers there were asked: 'Do you think being a Christian involves a responsibility to share in meeting the needs of people in developing countries?' Most respondents replied either 'Yes, and I am involved this way' (42%) or 'Yes, but I currently have no involvement in this area' (48%). Here it was members of more conservative denominations who typically gave the first response, Salvation Army (56%) and Baptists (48%), whereas the lowest first responses were given by the Lutherans (33%), Anglicans (35%) and Uniting Church (39%). Those identified as biblical literalists also had a high level of first responses (52%). There is certainly scope for much more research in this area.

To return to data about churchgoers as a whole, it might seem from the lottery questions that they are less concerned than other people about the non-human environment. In turn, this might confirm the much discussed Lynn White thesis, to the effect that Judaism and Christianity have been responsible for fostering a negative and destructive view of the natural environment. In words that have been repeated many times over within the ecological movement, White (himself a churchgoer) concluded:

> Especially in its Western form, Christianity is the most anthropocentric religion the world has seen. As early as the 2nd century both Tertullian and Saint Irenaeus of Lyons were insisting that when God shaped Adam he was foreshadowing the image of the incarnate Christ, the Second Adam. Man shares, in great measure, God's transcendence of nature. Christianity, in absolute contrast to ancient paganism and Asia's religions (except, perhaps, Zoroastrianism), not only established a dualism of man and nature, but also insisted that it is God's will that man exploit nature for his proper ends.[25]

[24] Kaldor and Powell, *Views from the Pews.*

[25] Lynn White, 'The Historical Roots of our Ecologic Crisis', *Science*, vol. 155, no. 3767, 10 March 1967, pp. 1203–7.

There is now a growing literature of international sociological research assessing whether or not White's thesis can be corroborated empirically.[26] Overwhelmingly, it has found no significant correlation between religious belief and belonging today with environmentally damaging beliefs, attitudes and behaviour.

It is unnecessary to discuss this thesis in depth again here,[27] but necessary to examine new data on churchgoers and environmental issues. Two pieces of evidence have already been noted. The first is that most weekly churchgoers (86%) in BSA 1993 agree that, 'Human beings should respect nature because it was created by God.' Sometimes it is forgotten in this debate that belief in a creator God might actually enhance rather than diminish respect for the environment. The second is that churchgoers in both BSA and BHPS are actually more likely than nonchurchgoers to be members of an environmental group. The lottery questions, too, suggest that churchgoers are just as concerned about the environment as other people. The only exception to this is the question about allocating money 'helping to prevent cruelty to animals in Britain'. In contrast, the option 'helping to protect the environment' suggests no significant difference between churchgoers and nonchurchgoers.

Other questions in BSA 1994 suggest that churchgoers are more likely than other people to act on environmental issues. In one scenario it was suggested that 'A housing development was being planned in a part of the countryside you knew and liked' and respondents were asked what if anything they might do

[26] See Andrew Greeley, 'Religion and Attitudes Toward the Environment', *Journal for the Scientific Study of Religion*, 32:1, 1993; Michael P. Hornsby-Smith and Michael Procter, 'Catholic Identity, Religious Context and Environmental Values in Western Europe: Evidence from the European Values Surveys', *Social Compass*, 42:1, 1995; Douglas Lee Eckberg and T. Jean Blocker, 'Christianity, Environmentalism, and the Theoretical Problem of Fundamentalism', *Journal for the Scientific Study of Religion*, 35:4, 1996; Alan W. Black, 'Religion and Environmentally Protective Behaviour in Australia', *Social Compass*, 44:3, 1997; and Paul Dekker, Peter Ester and Masja Nas, 'Religion, Culture and Environmental Concern: An Empirical Cross-national Analysis', *Social Compass*, 44:3, 1997.

[27] See further Michael S. Northcott, *The Environment and Christian Ethics*, Cambridge University Press, Cambridge, 1996, and section four of my *A Textbook of Christian Ethics*.

about this. Churchgoers differed from nonchurchgoers in that they said that they would contact their MP or councillor (47%, 41%, 37%, 29% and no-religion 29%) and contact a government or planning department (21%, 11%, 20%, 12% and no-religion 12%). In a second scenario it was suggested that 'A site where wildflowers grew was going to be ploughed for farmland.' On this, too, churchgoers appeared different in that they 'would take action' (15%, 5%, 8%, 9% and no-religion 4%). Asked more bluntly what they had actually done 'to help to protect the countryside', more churchgoers than nonchurchgoers said that they had contacted their MP or councillor (16%, 7%, 10%, 6% and no-religion 6%). These patterns do not suggest that churchgoers are particularly apathetic about, let alone hostile to, environmental issues.

In the Authorised Version of the Bible, on which older churchgoers were nurtured, Faith, Hope and Love were, of course, Faith, Hope and Charity. Although it would be a mistake to reduce Christian altruism to 'charity' in its modern sense, the latter clearly does play a distinctive part in the culture of churchgoing. Much more research is needed in this area as well as in that of voluntary service. At present too little is known about the outside charitable giving of churchgoers or about the motives underlying this giving. Most available information is about patterns of giving within churches, but even that requires more rigorous and comparative analysis. The economics of religion is as yet in its infancy.

As the beginning of this chapter emphasised, attitude surveys are far too crude to reveal the depths and complexities of moral character. Yet, taken together, BSA and BHPS data do appear able to sketch some of the distinctive moral outlines of churchgoers.

Faith, Hope and Love have, it seems, still left discernible, even if sometimes puzzling, reflections amongst churchgoers today.

PART THREE

The implications

CHAPTER 8

Churchgoing and Christian identity

At last it is possible to return to the issue of identity. More than enough data have been collected on the culture of churchgoing today to sketch its broad outline. It is time now to set this outline into a more specifically theological and qualitative context which supplements what can be learned from purely quantitative sociological investigation.

The mass of new data shows that churchgoers are indeed distinctive in their attitudes and behaviour. Some of their attitudes do change over time, especially on issues such as sexuality, and there are obvious moral disagreements between different groups of churchgoers in a number of areas. Nonetheless, there are broad patterns of Christian beliefs, teleology and altruism which distinguish churchgoers as a whole from nonchurchgoers. It has been seen that churchgoers have, in addition to their distinctive theistic and christocentric beliefs, a strong sense of moral order and concern for other people. They are, for example, more likely than others to be involved in voluntary service and to see overseas charitable giving as important. They are more hesitant about euthanasia and capital punishment and more concerned about the family and civic order than other people. None of these differences is absolute. The values, virtues, moral attitudes and behaviour of churchgoers are shared by many other people as well. The distinctiveness of churchgoers is real but relative.

This is exactly the picture that Alasdair MacIntyre paints in *After Virtue*. Unlike the dichotomy, seen in chapter one, between church and society increasingly present in the writings of Stanley Hauerwas and others, MacIntyre avoids idealised depictions of churches. For him society at large contains a 'conceptual *mélange* of moral thought and practice . . . fragments from the tradition – virtue concepts for the most part – are still to be found alongside characteristically modern and individualist concepts such as those of rights or utility'.[1] He recognises that, even in pluralistic American society, there are still religious communities – Catholic Irish, Orthodox Greeks and Orthodox Jews – which are relatively less fragmented. Yet, 'even however in such communities the need to enter into public debate enforces participation in the cultural *mélange* in the search for a common stock of concepts and norms which all may enjoy and to which all may appeal . . . in search of what, if my argument is correct, is a chimaera'.[2] This produces a curious mixture of historically and culturally contingent communities misguidedly searching for moral consensus. MacIntyre argues that 'moral philosophies, however they may aspire to achieve more than this, always do articulate the morality of some particular social and cultural standpoint'. As a result, modern, pluralistic societies cannot hope to achieve moral consensus. Rather, 'it is in its historical encounter that any given point of view establishes or fails to establish its rational superiority relative to its particular rivals in some specific contexts'.[3] A pattern, then, is to be expected: churches today may well be distinctive, but they will still overlap at many points with 'secular' communities.

The real but relative distinctiveness of churchgoing communities is important for the issue of identity. In his account of moral communities in pluralistic societies, the distinguished professor of law and sociology, Philip Selznick, argues that 'identity' is a key feature. For him:

A shared history tends to produce a sense of community, and this sense is manifested in loyalty, piety, and a distinctive identity. Every effort to create a community fosters such feelings and perceptions. A formed identity is the natural product of socialization, a process that

[1] Alasdair MacIntyre, *After Virtue: A Study of Moral Theory*, Duckworth, London, 1985, p. 252.
[2] *Ibid.* [3] *Ibid.* pp. 268–9.

is carried out not only in families but in most other institutions of self with others, with locality, and with association.[4]

Yet such 'identity' is also one of the most problematic features of communities. Whether this identity is local, religious or ethnic, it is prone to parochialism and virulent antagonisms. Selznick maintains that, in a properly balanced moral commonwealth, 'the gains in security and self-esteem must be balanced against the loss of more comprehensive, more inclusive, more integrated attitudes'.[5] Identity can too readily become exclusive. This will be one of the crucial questions to be explored in chapter nine. How can inclusive churches cope with sharp moral disagreements without becoming coercive and exclusive themselves?

Despite areas of considerable disagreement, a shared moral life and worship were important sources of identity for the earliest Christians. Whether the language is that of the Synoptic Gospels about 'entering the Kingdom of God' or that of Paul about 'being in Christ' and becoming a 'new person', a new life and identity follow. This is captured graphically in Acts:

> Peter replied, 'Repent and be baptised, every one of you, in the name of Jesus Christ so that your sins may be forgiven. And you will receive the gift of the Holy Spirit. The promise is for you and your children and for all who are far off – for all whom the Lord our God will call.' With many other words he warned them, 'Save yourselves from this corrupt generation.' Those who accepted his message were baptised, and about three thousand were added to their number that day. They devoted themselves to the apostles' teaching and to the fellowship, to the breaking of bread and to prayer.[6]

Worship is a key element here in the new identity of all those called by God in the name of Jesus Christ with the gift of the Holy Spirit. Specifically Christian worship involving 'the breaking of the bread' is a distinctive feature of their new fellowship. And it is within this fellowship that Christian identity can be nurtured.

[4] Philip Selznick, *The Moral Commonwealth: Social Theory and the Promise of Community*, University of California Press, Berkeley, 1992, p. 361.

[5] *Ibid.* p. 362.

[6] Acts 2.38–42 (NIV).

CAUSE OR EFFECT?

At several points in this book a crucial issue has been discussed. Can a causal relationship be established between churchgoing and the distinctive virtues that regular churchgoers hold to a greater degree than other people? Several pieces of evidence have been given suggesting that there really is a causal relationship here. There is the sheer extent of the data connecting churchgoing and distinctively Christian virtues. In almost any other area of sociology a variable which tested as so consistently significant (for example gender or social class) would be taken very seriously as an independent variable. In less technical language, it would simply be assumed that it is a key factor in shaping the values held by an individual. Again, there is the evidence that across several different cultures regular churchgoing appears to be closely connected with distinctive virtues. Comparative data have been reviewed from Australia and from several different European countries. There is also the range of statistical tests that have been used on the new British data. Particularly, ordinal by ordinal directional analysis has been used on all of this data, showing that the more regularly individuals go to church the more likely they are to share and practice distinctively Christian virtues. While these virtues are not absent from the broader society, they are found disproportionately amongst churchgoers and especially amongst the most regular churchgoers.

Of course it is still possible that, although there is a causal relationship here, it works from virtues to churchgoing rather than from churchgoing to virtues. That is to say, individuals who already share a number of Christian virtues are more likely than other people to go regularly to church and then to remain regular churchgoers. For example, some individuals may stop going to church precisely because their values differ from those of other churchgoers. Amongst American sociologists of religion there has been considerable discussion about this phenomenon affecting so-called 'baby boomers'. This generation, born between about 1945 and 1960, experienced a culture of permissive sexuality and drug taking in the 1960s and 1970s which put them at odds with the virtues of older churchgoers. As a result, so it is argued, they often stopped going to church.[7] Applying this theory to British data on church-leavers, Philip Richter and Leslie Francis conclude:

> We have suggested that, rather than losing their faith, leavers may have adopted a *different* style of faith, less conducive to church going, in response to these cultural shifts. We have noted that people born since 1945 tend to be a 'generation of seekers', with a distinctive set of values: they have an intrinsic tendency to be suspicious of all institutions, including the Church; they are drawn to more mystical beliefs; they prioritise experience above belief; and they tend to 'shop around' widely to satisfy their needs for personal authenticity and spiritual growth. As we have seen, church leaving by those born since 1945 can only be fully understood in this context.[8]

Important as this theory is, it does not explain all of the evidence uncovered in earlier chapters. Richter and Francis certainly do not see it as the only factor involved in church-leaving. It was noted in chapter two that Francis also supplies abundant evidence elsewhere[9] that teenage churchgoers today often hold views on sexuality which are closer to those of the rest of their generation than to those of older churchgoers. If some young people leave churches because they hold radically different values to older churchgoers, others remain within churches despite holding these different values. For example, it has been noted that BSA and BHPS both supply evidence that, whatever their congregations might think, some unmarried regular churchgoers live as married couples.

However, the strongest evidence for churchgoing as a causal factor is given in table 11. Comparing the BSA 1991 responses of two groups of nonchurchgoers – the one originally brought up going to church almost every week and the other never going in childhood at all – this evidence relates more to Christian beliefs

[7] See Wade Clark Roof, *A Generation of Seekers: The Spiritual Journeys of the Baby Boom Generation*, Harper, San Francisco, 1993, and Wade Clark Roof, Jackson W. Carroll and David A.Roozen, *The Post-War Generation and Establishment Religion*, Westview, Oxford, 1995.

[8] Philip Richter and Leslie J. Francis, *Gone But Not Forgotten: Church Leaving and Returning*, Darton, Longman & Todd, London, 1998, p. 52.

[9] See Leslie J. Francis and William K. Kay, *Teenage Religion and Values*, Gracewing, Fowler Wright Books, Herefordshire, 1995.

than to moral values or behaviour. Of course it would be good to have more data on the latter, yet it was seen in chapter five that there are at least some indications of moral differences between the two groups. This is an area which would be well worth exploring further in future research. Yet, limited as it is, this finding already offers powerful evidence for the cultural theory of churchgoing. It suggests that the effects of involuntary churchgoing as a child can still be traced in the relative strength of the Christian beliefs of adult nonchurchgoers. Compared with nonchurchgoers who never went to church as children, those adult nonchurchgoers who went regularly as children show twice the level of Christian belief. In addition, the latter are more likely to hold moral attitudes on personal honesty and sexuality which are closer to those of regular churchgoers.

What is still missing from this is a convincing account of why this is so. Once all of the connections in the data have been tested as rigorously as possible, it is still important to provide a credible explanation about how these connections might be causally related. Every sociologist has some witty anecdote for use in class to show students that statistical connections can be made between manifestly unrelated phenomena (lions and tigers, or polar bears and penguins). It is not sufficient simply to point to the data. Beyond the data, can a convincing explanation be given about why two phenomena are causally related?

Of the three rival theories of churchgoing – secularisation, persistence or separation – it is secularisation theories which offer the most convincing explanations.[10] The latter tend to trace links between the profound changes in culture effected by Darwin, Freud and others with the increase in popular scepticism, itself giving rise to doubts about the veracity of Christian practice. In such a sceptical environment, so it is argued, it is scarcely surprising that churchgoing has tended to wither within most societies affected by Western culture. A crisis of plausibility has gradually eroded most forms of religious belief and practice. Whatever reservations were raised in chapter

[10] E.g. Bryan Wilson, *Religion in Secular Society*, C. A. Watt, London, 1966, and *Contemporary Transformations of Religion*, Clarendon Press, Oxford, 1974, and Steve Bruce, *Religion in the Modern World*, Oxford University Press, Oxford, 1996.

three about the congruity of secularisation theories with all of the data, they do at least seek to give an explanation which goes beyond data. They typically deploy an account based upon a history of ideas and suggest that there is a relationship between academic scepticism and popular scepticism. As a result, if churchgoing assumes a certain level of Christian belief for its credibility, then an erosion of that belief in many modern societies is judged likely to result in a gradual decline in churchgoing.

A cultural theory of churchgoing suggests a very different predominant relationship between Christian belief and practice. Of course there are some individuals who leave churches because of scepticism about Christian beliefs or values. There are also individuals who go regularly to church and yet dissociate themselves from the beliefs and values held by most other churchgoers. But for the most part it is within churches that people learn to share distinctively Christian beliefs and values. This is the central claim of a cultural theory of churchgoing. And it is this which needs a credible explanation. What exactly is it about churchgoing which fosters the distinctively Christian virtues of faith, hope and love? This is as much a theological question as a sociological one.

Theologically speaking churchgoing is such an odd activity. Its ritual antecedents in Judaism and beyond are clear enough. As Durkheim pointed out so forcefully, most people across time and within time gather together on occasions for ritual celebrations. Even if modern forms of communication mean that physical presence is not always required, human beings are eminently social in character. The large gathering unmistakably has an 'effervescence' for all but the most determined individualist. Crowds, audiences, gatherings and congregations can all share this sense of effervescence. Individuals who take part in them can be stirred, excited and inspired in ways that eminently confirm our social status. Mass evangelists, popular comedians and fascist politicians alike know this only too well. There is little mystery from a sociological perspective about the importance of mass gatherings for religious institutions. Yet from a theological perspective the significance of churchgoing is by no means so clear, since most of the features of public worship can be replicated in private prayer and meditation. Scripture readings, psalms and canticles, intercessions, praise and repentance can all take place in private. In some ways the public reading of Scripture or a public delivery of a sermon may actually carry less cognitive content for the assiduous individual than a private reading of the Bible, a biblical commentary, a published meditation or a theological monograph. In a private reading of the latter the individual can slow down, re-read, or even skim the familiar, in ways that are impossible in public worship. Without the distraction of variously attentive fellow worshippers, the individual can be engaged so much more fully in private prayer and meditation. It is hardly surprising that the individual mystic – wisely identified by Troeltsch as a type distinct from church or sect – has not always made a very enthusiastic churchgoer.

Perhaps this is too cerebral. In the Synoptic Gospels the Kingdom of God – the 'rule' of God within the world and beyond, or perhaps simply the 'dynamic, purpose-filled presence' of God reaching out to the world in Jesus Christ – is portrayed, not in analytical and cerebral terms, but in the form of artful and often humorous stories. In Paul's writings the organic language of body and analogies from nature depict the Christian life. And, at the close of the New Testament, Revelation depicts this life as the New Heaven and New Earth surrounded by apocalyptic imagery. All of these terms and metaphors are social in character. However much the individual may think and learn about God in private, it is together that we are finally caught into the presence of God in Christ through the Spirit.

An analogy with music making might be helpful at this point. There is a superficial danger that the perfections of the CD might make concert going and public music making superfluous. After all, for a few pounds or dollars I can have Yo-Yo Ma playing the Bach Cello Sonatas and Partitas in my own living room as often as I wish. I can sit listening with a glass of my favourite Pinot Noir and without the irritations of a fellow concert goer who sniffs or another who has been forced to go against his will (and who actually hates Bach and/or the cello). Having heard Yo-Yo Ma playing all of these pieces in the Edinburgh Festival, I am also aware that he plays them more perfectly on a CD. The minor imperfections which resonated around Greyfriars Kirk have been thoughtfully eliminated by the recording studio. The stunning results make even Cassals or Rostropovich sound flawed. A level of quality and reproduction is reached which the concert hall can never replicate. And to add to this, if my attention is distracted, a button on my CD player allows me instantly to repeat that section. As long as the phone is off the hook, the family is well in control and I do not fall asleep, I can commune incomparably with the glories and transcendent qualities of Bach's music. In short, live music making is no longer necessary.

Because this is a musical and not a religious analogy it is manifestly rubbish. If Yo-Yo Ma plays, the concert hall is full. Many in each audience will be very familiar with his recordings, but will be well aware that music making is as much about physical presence and activity as it is about sound. The regular CD gives access to the latter but denies access to the former. Even the visual CD gives little of the ambience and excitement of this physicality. Far from decreasing attendances at concerts, the perfections of a modern CD have actually encouraged many people to attend concerts, especially the concerts of those already recorded on CD. In addition, within a live performance 'imperfections' can add to the individuality of a concert. Waiting, anticipation, silence and gaps are also part of the texture of live music making. Concerts that must be booked months in advance can be endowed with meaning quite different from a CD which can be reached at whim from the rack. The social webs surrounding live music making – travel, transport, company, eating, interval drinking and departures – can also be an important part of its enjoyment.

When participation is added to all of this, then the differences between a CD and live music making become even more obvious. Sadly I have no idea what it is like to be Yo-Yo Ma. Yet many of us do know what it is like to play in public (however badly) and most of us know what it is like to sing in the company of others. Individuals who would not normally sing solo in public, or perhaps even in private, know the vigour, depth and excitement that can come from singing with other people. As it happens such corporate singing is a key feature of many forms of Christian worship. It is the point at which this analogy turns into the thing itself. Communal singing and public worship, although distinct in many contexts, become fused for many churchgoers. Singing hymns or canticles is not something that most of us do comfortably on our own. At least here we can see that worshipful singing belongs more to public churchgoing than to private devotion. Furthermore it does have its own peculiar meaning and religious significance.

HYMNS AND CHRISTIAN IDENTITY

Hymns provide a useful point of entry into my question. They offer a clue about the distinctiveness of churchgoing and the specific ways that it might shape Christian identity. Although any number of examples could be given, a single one will be sufficient to ground the discussion here within actual worship. After the formation in 1972 of the United Reformed Church in Britain there was much discussion about producing a unified hymn-book. The publication of the Presbyterian *The Church Hymnary* in 1973 and the possibility of an ecumenical hymn-book to be produced by the Methodist Church delayed these plans. However in 1985 the General Assembly of the United Reformed Church finally decided to produce its own hymn-book, reflecting the different traditions of its three founding denominations (Presbyterian, Congregationalist and Churches of Christ). The result was the publication in 1991 of *Rejoice and Sing*, which was intended to present 'the best from all parts of the Church in many lands and across the centuries . . . a freely "catholic" selection of hymns which, in addition to Watts, Wesley, and other classic hymn-writers, includes great hymns of earlier centuries as well as contemporary hymns and some from the world Church'.[11]

[11] United Reformed Church, *Rejoice and Sing*, Oxford University Press, Oxford, 1991, p. viii.

Over six hundred hymns, old and new, are collected together in *Rejoice and Sing*, in addition to prayers and psalms. It is striking that half of these hymns are collected under the broad heading 'God's Creating and Redeeming Love'. Set out in the pattern of a Trinitarian creed – 'God the Creator', 'God Incarnate' and 'God the Life-Giver' – it also reflects the emphasis of the historic creeds upon Christology since it is the 'God Incarnate' sub-section which is by far the longest. The theological assumptions behind this presentation are clear: this hymn-book, like its predecessors, is at once both theocentric and christocentric.

Indeed most of the hymns in this first section refer to God and/or Jesus Christ in the very first line. So, just to take examples from the first twenty hymns in this section:

All creatures of our God and King (39)
I sing the almighty power of God (43)
Lord of the boundless curves of space (44)
O praise him! O praise him! O praise him! (46)
O worship the King (47)
Sing praise to the Lord! (49)
Praise ye the Lord, 'tis good to raise (50)
To God who makes all lovely things (52)
To thee, O Lord, our hearts we raise (53)
A sovereign protector I have (54)
All as God wills, who wisely heeds (55)
Creating God, your fingers trace (56)
Eternal Father, strong to save (58)

The opening Advent hymns of the sub-section 'God Incarnate' present a similar pattern:

O come, O come, Immanuel (126)
Hail to the Lord's Anointed (127)
The Lord will come and not be slow (128)
Behold the mountain of the Lord (130)
The voice of God goes out to all the world (131)
Joy to the world, the Lord is come! (135)
Hark, the glad sound! The Saviour comes (137)
Come, thou long-expected Jesus (138)
O Lord, how shall I meet you (140)
Make way, make way, for Christ the King (141)

United Reformed Church congregations using this hymn-book are saturated with theocentric and christocentric images and language. The effervescence of corporate singing is, by design, intimately bound up with theological intentions and assumptions.

If anything, the twentieth-century hymns introduced into United Reformed Church worship by *Rejoice and Sing* increase this theocentric and christocentric emphasis:

Great is thy faithfulness, O God my father (96)
O Lord my God, when I in awesome wonder (117)
Lord of the dance (195)
Were you there when they crucified my Lord? (227)
Spirit of the Living God (308)
Lord Jesus Christ, you have come to us (373)
Seek ye first the Kingdom of God (512)
From heaven you came, helpless babe (522)
Tell out my soul, the greatness of the Lord (740)

It is sometimes imagined by critics that 'new' hymns are too preoccupied with mundane matters and give insufficient attention to the divine. In reality, 'new' hymns are characteristically both theocentric and christocentric. Few repetitive charismatic choruses have been included in *Rejoice and Sing*. This is a cautious hymn-book designed to be still acceptable to largely middle-aged and elderly congregations. So, although the language it uses in the hymns tends to be inclusive when referring to people, it remains masculine when referring to God. In addition, not all mentions of 'thee' are replaced by 'you'. However, had *Rejoice and Sing* taken more account of younger, charismatic congregations, it would almost certainly have remained just as theocentric and christocentric.

All of this suggests that to be involved in hymn-singing is to be reminded at every stage that this is an activity directed to God in Jesus Christ. Hymns well illustrate that worshipping communities remain today, as once they were for the earliest Christians, crucibles of Christian doctrine.[12] A high Christology and a strong sense of the centrality of God are implicit within

[12] See Geoffrey Wainwright, *Doxology: The Praise of God in Worship, Doctrine and Life: A Systematic Theology*, Clarendon Press, Oxford and New York, 1980.

Rejoice and Sing and, indeed, within most other hymn-books used by congregations across apparently different denominations. Christian hymn singing acts as a powerful carrier of implicit theology.

What hymns offer is not just another way of conveying Christian beliefs. At best they can also add textures and emphases to these beliefs which cannot be captured adequately in sequential prose. This surely is the reason for the popularity today of 'Great is thy faithfulness, O God my Father'. Written in the 1920s, as the use of 'thy ' and 'thou' throughout indicates, this American hymn became popular in Britain with its inclusion in *Mission Praise* in 1983 as well as by featuring regularly in *Songs of Praise* on BBC television. The phrase 'Great is thy faithfulness' is repeated ten times in the course of the short hymn, once in the opening line and then three times in each of the choruses. It thus sets the theme unambiguously. This is clearly a declaration of praise, celebrating the great faithfulness of God. It is also a purely theistic hymn and could be sung equally by Jews and Muslims. Chisholm's words are given a musical climax by Runyan's tune Faithfulness. A separate crochet is used for the three words 'great', 'is' and 'thy' on each of the occasions the phrase is used. A dotted crochet followed by a quaver is used to emphasise 'faithfulness' in the opening line. This is given extra speed in the first line of the chorus with a dotted quaver followed by a quaver for both uses of 'faithfulness' there. Then the final line of the chorus slows the pace slightly, returning to a dotted crochet followed by a quaver for its use of 'faithfulness'. Pitch as well as pace is used for emphasis. Each time the full phrase occurs the pitch is raised slightly.

If praise of God is the dominant theme of this hymn, the sinfulness and dependence of human beings is the sub-theme, which in turn serves to highlight the dominant theme. The first verse focuses upon the unchanging faithfulness of God. It is God my Father who is unfailingly faithful and compassionate. The chorus too emphasises the faithfulness and new mercies of God, which are 'all I have needed'. The second verse sees continuities in the seasons, in the heavens and in nature as witnesses to God's faithfulness. The third and final verse, however, stresses the human, seeing God as the source of pardon, peace, guidance, strength and hope – 'blessing all mine'. The tune, too, helps to emphasise the contrast between the faithfulness of God and the dependence of me as a human being. In the final line of the chorus 'great is thy faithfulness' is set several notes higher than the concluding 'Lord, unto me'.

It matters very little whether or not congregations are aware of the poetic and musical devices that are used in this hymn to emphasise the faithfulness of God. A mixture of contrast and repetition, pitch and pace is used to achieve this. Doubtless many audiences also ignore the musical devices, especially using trumpets and drums, which Bach's cantatas characteristically use to emphasise the glory of God. An appreciation of art, poetry or music is certainly not dependent upon technical analysis. Even the expert may feel hard pressed to explain exactly why this particular picture, poem or piece of music actually works. At some point art becomes more than configurations of paint on a canvas, poetry becomes more than words placed oddly on a page, or music becomes more than different sounds, rhythms and spaces in conjunction. Hymns, too, are not to be reduced simply to technical devices which can be translated point-by-point into sequential prose. For most churchgoers they are much more than that. They are irreplaceable means of expressing praise to God.

This surely explains why hymns can become such issues of contention within congregations. The compilers of *Rejoice and Sing* are well aware that by producing a hymn-book for the new United Reformed Church they are engaged in a contentious enterprise:

> Hymns have always been particularly important to those traditions represented by the United Reformed Church, whether Congregational, Presbyterian, or Churches of Christ, for they have enabled congregations to express together their worship and praise, their wonder at the almighty power and grace of God.[13]

[13] *Rejoice and Sing*, p. vii.

Not only that, in traditions having no formal written liturgy to be followed by members of a congregation, the hymn-book is often *the* congregational book. It has in effect occupied a role held by the *Missal* in traditional Roman Catholic congregations or the *Book of Common Prayer* in Anglican ones. Just as changes in liturgical text have proved so contentious in recent decades for Roman Catholics and Anglicans, so changes in hymn-book are likely to prove contentious for Free Church members. Added to this, the United Reformed Church faces a special problem in bringing together three separate denominations with very different traditions of hymnody. The compilers of *Rejoice and Sing* are very conscious of the potential sources of conflict here:

> The presence of three different traditions in the Church also means that where versions of a hymn or the customary tune differ, no particular version or tune has an established claim. The Words Sub-committee has tried, so far as possible, to establish the original text of each hymn, and in many cases has preferred that text to later amended versions. The Music Sub-committee has sometimes paired tunes from different traditions and sometimes chosen completely new tunes.[14]

As a result 'Guide me, O thou great Jehovah' remains just that, and not 'Guide me, O thou great Redeemer'. Some of the antique language of this perennial hymn remains ('thou', 'whence' and 'doth'), but some has been removed ('Feed me till my want is o'er'). Even the remaining uses of 'thou' have been altered to lower case. Doubtless to the amusement of English congregations, it is also printed in full in both English and Welsh. In addition, the only tune set is now *Cwm Rhondda*. The two tunes set in the old *Church Hymnary*, namely Mannheim and Caersalem, have not been included. Given the iconic status of this hymn, and its separate history in each of the three former denominations, these must have been extremely tricky decisions for the compilers to make.

My point is not, of course, to criticise these changes, but rather to note their significance. For many churchgoers hymn singing is not a peripheral activity. It is a central feature of worship which cannot readily be replicated in private. It adds

[14] *Ibid.* p. viii.

textures and emphases to Christian faith in a way that is distinctive and unique. In such a context, changes in hymn-books potentially threaten churchgoers with the possibility of a change of denominational, or even Christian, identity. The compilers of *Rejoice and Sing* are consciously engaged in a task of producing a fresh identity for the United Reformed Church. Whether URC congregations welcome this or resist it fiercely, they too are implicitly aware of the connection here between hymns and identity.

The theocentric and christocentric nature of many hymns also has important moral significance. Although he gives little consideration to hymns, Stanley Hauerwas' colleague at Duke University, Harmon Smith, argues that worship and Christian ethics are inextricably connected with each other. Unlike Hauerwas in his recent writings, Smith pays more attention (albeit critically) to actual rather than idealised churches and to the worship that they typically present. He argues that the overall shape of this worship, across different denominations, is indeed intimately connected with ethics:

> Both Christian worship and Christian ethics are marked by a dyadic, or two-sided, complementarity. On the one hand is an attitude of complete submission to and exaltation of God; on the other hand is the act of a whole life faithfully lived and acted out in passionate obedience and fidelity to God.[15]

Exactly this point can be seen in the contrasts made in 'Great is thy faithfulness'. The moral faithfulness of God serves to highlight both human inadequacy and, in turn, the moral human need for divine grace. In the final verse the conclusion is reached that it is the faithfulness of God which is 'pardon for sin and a peace that endureth' and it is God's presence which guides, strengthens and offers 'hope for tomorrow'.

Harmon Smith maintains that:

> No more than Christian faith can be reduced to doctrinal formulae can Christian identity be comprehended apart from prayer and worship within community . . . Christians are a people whose vision of the moral life is formed by adoration and praise, by penitence and

[15] Harmon L. Smith, *Where Two or Three are Gathered Together: Liturgy and the Moral Life*, Pilgrim Press, Cleveland, 1995, p. 43.

pardon, by thanksgiving and offering, by petition and intercession, by revelation and confession . . . and by all of these ascribed and supplicated to the God whom we know through Jesus. When our vision of the moral life is formed in these ways, we Christians will know that we worry about war and sexuality and racism and the rest *soli Deo gloria*.[16]

Once again *Rejoice and Sing* illustrates this point clearly. The theme of the first half of the hymn-book is 'God's Creating and Redeeming Love', but that of the second is 'Creation's Response to God's Love'. Within this second section there are again three sub-sections: 'The Gospel', 'The Church's Life and Witness' and 'The Gospel in the World'. And within this third sub-section several moral themes are offered: 'Christ for the World', 'Love in Action', 'Justice and Peace', and 'Healing and Reconciliation'. The first lines of some of the most popular hymns clearly connect worship and morality:

Will your anchor hold in the storms of life (598)
Forth in the peace of Christ, we go (602)
Am I my brother's keeper? (609)
Beloved, let us love; for love is of God (610)
For the healing of the nations (620)
Make me a channel of your peace (629)

Just as congregations using *Rejoice and Sing* are bombarded with references to God and Christ, so they are also prompted repeatedly to relate Christian faith to morality and morality back to Christian faith. Harmon Smith's general points about the connection here apply very specifically to hymn singing within worship. Hymns not only carry an implicit theology but also an implicit Christian ethic. Specifically Christian virtues are weaved closely into this hymn-book, just as they are weaved into Smith's own American Episcopal Church's *The Hymnal 1982* (with very similar sub-headings).

There is more to say about this connection. *Rejoice and Sing* has several strongly teleological features. Of course hymn singing as a whole is typically related to a sense of 'order'. Congregations feel comfortable with familiar hymns and are notoriously suspicious of ministers who persistently wish to

[16] *Ibid.* pp. 2–3.

introduce new ones. Oft-told stories and anecdotes have particular significance within families. These may be about crucial points in the life cycle – photographs, stories and anecdotes about the birth, marriage or death of relatives. Or perhaps it is just the idiosyncratic trivia carried in the memories of active family members, bound together at least in part by these shared memories. In a similar way, the repetition of familiar hymns serves to reinforce identity within many Christian congregations. Worshipping communities, like other face-to-face communities that survive from one generation to the next, do need to have some carriers of continuity, some marks which distinguish their particular activity from the rest of life. Constantly repeated hymns are ideal carriers.

Ironically, many of the older hymns contained in hymn-books like *Rejoice and Sing* originate from mutually excluding campaigns and missions. In producing a hymn-book which has 'the best from all parts of the Church in many lands and across the centuries', the compilers succeed in placing together an irenic mixture of antagonisms. Tractarian and conservative evangelical hymn-writers from the nineteenth century, with their quite opposite theological intentions, now appear alongside each other. Medieval sentiments about death, heaven and hell jostle with more liberal theological interpretations of eschatology. In the process, an ecumenical order of sorts is imposed upon these divergent theological traditions. Unlike the hymn-book of a specific mission, the hymn-book of the United Reformed Church needs to be 'catholic' in the widest sense. If possible it must appeal to congregations from a variety of theological approaches who can choose from within it as they wish.

There are also two other important carriers of order in *Rejoice and Sing*. It introduces a written (but, of course, optional) liturgical framework and it offers guidance for the choice of hymns at different points in the liturgical year. The compilers are aware that it is the first of these which is likely to be the most contentious:

> The feature which will probably be most novel is the inclusion of prayers and responses for congregational use . . . in order to maintain the freedom and variety in worship which has characterized our

tradition, we wished to provide material which could be used in different ways. Hence the book begins with an outline order of worship, and contains a numbered sequence of prayers and ancient hymns which will be particularly useful for Communion but can be used at other times as well . . . In the body of the book there is also a section of prayers and responses, and single verses which may be repeated several times . . . Confessions of faith and statements of faith, which may be used at baptisms and ordinations, appear at the end of the book.[17]

For Roman Catholics, Anglicans or Lutherans none of this will be at all surprising. Yet for many former Congregationalists and Presbyterians it is a major innovation. Having resisted Anglican pressures to have a congregational prayerbook and corporate responses for so long, features of both now appear in *Rejoice and Sing*. And with this comes a new sense of liturgical order which Harmon Smith believes to be so important for Christian ethics.

The liturgical year does not play nearly such a central role in *Rejoice and Sing* as it does in a corresponding Anglican hymn-book (half of the hymns in *The Hymnal 1982* are ordered on this basis). Nonetheless it is still present. The long christological section, 'God Incarnate', is presented in sequence from Advent to Ascension, and is followed immediately by 'The Coming of the Holy Spirit'. In addition, the compilers report that they made an effort 'to ensure that the book contains sufficient psalms for every Sunday of the liturgical year'.[18] The rhythms within the liturgical year, with some hymns that can be sung at one point and not another (especially Christmas and Easter hymns), and the slower rhythm of one liturgical year following the next, are important agents of a sense of order.

Of course such rhythmic, annual order is not entirely absent from secular society. The seasons themselves bring their own natural rhythms and, in turn, impose rhythms upon different sports and outdoor public entertainment. International sport has annual, biennial and even quatennial rhythms. There are also the politically constructed rhythms of liberated countries, such as the American Independence Day or Thanksgiving, the

[17] *Rejoice and Sing*, p. ix. [18] *Ibid.* p. viii.

French Bastille Day, or the British VE Day. For countries with monarchies there are Coronation Days and periodic times of royal mourning or celebration. And, increasingly, music festivals, such as Glastonbury, provide a cultic and perhaps even mystical rhythm for many. Nevertheless, churchgoers are unusual in being so regularly and systematically part of a voluntary, rhythmic order. Each Sunday, especially between Advent and Pentecost, they are likely to be reminded in their service of whatever denomination about the point in the liturgical year that has now been reached. Even their hymn-book reminds them of this.

Teleology is well represented in *Rejoice and Sing*, and so is altruism. The compilers summarise the aims of the final section of the hymn-book:

> The second is concerned with the Church's life and witness, containing hymns for Sunday worship and the sacraments, and for the significant moments in the life of the people of God – their growth in faith and discipleship, the proclamation of the Gospel and the Church's continuing hope. The third is concerned with the way the Gospel becomes effective in the world, introducing such themes as love in action, justice and peace, and healing and reconciliation.[19]

Themes of justice and altruism can be found in both older and more recent hymns in *Rejoice and Sing*. The Victorian Anglican hymn 'Thy kingdom come, O God' (638) appears alongside modern hymns on the theme of justice by Brian Wren ('This we can do for justice and for peace' 639) and Fred Kaan ('For the healing of the nations' 620) in this final section.

First published in 1867 in his collection *Hymns for the Minor Sundays from Advent to Whitsuntide*, Canon Lewis Hensley's 'Thy kingdom come, O God' soon became a standard hymn in both Anglican and Free Church hymn-books. For example, it appeared in *The Church Hymnary*, using the familiar tune St Cecilia, long before *Rejoice and Sing* was published. It provides a point of contact between churchgoers of many different denominations. Throughout it has a strong emphasis upon justice, asking 'Where is thy reign of peace and purity and love? When shall all hatreds cease, as in the realms above?', and longing for a time

[19] *Ibid.* pp. ix–x.

'that war shall be no more' and there is no more 'lust, oppression, crime'. The penultimate verse captures this with the words: 'By many deeds of shame we learn that love grows cold.' Of course the way that the original words of this famous hymn sees justice in the world is inescapably Victorian. *Rejoice and Sing* attempts to correct this by changing the first two lines of the final verse from 'O'er heathen lands afar thick darkness broodeth yet' to late-twentieth-century political correctness, 'O'er lands both near and far thick darkness broodeth yet.'

Brian Wren's hymns make an interesting modern contrast to 'Thy kingdom come, O God'. He is unusual in that he writes both tunes and words and publishes theological books on the issue of justice. Strongly committed to overseas aid and justice he sees his whole ministry predominantly in these terms. *Rejoice and Sing* includes two of his hymns: 'This we can do for justice and for peace' and 'We are not our own. Earth forms us' (482). The second of these hymns makes altruistic links at several levels. It opens with a concern about the earth, then gradually and skilfully points to family, friends, neighbours and strangers. All serve to remind us that 'we are not our own'. The prayers of the saints finally surround us in 'love's encounters' with other people. Even if congregations may still find his hymns difficult to sing, the words that he offers are unusually thoughtful and theologically sophisticated. It is possible that in time they may gain a more central place in hymn-books.

Taking this evidence about hymn singing as a whole, it soon becomes clear that this is an activity rich in implicit theology, teleology and altruism. So much attention has been given to hymns here precisely because they form a generic and highly distinctive feature of most forms of Western churchgoing. Roman Catholics, Anglicans and the Free Churches all use hymns in their church services. Even though there is a wide variety of hymns used across different denominations, the broad characteristics of hymns that have been isolated are not specific to any of these denominations. Hymn-books of whatever church are typically theocentric and christocentric, teleological and altruistic. It may not be too surprising, then, that regular churchgoers who sing hymns together with other worshippers week by week and over many years are likely to assimilate these distinctive features.

It seems likely that a culture of hymn-singing churchgoing will at least sensitise churchgoers to these aspects of faith, hope and love. Ephesians talks about those in Christ being 'renewed in the spirit of your minds' and makes a sharp contrast between the old nature and new nature:

> Now this I affirm and testify in the Lord, that you must no longer live as the Gentiles do, in the futility of their minds; they are darkened in their understanding, alienated from the life of God because of the ignorance that is in them, due to their hardness of heart; they have become callous and have given themselves up to licentiousness, greedy to practise every kind of uncleanness. You did not so learn Christ! – assuming that you have heard about him and were taught in him, as the truth is in Jesus. Put off your old nature which belongs to your former manner of life and is corrupt through deceitful lusts, and be renewed in the spirit of your minds, and put on the new nature, created after the likeness of God in true righteousness and holiness. Therefore, putting away falsehood, let every one speak the truth with his neighbour, for we are members one of another. Be angry but do not sin; do not let the sun go down on your anger, and give no opportunity to the devil. Let the thief no longer steal, but rather let him labour, doing honest work with his hands, so that he may be able to give to those in need. Let no evil talk come out of your mouths, but only such as is good for edifying, as fits the occasion, that it may impart grace to those who hear. And do not grieve the Holy Spirit of God, in whom you were sealed for the day of redemption. Let all bitterness and wrath and anger and clamour and slander be put away from you, with all malice, and be kind to one another, tenderhearted, forgiving one another, as God in Christ forgave you. Therefore be imitators of God, as beloved children. And walk in love, as Christ loved us and gave himself up for us, a fragrant offering and sacrifice to God.[20]

This depiction of the Christian life is also at once both theocentric and christocentric. The final sentences set the moral virtues that make up the Christian life firmly into this theological context. It is because God in Christ first forgave and loved us that we, in turn, should behave in a forgiving and loving way to other people. It is because we are created

[20] Ephesians 4.17–5.2 (RSV).

in the likeness of God's righteousness and holiness that we too should be righteous and holy. And it is finally in Jesus Christ that we can 'learn'. A culture of theocentrism and christocentrism, expressed so emphatically by hymns, is an essential feature of the distinctively Christian life, allowing those taking part regularly in this culture to renew the spirit of their minds.

The moral features flowing from this theocentric and christocentric culture in Ephesians are a mixture of personal and social virtues. At the personal level the Christian should be righteous and holy, putting off deceitful lusts, hardness of heart and every kind of uncleanness. At the social level the Christian should give to those in need, be truthful to others, labour and not steal from others, avoid wrath, bitterness and slander, and forgive and love one another. Wayne Meeks points out[21] that such virtues would have also been readily affirmed by many good pagans at the time. Similarly they are not confined to churchgoers today. Nonetheless, the theological basis upon which they are justified in Ephesians does provide these virtues with a renewed emphasis. More than that, 'members one of another' of the body of Christ share a community of virtue shaped by worship and hymn-singing:

> Be filled with the Spirit, addressing one another in psalms and hymns and spiritual songs, singing and making melody to the Lord with all your heart, always and for everything giving thanks in the name of our Lord Jesus Christ to God the Father.[22]

Those holding a theocentric and christocentric faith should be drawn naturally to these virtues. Indeed, those living out their lives in a theocentric and christocentric culture – singing together the hymns of this faith – are likely to be distinctively sensitised to these virtues.

At first sight hymn-singing might appear to be relatively free of values. After all, football crowds in the recent past have often been celebrated for their purely emotional rendering of hymns at important matches. Although such crowds are undoubtedly

[21] Wayne A. Meeks, *The Origins of Christian Morality: The First Two Centuries*, Yale University Press, New Haven and London, 1993.

[22] Ephesians 5.18–20 (RSV).

engaged in forms of public ritual,[23] it is difficult to imagine that they are engaged in anything approximating to worship. In any case, as a new generation has arrived at football matches, with little or no previous experience of Christian worship, so the National Anthem and Rule Britannia have increasingly come to replace 'Abide with me' in this corporate singing. Meanwhile hymns for churchgoers act as carriers of both implicit theology and distinctive virtues.

Nevertheless, the features of teleology and altruism in hymns are necessarily set at a fairly general level. Even Brian Wren's stress upon social justice is very generalised. If nothing else, hymns are usually designed to last for some time and must therefore be applicable to a variety of situations and contingencies. 'Thy kingdom come, O God' was first published between the Crimean and Franco-Prussian wars and between the first and second Afghanistan wars. Had it referred directly to any of these it would scarcely have endured for so long. In contrast, perhaps it is too specific a reference in the hymn 'O Valiant Hearts' to the 'little calvaries' of those soldiers who died in the First World War that makes it so unpopular today amongst many ordained ministers (despite its enduring popularity amongst war veterans).

WORSHIP AND CHRISTIAN IDENTITY

Yet there are other generic features of churchgoing across denominations which can make worship highly specific. If effective hymns need to be generalised, effective sermons and intercessions may need to be specific. Even within highly formalised liturgies, sermons and intentions within intercessions are frequently personalised moments. Indeed, sociological research on sermons[24] suggests that there is typically quite a

[23] See Robert Bocock, *Ritual in Industrial Society: A Sociological Analysis of Ritualism in Modern England*, George Allen and Unwin, London, 1974.

[24] See Marsha G. Witten, *All is Forgiven: The Secular Message in American Protestantism*, Princeton University Press, New Jersey, 1993; Robert Wuthnow, *Rediscovering the Sacred: Perspectives on Religion in Contemporary Society*, William Eerdmans, Grand Rapids, 1992; William O. Avery and A. Roger Globbel, 'The Word of God and the Word of the Preacher', *Review of Religious Research*, 22: 1, 1980.

large gap between what the preacher intends and what members of a congregation perceive. Whereas the preacher may well have a careful plan and structure for a sermon, members of the congregation are likely to retain little more than a number of images and anecdotes. In some city-centre, eclectic churches, especially those which are famed for their preaching and attract large numbers of students, members of a congregation may follow a sermon using an open Bible and taking notes. But more often members of a congregation will value the spiritual and emotional content of a sermon more highly than its cognitive content. Relevant stories told well will be treasured more highly than systematic theology. Because sermons seldom present opportunities for immediate responses and, in turn, the preacher has little feed-back except short comments or perhaps just general evaluations as people leave the church, the sermon seldom resembles the student lecture. Most sermons are not obvious occasions for imparting information. Their function is more to ground Scripture and worship in the actual lives of congregations. Sometimes this grounding may be related to faith, sometimes to hope and sometimes to love. The sermon, unlike the hymn, can be a very specific way of imparting and sharing distinctively Christian virtues.

Intercessions, too, can have a similar function. They are typically offered to God in Christ through the Spirit and thus share the implicit theology of hymns. Yet they can have a very specific *telos* and concern for other people. In many congregations lay people lead or actively join in intercessions. Sometimes there is a pause when names are invited from the congregation for those in special need of prayer. In most churches those who are ill or dying, as well as those who are mourning, will be specifically named in intercessions. Again, there will often be reference in intercessions to specific items from the world news which are of particular concern to the congregation at the moment. Increasingly ecological issues are also mentioned in intercessions. Or perhaps it is a local event or concern which receives specific attention. Whether intercessions take the form of litanies and responses or the style of extemporary prayers, they do typically contain items which are very specific and which are grounded in the needs and concerns of that particular congregation.

One issue which illustrates this process very well is that of overseas aid. It was noted in chapter seven that BSA data suggest that regular churchgoers are far more likely than others to show concern about medical supplies to Africa, starving people in poor countries, and charitable money going to those in need overseas. Given the recurrent themes of intercessions in many churches this is hardly surprising. To be a regular churchgoer in most denominations is to be part of a worshipping community which prays regularly for those in need overseas. Some of the hymns (and presumably the intercessions) of the Victorians may appear patronising and imperialistic today, yet there cannot be any doubt about Victorian concerns. Many churchgoers then, as now, were deeply concerned to extend prayers and charitable giving beyond their fellow citizens. For churchgoers intercession remains an important way of enacting this.

From a theological perspective, intercessions are not simply about articulating local needs and concerns, important as this is. Intercessions are intended also to effect change. By bringing the needs and concerns of the ill, the vulnerable and those who mourn to God in Christ through the Spirit, the worshipper also seeks to be open to the divine grace which can effect real change. Whereas the secularist may read, worry or even lobby about world events, but believes that there is nothing else the non-politician can do, the churchgoer believes that, apart from reading, worrying and lobbying, within intercession these events can become open to divine grace and change. So, having prayed year after year for the people of South Africa and Northern Ireland, many churchgoers really do believe that their prayers have been an important part of the political changes there. Without adopting a crudely instrumental view of intercession (many intercessions will, in any case, contain the theological caveat that 'thy will not my will be done'), few worshippers who engage in intercession will believe that it is nothing more than a public articulation of needs and concerns.

Nor will most churchgoers believe that confession and absolution are simply about articulation. In contrast, most will believe that involved in confession and absolution, properly understood, is God's forgiveness. This is the connection that Ephesians makes: human forgiveness is directly related to divine forgiveness, since just as God first forgave us so we should forgive each other. So the order becomes: God's love, our confession, God's forgiveness, our forgiveness. It is an order which is constantly repeated in worship. Typically within acts of worship there is a rhythm. Starting with praise and thanksgiving, congregations are reminded of the greatness of God and then led to remember their own contrasting sinfulness. Confession follows. Absolution is offered. Praise and thanksgiving can then return. Next the rhythm may be taken up by intercession. The world, too, needs God's forgiveness and grace and we, in turn, need to be reminded that God's forgiveness should be extended by us to other people. Praise and thanksgiving can then return once more. The service concludes with blessing and dismissal. Rhythms which are formalised in written liturgies are still manifestly present in those which are not. Within both patterns of worship, public confession and absolution are central features of this rhythm.

This rhythm of confession, absolution and renewal has important moral implications. Harmon Smith again summarises this:

> Christians would do well to be more self-conscious of the potency and actual leverage which gathering, in and of itself, generates. If we remember that this action is a moral act, that it is a distinguishable act, that it is a hermeneutical act, we will recognize that it is, in a phrase, our first move toward learning to see ourselves and the world aright. Of course, this means to see the world and the church as God intends, as all subject to and belonging to God. The tie that binds all together with God invites us to reflect briefly on confession, repentance, penance, reconciliation, forgiveness, pardon, and absolution, because they are the means by which Jews and Christians understand the estranged creation to be re-ligated to its Creator and Sovereign Lord.[25]

[25] Smith, *Where Two or Three Are Gathered Together: Liturgy and the Moral Life*, p. 82.

This is a moral act at several different levels. Regular churchgoing in itself may at times become a moral act. Most people who have maintained long periods of weekly churchgoing will be aware of times when this is sustained less by a sense of personal identity than by a concern for other people. There are times when many continue to be regular churchgoers despite their minister, despite other members of their congregation, or despite some crisis in their personal faith. In their own perception, churchgoing then becomes a 'duty' and little more. Perhaps it is a duty to God, to themselves, to others in the community or to members of their family, or perhaps it is a mixture of these. Whatever, churchgoing in these circumstances is accompanied by little personal sense of joy, praise or thanksgiving. For them confession may be real enough but lacks any accompanying sense of assurance of absolution. The 'habit' of churchgoing is maintained with, at best, a hope that its fuller meaning may be recovered at some point in the future. Such perseverance is surely a moral act. In theological terms, faithfulness may at times require us to act in faith rather than through faith, trusting only that 'then' shall I understand 'even as I have been fully understood'.

However, once the fuller meaning of confession and absolution within worship is recovered, then an important teleological feature emerges as Harmon Smith observes. Within confession and absolution we can learn 'to see ourselves and the world aright'. The order that is broken through sin is restored by God through confession and absolution. So understood, confession and absolution are concerned with moral re-ordering, with 're-ligating', albeit through divine grace. The broken human order is viewed, *sub specie aeternitatis*, in the light of God's intended order.

It is, of course, important to be conscious of the brokenness before becoming aware that this is indeed a re-ordering. And it is regular worshippers who, far more often than other people, are reminded of their sinfulness. The findings, noted in chapter two, of the European Value Systems Study Group that European churchgoers are significantly more likely than other people to believe in the reality of 'sin' are only to be expected.

Their liturgies and forms of worship remind them of the reality of sin, Sunday by Sunday. To take a single example, *Rejoice and Sing*, adapting words familiar to Anglicans, Roman Catholics and many others, reinforces this with the following preface to its optional forms of confession:

> If we say we have no sin, we deceive ourselves.
> If we confess our sins, God is faithful and just
> and will forgive our sins
> and cleanse us from every kind of wrong.

Public confession on a weekly basis itself carries a sense of order and regularity. The reality of human sin is acknowledged every week, as is the need for repentance and the assurance of forgiveness. A process of contrition, which can in moments of human frailty, bereavement and vulnerability be heart-felt and intense, for the most part becomes 'routine'. To depict it in this way is not necessarily to trivialise this process. Some routine, even within apparently extemporary worship, is probably both inevitable and reassuring. Like the familiar hymn and biblical story, it helps to generate and sustain Christian identity. To be an active Christian is to confess regularly and then to be absolved. Naturally this is a process which can be abused, notoriously so in Luther's times. Yet, properly understood, it may be an important signal of order and *telos*.

Confession also has an important altruistic dimension. Within many forms of worship congregations are invited to confess their sins, not just against God, but also against other people and, in some congregations today, against the planet itself. Just as the request for forgiveness by God is linked in the Lord's Prayer with an injunction to forgive others, so public confessions in worship typically link divine and human forgiveness. Confession is thus not only a re-ordering of lives to God but also a re-ordering of lives to other people and, beyond people, a re-ordering of human lives to animal lives as well as to the wider environment. Absolution, in turn, is the assurance of this re-ordering. Through absolution we are assured of God's love to us on the understanding that our love for other people (and perhaps for the planet) is also re-ordered.

Ecological sensitivities have certainly become more evident in some congregations. Hymns were always an important source of ecological awareness, with those about nature, the seasons, and the harvest being amongst the most enduring. Increasingly intercessions and confessions in worship also have an ecological dimension. In part, as noted earlier, this may be a response to environmentalists' use of the Lynn White thesis. It may also reflect the fact that churchgoers, like others in Western society, are themselves becoming more conscious of ecological issues. Whatever the reason, ecologically conscious intercessions, confessions and even liturgies (of which the 1989 Anglican *A New Zealand Prayer Book/He Karakia Mihinare o Aotearoa* is amongst the most striking) are becoming more common. Again this fits the BHPS and BSA evidence suggesting that relatively high environmental concerns are evident today amongst regular churchgoers.

Hymns, sermons, intercessions and public confessions are all key ingredients of most forms of Western Christian worship. They feature abundantly and rhythmically in the distinctive culture of churchgoing and act as crucial carriers of Christian identity. Each is theocentric and christocentric. Each also has clear moral significance, characterised by both teleology and altruism. Together they supply the evidence which has been so far absent from the survey data. The latter show that churchgoing and Christian beliefs and virtues are all significantly related to each other. Yet they do not of themselves demonstrate why this is so. A more theological account of churchgoing – in terms of hymns, sermons, intercessions and public confessions – provides a much clearer connection. It suggests that these key ingredients sensitise and shape the beliefs and behaviour of regular churchgoers. Surrounded by a culture imbued with Christian beliefs and virtues, it is entirely plausible that regular churchgoers adopt them for themselves. It is also plausible that adult nonchurchgoers, who nonetheless went regularly to church as children, still retain significant traces of these Christian beliefs and virtues. The reason for this is simple: once they were part of this distinctive culture of churchgoing and were thus sensitised and shaped by its key ingredients.

There are, however, two ingredients of worship across denominations which have so far been mentioned only indirectly. Many churchgoers will regard these as the most important features of worship, namely the public reading of Scripture and the celebration of the Eucharist. In a sense the theological and moral significance of both is so obvious as not to need much elaboration. Scripture shapes many hymns and intercessions and most sermons. The Eucharist for many regular churchgoers is the very centre of our worship. Both are clearly theocentric and christocentric. Scripture has already provided an authoritative basis for the Christian virtues discussed in this book. And the Eucharist combines a strong sense of repeated action and order with a firm direction for communicants to go out and serve the world.

Yet there is a danger in modern theology that they come to be regarded as the only theologically significant ingredients of worship. Elsewhere[26] I have argued that George Lindbeck's highly influential *The Nature of Doctrine* is in danger of identifying Christian culture too exclusively with canonical Scripture. In the process he tends to underestimate those forms of worship which have been as much shaped by other ingredients. But having made this criticism, his work is still highly informative about the social and communal significance of Scripture. Lindbeck connects Scripture, identity, theology and morality as follows:

> It is possible to specify the primary function of the canonical narrative (which is also the function of many of its most important component stories from the Pentateuch to the Gospels). It is 'to render a character . . . , offer an identity description to an agent,' namely God. It does this, not by telling what God is in and of himself, but by accounts of the interaction of his deeds and purposes with those of creatures in their ever-changing circumstances. These accounts reach their climax in what the Gospels say of the risen, ascended, and ever-present Jesus Christ whose identity as the divine-human agent is unsubstitutably enacted in the stories of Jesus of Nazareth. The climax, however, is logically inseparable from what precedes it. The Jesus of the Gospels is the Son of the God of Abraham, Isaac, and Jacob in the same strong sense that the Hamlet of Shakespeare's play is Prince of

[26] See my *Moral Leadership in a Postmodern Age*, T. & T. Clark, Edinburgh, 1997, pp. 51f.

Denmark. In both cases, the title with its reference to the wider context irreplaceably rather than contingently identifies the bearer of the name.[27]

Within the culture of churchgoing Scripture is repeatedly and authoritatively read aloud. Its familiar stories and sayings provide a crucial part of the distinctive Christian identity. The Jewish Bible, in this context, becomes the Old Testament and its prophets are presented as if they foresaw the birth, death and resurrection of Jesus Christ.[28] Here, too, the New Testament, and especially the words and parables attributed to Jesus, is given special and authoritative moral status. Viewed from the outside, the moral significance of Scripture within Christian worship must be obvious.

Likewise the moral significance of the Eucharist must be obvious. Whether celebrated at least weekly, as in Roman Catholic and many Anglican churches, or at key moments in the year, as in much Free Church worship, the Eucharist is a central focus for many regular churchgoers. For us it is the fusion within worship of Christian faith and life. It is surely no accident that the earliest account of the Last Supper is given as a sharp contrast to the lax moral behaviour of the Corinthian Christians:

When you assemble as a church, I hear that there are divisions among you . . . in eating, each one goes ahead with his own meal, and one is hungry and another is drunk. What! Do you not have houses to eat and drink in? Or do you despise the church of God, and humiliate those who have nothing? What shall I say to you? Shall I commend you in this? No, I will not. For I received from the Lord what I also delivered to you, that the Lord Jesus on the night when he was betrayed took bread, and when he had given thanks, he broke it, and said, 'This is my body which is for you. Do this in remembrance of me.' In the same way also the cup, after supper, saying, 'This cup is the new covenant, in my blood. Do this, as often as you drink it, in remembrance of me.' For as often as you eat this bread and drink the cup, you proclaim the Lord's death until he comes. Whoever, therefore, eats the bread or drinks the cup of the Lord in an unworthy

27 George A. Lindbeck, *The Nature of Doctrine: Religion and Theology in a Postliberal Age*, Westminster Press, Philadelphia, and SPCK, London, 1984, p. 122.

28 See Gerard Loughlin, *Telling God's Story: Bible, Church and Narrative Theology*, Cambridge University Press, Cambridge, 1996.

manner will be guilty of profaning the body and blood of the Lord. Let a man examine himself, and so eat of the bread and drink of the cup. For any one who eats and drinks without discerning the body eats and drinks judgment upon himself.[29]

The moral vices connected here with this bad behaviour at the Eucharist are factiousness, greed, gluttony, drunkenness, unconcern for those in need, profanation and bringing judgment upon oneself. The contrasting moral virtues are presumably peacemaking, self-control, restraint, sobriety, care for those in need, holiness and righteousness. It is the virtues not the vices which should result from a proper sharing of the Eucharist together.

Doubtless there has always been a gap between the exalted fruits of the Christian life which should result from a regular sharing of Christian worship and the impoverished fruits which are actually evident amongst churchgoers. Yet there are many indications from the data in previous chapters, thankfully, that most churchgoers today do not behave as appallingly as those early Corinthians. Instead, significant traces of faith, hope and love have been detected amongst those most exposed to the culture of churchgoing. The staple ingredients of this culture – hymns, sermons, intercessions, public confessions and, above all, readings of Scripture and celebrations of the Eucharist – all act as carriers of this distinctive culture. Together they continue to shape the lives – however imperfectly – of faithful worshippers.

[29] 1 Corinthians 11.18, 21–9 (RSV).

CHAPTER 9

Churches and moral disagreement

In the previous chapter it was suggested that the staple ingredients of regular worship act as carriers of the distinctive Christian culture of faith, hope and love. Yet a final paradox remains. This culture provides churchgoers both with a shared means of philosophical justification and with an apparently interminable potential for disagreement on particular moral issues. Precisely because these Christian virtues of faith, hope and love are set at a general level, they can unite churchgoers. Yet once they are particularised and related to actual moral decision-making in a pluralistic society, they soon expose bitter and passionately held moral differences amongst churchgoers and within and between different churches. An account of Christian ethics which emphasised only points of moral unity amongst churchgoers, and which failed also to explore radical moral disagreements, would surely be inadequate.

This final chapter will examine some of the theological and institutional implications of this paradox, using an extended example of troublesome moral decision-making. The thirteenth Lambeth Conference of Anglican Bishops was held on the campus of my own university in the summer of 1998. Since I was involved as a theological consultant on ethics both in the Conference itself and in its lengthy preparation process, I could share and observe at first hand what proved to be a difficult and fractious series of moral debates within and across different provinces of the Anglican Communion. I will, of course, be careful to use only information which is already in the public domain – it would be quite wrong to disclose confidential negotiations. However, a broad understanding of these debates may help to put some of the moral differences amongst churchgoers already noted in earlier chapters into a more adequate theological and sociological framework. It will soon become evident that virtue ethics is only the beginning of moral wisdom. A focus upon moral character and community does not eliminate continuing conflicts about moral decisions.

MORAL AGREEMENT AND CONFLICT

At the outset it is worth noting some general points – especially those raised by earlier monographs in this series *New Studies in Christian Ethics* – about moral agreement and conflict within Christian culture. The moral unity created by a shared sense of faith, hope and love is important for Christian ethics. To return to arguments noted in the Introduction, Christian faith does, as Kieran Cronin insists, offer 'a specifically religious justifying reason for acting morally'.[1] So, once convinced of the dynamic, purpose-filled presence of God reaching out to the world in Jesus Christ, the Christian is given a powerful justifying reason for both hope and love. Teleology is not simply a matter of us choosing to endow meaning to an otherwise meaningless existence and altruism is not simply an act of defiance in an amoral world. Rather both teleology and altruism – hope and love – are seen as fitting human responses to divine grace. For the Christian, God in Christ endows the universe with purpose and love from the moment of creation. The divine Logos is simultaneously Logos as purpose, hope and meaning and Logos as active love.

Ian Markham makes a similar point, although one which could apply equally to Jews and Muslims, when depicting a theistic explanation for morality:

> The often discussed difficulties with a religious foundation for ethical assertions often presuppose a crudely anthropomorphic God. So let me repeat what exactly the theist is trying to claim. For the naturalist the universe is an inanimate entity that through remarkable chance has generated mind and consciousness. The main theistic claim is the

[1] Kieran Cronin, *Rights and Christian Ethics*, Cambridge University Press, Cambridge and New York, 1992, p. 233.

opposite: at the heart of the universe is goodness and love enabling all to be. This is what we mean by God. We find ourselves in awe and reverence placing the ultimate value on this being at the heart of the universe. As I have already said worship is not pandering to a giant ego saying 'Oh God, you are jolly big.' Instead as we focus on God – the ultimate beauty, love, goodness, and joy – we start to appreciate the appropriate value of everything else. Worship is the realization of the location of ultimate value. Such a disposition forces one to monotheism. Further reflection on God establishes the crucial nature of interpersonal relations both with each other and between God and us. The claim that the universe is ultimately personal points to the moral dimension. These moral truths are grounded in the character of God.[2]

Belief in God, properly understood, is seen as the most fitting response to a world which already shows evidence of moral and physical order and love. Within worship this belief is shaped and strengthened.

Michael Northcott extends this line of argument into the ecological debate. He believes that the 'doctrines of creation, Trinity, incarnation, redemption and eschatology can in fact provide us with a powerful model of embodied human life, and of self-in-relation, which challenges the atomistic and denatured self of the post-Enlightenment utilitarian individualism.[3] He believes that a recovery of a proper sense of the natural, created order is crucial for the ecological debate. This, he argues, offers a much stronger way of arguing for the preservation of the environment than a secular argument based purely upon human interest and human welfare. For Northcott 'the recovery of a more objective and naturally located basis for human moral life would seem to be a prerequisite for reordering human life towards a more relational social order in which the richness of human goods is more fully pursued, and in which the goods of the non-human world are also affirmed and conserved'.[4] Again, like Markham, Northcott concludes that it

[2] Ian S. Markham, *Plurality and Christian Ethics*, Cambridge University Press, Cambridge and New York, 1994, pp. 166–7.

[3] Michael S. Northcott, *The Environment and Christian Ethics*, Cambridge University Press, Cambridge, 1996, p. 163.

[4] *Ibid.* p. 256.

is specifically within worship that these theological and moral convictions can be shaped and strengthened:

Green consumerism, ecocracy, even environmental protest movements, ultimately cannot succeed in radically changing the direction of modern civilisation so long as they avoid the moral and spiritual vacuum which lies at its heart. The ecological repristination of the natural law tradition argues for a fundamental connection between the reorientation of society towards the common good of humanity and cosmos and the situation of persons in moral and worshipping communities where the quest for the common good is enriched and legitimated by the spiritual quest . . . The fundamental good is the orientation of life towards God as the giver of life, an orientation which is expressed in the first commandment of the Decalogue, which is the revealed form of the natural law, the commandment to worship God and God alone, and not to idolise – and hence abuse – any other feature of created reality. The centrality of worship in this vision of ethics points to the moral significance of worshipping communities in which the dependence of all life on God, and the gifted and relational character of all forms of life on earth, are celebrated and affirmed, and in which those values or virtues, which make for the good life, and the common good, of both human life and the land, are pursued and legitimated.[5]

For some theologians these primary insights about teleology and altruism can be seen, not just in Christian faith, but also in many of the world's historic faiths. Hans Küng, for example, argues[6] that religious-based forms of ethics are essential for responsible politics. The latter is not simply about the self-interests of states, let alone about some brute will-to-power. A global economy, especially, involves ethical as well as empirical considerations. In both responsible politics and economics Küng believes that there is an important role for religious faith. Because these issues are global and not simply national, dialogue across religious traditions and, indeed, across religious and secular traditions, is essential. This fierce opponent of Vatican hegemony is equally strident in dismissing any form of religious imperialism, still a cause of too much hatred, abusive power and war in the world.[7] He believes that it is possible to

[5] *Ibid.* pp. 312–14.

[6] Hans Küng: *A Global Ethic for Global Politics and Economics*, SCM Press, London, 1997.

[7] See also Lawrence Osborn and Andrew Walker (eds.), *Harmful Religion: An Exploration*

build up a global ethic, based upon shared rights and responsibilities, which complements but does not eliminate the need for the particularities that specific religious traditions offer.

These overviews suggest that there really can be a shared and distinctive moral vision amongst churchgoers – and perhaps, on some points, more widely amongst worshippers across different faith traditions. Inevitably this will be a broad vision. As such it may be particularly appropriate for global issues where human beings from many different cultures and heritages do need to cooperate and find new ways of living peacefully and responsibly together. The broad teleological and altruistic moral vision of churchgoers offers an important contrast to secular forms of utilitarianism, individualistic autonomy, moral relativism or simply moral nihilism. Senses of the need for both moral order and moral action beyond self-interest are held most strongly by regular churchgoers. Both are distinctive features of a churchgoing culture. And both offer a critical challenge to some of the 'shortcoming and effects' of secular orthodoxies.[8]

Yet what about more specific, contentious and particularised moral issues? How can moral visions be shared in contexts of radical conflict? How can churchgoers, even when they agree about the general virtues that they share, reach a common mind in areas of sharply polarised moral decision-making?

One modern theologian who has done more than any other to treat conflict seriously within the church is Stephen Sykes. He argues at length that conflict has been a feature of the Christian church from the very outset and will remain a feature until the eschaton. Given the nature of the Christian Gospel, conflict is inevitable and can, properly, be contained within boundaries but can never be eliminated without also disrupting the essential ambiguities and tensions of Christian identity. So, having reviewed the conflicts itemised by Paul in Galatians and 1 Corinthians, he concludes:

of Religious Abuse, SPCK, London, 1997. For a balance see also David Martin, *Does Religion Cause War?*, Oxford University Press, Oxford, 1997.

[8] See David A. S. Fergusson, *Community, Liberalism and Christian Ethics*, Cambridge University Press, Cambridge, 1998. See also E. Clinton Gardner, *Justice and Christian Ethics*, Cambridge University Press, Cambridge and New York, 1995, and Stanley Rudman, *Concepts of Persons and Christian Ethics*, Cambridge University Press, Cambridge, 1997.

What these examples show is the reality of conflict in the Pauline church. The conflict concerned not merely moral questions, which invariably entail ambiguities of intention, circumstance and consequence. Rather we find controversies about Paul's authority, based, he believed, on a misunderstanding of the gospel, controversies about the continued applicability of the legal traditions of Judaism, and controversies about his own attempt to mediate between the Jewish and Gentile elements in the Christian movement. The point to be made clear is that these are not in every case external trials brought about by some implacably or demonically hostile agency. They constitute rather a continuous spectrum of difficulty apparently inherent in the complexity of what was being attempted. The Christian movement was the cause of its own dissensions.[9]

Far from seeing conflict as essentially harmful to the church, Sykes argues that it can have an important and positive function. For him 'Christian identity is . . . not a state but a process; a process, moreover, which entails the restlessness of a dialectic, impelled by criticism.'[10] Like Markham and Northcott in *New Studies in Christian Ethics*, it is finally in worship that Sykes believes that this identity is to be located. For all three Anglican theologians, worship shapes and legitimates moral and theological vision. Within worship, Sykes argues, Christians can find unity despite their many conflicts and sharp disagreements. The latter, although often distressing for churchgoers themselves, have a constructive and dynamic role within the church.

Several of the monographs in *New Studies in Christian Ethics* suggest areas of potential conflict between Christians engaged in moral issues. Jean Porter, especially, states the problem here clearly. At the end of her careful and finely nuanced study of the different virtues which contribute to Christian character, she asks:

How are we to balance the competing claims of mercy and justice, caring and conscientiousness? We realize by now that there can be no simple formula for doing so. This balance must be attained through the process of intelligent action in situations of tension among these diverse ideals; this process, in turn, will partially presuppose, and further clarify, some more or less conscious conception of the differing

[9] Stephen Sykes, *The Identity of Christianity*, SPCK, London, 1984, p. 17.
[10] *Ibid.* p. 285.

claims of self, other, and the community as a whole, their relative weights, and the correct ordering of priority among them. Once again, we find ourselves at the same conclusion: the person who is able consistently to achieve a felicitous balance between the demands of caring and the demands of conscientiousness will necessarily be a prudent person, whose wisdom is grounded in a sound and reflective conception of the human good.[11]

In terms of virtue ethics, there is a critical gap between a community that is shaped by distinctive Christian virtues and a community which agrees without dissent about specific moral decisions in contentious areas. Just supposing that Christian virtues could be stated and agreed upon without ambiguity, the balance and tension between them, as well as their specific implications, would always be a matter of fine moral judgment, prudence and wisdom. Even the great, the good and the wise have strong moral disagreements in free societies.

Indeed, from the mass of data reviewed in previous chapters it is difficult to find measurable evidence of a single moral area in which churchgoers make unanimous moral decisions. Naturally opinion surveys tend to ask respondents about moral choices which are disputed in society at large. In the process, areas which might receive moral unanimity (about genocide, child abuse, or whatever) tend to be ignored in these surveys, so it would be a mistake to leap to dogmatic conclusions about moral relativism on this basis. Nevertheless, large areas of moral disagreement amongst churchgoers clearly are revealed in the surveys.

At the 1998 Lambeth Conference, too, strong and sometimes bitter moral disagreements quickly became evident. Had the bishops taken full account of the different feminist critiques of moral decision-making analysed by Susan Parsons,[12] or the

[11] Jean Porter, *Moral Action and Christian Ethics*, Cambridge University Press, Cambridge and New York, 1995, pp. 195–6. See also Garth L. Hallett, *Priorities and Christian Ethics*, Cambridge University Press, Cambridge and New York, 1998. For an important empirical account of conflict at congregational level see Penny Edgell Becker, *Congregations in Conflict: Cultural Models of Local Religious Life*, Cambridge University Press, Cambridge and New York, 1999.

[12] See, Susan Frank Parsons, *Feminism and Christian Ethics*, Cambridge University Press, Cambridge, 1996, and Lisa Sowle Cahill, *Sex, Gender and Christian Ethics*, Cambridge University Press, Cambridge and New York, 1996.

range and complexity of different styles of biblical interpretation analysed by Ian McDonald,[13] these disagreements might have been sharper still. Both authors in *New Studies in Christian Ethics* successfully show that complex and probably incommensurable choices are involved in these two huge areas of scholarship – choices which have radical implications for the discipline of Christian ethics. Given the difficulty of these choices, Sykes' judgment does seem to be correct. Conflict appears to be inevitable.

CONFLICT AND COERCION

Coercion is an obvious way to resolve moral conflict within churches. As was noted in the Introduction, James Mackey's monograph for the series pays particular attention to this option. He defines power as 'that which makes things happen, which enables states of affairs to come about'[14] and sees power as located between two extremes; pure moral authority at one end and force or coercion at the other. Churches typically view their own power as consisting only of moral authority. Mackey is highly sceptical of this claim and seeks to show at length that, like secular authorities, those in power within churches find coercion difficult to resist, especially when moral issues are at stake. Given sufficient power, church leaders do seem to find the enforcement of morality upon other people, whether they are Christian or not, extremely tempting.

James Mackey takes two extended examples of ecclesiastical power as force, the first drawn from his own Roman Catholic Church and the second, more surprisingly, from the Church of Scotland. Although he offers only passing hints, he is also aware that the Church of England suffers from the same temptation. He finds the widespread claim that churches have only spiritual not secular power particularly disingenuous:

[13] See J. I. H. McDonald, *Biblical Interpretation and Christian Ethics*, Cambridge University Press, Cambridge, 1993.

[14] James P. Mackey, *Power and Christian Ethics*, Cambridge University Press, Cambridge, 1994, p. 35.

amongst the factors that count against this impression there is not just the fact that in Western civilisation Christian churches have constantly engaged with secular powers on similar if not identical terms, there is also the fact that the terminology and understanding of power in the West is common to church and civil society . . . the essence of power is the same in church and state.[15]

Fourteenth-century Catholicism provides an obvious example of this identification of ecclesiastical and civil power as force. Mackey refers specifically to Pope Boniface's Bull *Unam Sanctam* to illustrate his theme, with its image of two swords, the spiritual and the temporal, both controlled by the church, with an insistence that 'sword must be subordinated to sword'. Although the coercive power of the Roman Catholic Church is much weakened in the modern world, Mackey argues that it can still be traced especially in countries such as the Republic of Ireland:

The Roman Catholic Church in Ireland has frequently affirmed through its highest office-bearers that it desires 'a clear distinction between Church and State and that the Constitution was for the people to decide and the laws for the legislators'. It has even more frequently claimed the right and the duty to form the consciences of its members on matters of moral import . . . But when the same church mobilises the vast Catholic majority in the Republic of Ireland to see through a particular constitutional amendment, as happened in the case of abortion in 1983, or to prevent the passing of legislation on divorce, as happened in 1987, there are some grounds for the accusation that it seeks to impose its own moral judgments on the state by abuse of the voting power of a majority . . . democracy does not guarantee the rejection of power as force, in favour of power as authority; majority rule can show a force as naked as any despot could exercise.[16]

Mackey believes that recent papal arguments about contraception, abortion and divorce are not just logically flawed but also demonstrate the true source and bleak effects of ecclesiastical power here. After *Humanae Vitae*, especially, it has become evident that 'in this piece of moral legislation, then, Rome simply got it wrong; and it would be foolish of anyone to try to say, in face of such a bad law, that the power behind it was

[15] *Ibid.* p. 18. [16] *Ibid.* p. 139.

sacred'.[17] More than that it has contributed directly to misery amongst churchgoing Catholics: 'it has brought a very great deal of unnecessary suffering on the few faithful ones who did try to live by it during their reproductive years, as on many others who suffered the painful wrench of conscience in risking, in this instance, the rejection of their spiritual leaders'.[18]

There is an extremely important point to note here. Several contributors to *New Studies in Christian Ethics* fear the temptation towards coercion in a context of moral pluralism.[19] However, James Mackey's example of the situation following *Humanae Vitae* demonstrates that attempted coercion within complex churches set in pluralistic societies may actually be counter-productive. In theory, the Roman Catholic Church has a united moral stance on contraception, abortion and divorce. The papal teaching on each seems to be clear. In reality, there are internal fault-lines in the teaching and a widespread rejection of it both amongst churchgoing Catholics and in the population at large. In addition, the obvious discrepancies here may in turn have contributed both to popular scepticism about papal authority[20] and to churchgoing decline amongst young Catholics.[21]

Mackey's claim about the moral despotism of democratic majorities allows him to include churches such as the Church of Scotland within his critique. The distinctly less democratic church, the Church of England, would have offered him many similar examples. Most recently, at the time of writing, there is the example of bishops voting in the House of Lords against legislation, which was supported by a large majority in the House of Commons, attempting to lower the age of consent for homosexuals. Under the previous government, Church of England bishops also tried to stop legislation on Sunday trading. In his detailed and scholarly study *Religions, Rights and*

[17] *Ibid.* p. 133. [18] *Ibid.* p. 95.

[19] See William Schweiker, *Responsibility and Christian Ethics*, Cambridge University Press, Cambridge and New York, 1995, and Markham, *Plurality and Christian Ethics.*

[20] See John Mahoney, *The Making of Moral Theology: A Study of the Roman Catholic Tradition*, Clarendon Press, Oxford, 1987.

[21] See Philip Richter and Leslie J. Francis, *Gone But Not Forgotten: Church Leaving and Returning*, Darton, Longman & Todd, London, 1998.

Laws, Anthony Bradney[22] concludes that in Britain mainstream Christianity, and especially the Church of England, is privileged by law, and members of minority faiths correspondingly disadvantaged, in five major areas; marriage and the family, education, blasphemy, work, and charitable status. In another extensive study, James Beckford and Sophie Gilliat[23] show that, despite major changes in the beliefs and religious allegiances of prisoners themselves, the Church of England still retains a very dominant role in prison chaplaincy. Each of these areas involves moral issues and in each the Church of England is given an advantage through force of law.

Coercive power within churches can take several forms. At its most extreme in the medieval church it sometimes took the form of torturing and even executing individuals for their lack of moral or theological 'orthodoxy'. In the modern world it is more likely to take the form of social exclusion. At various points in the last few years the Roman Catholic Church has attempted to silence or disown some of its own leading theologians – Hans Küng, Edward Schillebeeckx and Leonardo Boff are all obvious examples. Even the Anglican Church worldwide has acted similarly. For example, the conservative evangelical Moore College in Sydney, Australia, recently dismissed a lecturer for becoming too 'liberal' in biblical studies. Indeed, many churches might seek to control their own theologians, not least by failing to appoint them to those lectureships within their control. Between these two forms of coercive power is the attempt, especially by established churches, to control civil legislation on moral issues.

James Mackey is adamantly opposed to all such ecclesiastical uses of coercive power on moral issues. He argues that for morality properly to be morality individuals must be free to choose evil as well as good. The attempt to enforce morality, however well intentioned, is a profound mistake. Just as God's creative action within the world and within Jesus Christ always

22 Anthony Bradney, *Religions, Rights and Laws*, Leicester University Press, Leicester, 1993.

23 James A. Beckford and Sophie Gilliat, *Religion in Prison: Equal Rites in a Multi-Faith Society*, Cambridge University Press, Cambridge, 1998.

treats people as moral agents who must choose and not be coerced, so churches too should properly wield power as moral authority and emphatically not as force or coercion.

This analysis of power as moral authority or coercion helps to reframe a classic debate within the sociology of religion, which, as noted in chapter one, has now entered the theological debate about Stanley Hauerwas. Following Weber and Troeltsch, sociologists of religion have long distinguished between 'churches' and 'sects', whilst insisting that the term 'sect' is not used normatively in a pejorative sense. Not all theologians have been so careful, sometimes accusing Hauerwas of sectarianism. Although there is still considerable debate even about the sociological distinction,[24] a notion of power in Mackey's sense offers fresh insights here.

On a scale from power as coercion to power as moral authority, the universal church and the thoroughgoing sect are on the coercive end and the liberal denomination and the cult on the opposite end. The first two tend to settle contentious moral issues through physical or social exclusion, whereas the last two contain ongoing moral tensions albeit sometimes with considerable difficulty. All can and do change their moral stances over time, but the tendency of the first two is to change sharply and sometimes traumatically, whereas the last two tend to change more smoothly in response to changes in society at large.

The thoroughgoing sect illustrates the first process most clearly in the modern world. An essential feature of consistent, exclusive moral conclusions amongst sectarian members is an exclusive membership. Moral deviants must be excluded. In those rare utopian sects which have withdrawn physically from the modern world, such as the Amish and earlier the Shakers in North America, a pure membership is a prerequisite of a pure moral stance. Amongst the Amish this still causes considerable anguish for families, since children must finally decide whether they are to follow the Amish ways and live within the community or follow the ways of the world and be physically excluded

[24] See Bryan Wilson, *Religion in Sociological Perspective*, Clarendon Press, Oxford, 1987, and *The Social Dimension of Sectarianism*, Clarendon Press, Oxford, 1990.

from the community and, indeed, from their own parents. Amongst late nineteenth century Shakers only a tenth of the orphans they raised accepted their total commitment to celibacy and remained Shakers as adults, nine-tenths left or were required to leave.[25] Sexual contacts could not be permitted within a utopian community which went to such lengths to ensure sexual abstinence. Exclusive Brethren and Jehovah's Witnesses today, although remaining within society, also go to great lengths to keep their membership pure. The social exclusion of deviant members and the social isolation of faithful members are essential means of maintaining their distinctive beliefs and values intact.

The cult, in some sociological accounts, presents a sharp contrast to the thoroughgoing sect, since it awkwardly combines distinctive and socially deviant beliefs with an inclusive approach to membership.[26] The New Age Movement currently provides a striking example of this. It combines a series of loosely related transcendent beliefs which, as shown in table 1, are held by a sizeable minority of the population. Anyone can hold these beliefs, buy books and magazines which support them, and take part periodically in New Age Festivals. As yet there is little attempt at formal organisation or control, other than through publishing copyright. As a result New Age beliefs and values can adapt, conflict and transform and individuals can pick-and-mix from them as they wish. Even some regular churchgoers are apparently influenced by them. Nobody is excluded physically or socially by the New Age Movement. It is an icon of postmodern eclecticism.

There has been a longstanding tendency to see churches as inclusive and sects as exclusive religious organisations. Weber, after all, saw a sect as 'a community of personal believers of the reborn, and only these', in contrast to a church 'as a sort of trust foundation for supernatural ends, an institution, necessarily including both the just and the unjust, whether for increasing

[25] See Priscilla J. Brewer, *Shaker Communities, Shaker Lives*, University Press of New England, New Hampshire, 1986.

[26] See Roy Wallis, *The Road to Total Freedom: A Sociological Analysis of Scientology*, Heinemann, London, 1976.

the glory of God (Calvinistic) or as a medium for bringing the means of salvation to men (Catholic and Lutheran)'.[27] Here Weber was influenced by his friend Ernst Troeltsch who also saw the sect as 'a voluntary society composed of strict and definite Christian believers bound to each other by the fact that all have experienced "the new birth" ' who 'live apart from the world', whereas the church 'is able to receive the masses and adjust itself to the world, because to a certain extent it can afford to ignore the need for subjective holiness for the sake of the objective treasures of grace and redemption'.[28] However, such a neat division works rather poorly in practice. Bryan Wilson has shown over many years that 'sects' differ greatly amongst themselves about the extent of their exclusivity.[29] The Quakers, for example, have remained remarkably inclusive despite holding views on warfare at odds with society at large. Similarly 'churches', especially the Roman Catholic Church, can at times be highly exclusive, especially in the use of coercive power to control members. Divisions within some traditional Catholic families, while seldom as polarised as those of the Amish, can certainly be very sharp across the generations. Catholic adult piety has long been at war with morally (and especially sexually) deviant youth and Catholic education has often been seen as an important buttress against a morally pluralistic world.

If coercion is used as a means of countering moral disagreement within some sects and churches, it is not without cost. The sect, often with a high degree of estrangement from society at large, may remain morally pure but tends to lack any social significance. It has, for example, become a matter of curiosity to many Americans that the Shakers renounced sexual intercourse or that many of the Amish still renounce cars in favour of buggies or tractors in favour of horse-drawn ploughs. Yet, however jaded Americans might feel about modern sexual

27 Max Weber, *The Protestant Ethic and the Spirit of Capitalism*, Unwin, London, 1930 (1904–5), pp. 144–5.

28 Ernst Troeltsch, *The Social Teaching of the Christian Churches*, Harper, New York, 1960 (1919), pp. 993–4.

29 Wilson, *Religion in Sociological Perspective* and *The Social Dimension of Sectarianism*.

permissiveness or mechanised, let alone biotechnologised, farming, they are unlikely to emulate these sectarians.

The cost to the exclusive church can be rather different. The sheer size of the Roman Catholic Church makes it impossible to control in the same way as a thoroughgoing sect. It inevitably has to cope with the problem of 'receiving the masses' and including 'both the just and the unjust'. The example of contraception has already shown the problems involved in attempting to apply a papal teaching so at odds with everyday experience. No matter how strongly a modern pope feels about such an issue he is ultimately powerless to compel churchgoing Catholics to comply. A chasm between official teaching and actual practice becomes inevitable. Worse than that, at some stage a future pope must contemplate change whilst attempting not to damage papal authority. Many believed that this was still possible for Paul VI. It has been widely rumoured that it was the intention of John-Paul I. How a future pope manages to achieve this with any degree of credibility remains to be seen. Firm moral teaching – even when it is manifestly flawed – is difficult to change without trauma. Yet change eventually it surely must.

In the modern world, then, the exclusive sect coerces its own members rather more effectively than the exclusive church. Yet it is the latter which is potentially more dangerous in society at large. It was noted earlier that repeated evidence from opinion surveys shows that members of the public remain deeply suspicious of church leaders becoming 'involved in politics'. Church leaders themselves, and indeed political theologians, often mock this suspicion, arguing that the Christian Gospel inescapably has social and political implications. Yet the instinctive grounds of this suspicion may be more secure than is sometimes realised. The radical political agenda of the Jehovah's Witnesses can safely be ignored since nowhere in the world is this sect in a position to enforce political change. In contrast, churches in the past have been in positions of coercive power over the 'just and the unjust' alike and, in some countries, still retain vestiges of this power. Indeed, mullahs in some Islamic States today retain very much more than a vestige. It is therefore perhaps not surprising that people in liberal democracies remain so adamant about the political neutrality of church leaders. Unlike their politicians, church leaders are not even subject to the discipline of facing repeated elections. Perhaps this explains why the political views of American church leaders receive so little media attention (compared, say, with the corresponding attention in Britain) despite high levels of American churchgoing. In this most democratic of countries, church leaders, even if initially elected, simply cannot be trusted with making accountable political judgments. In more patrician countries, such as Britain, church leaders are apt to forget this.

In this respect the Church of England is unusual within the Anglican Communion. Uniquely it remains an established and national church, with both monarch and prime minister involved in its governance and with senior bishops still sitting in the House of Lords. Disestablished elsewhere in Britain and emphatically denominational in other parts of the Communion, Anglicanism is predominantly inclusive in character. Even the Lambeth Conference and its president, the Archbishop of Canterbury, has only an advisory status. The Conference can encourage or condemn political regimes, but it has no power to effect political change. Nor does it even have power to enforce change within the Communion. In 1988 the ordination and consecration of women within the Communion was a major and contentious issue. Yet the Conference itself could neither prevent such ordinations and consecrations nor enforce them. At most it could advise and exhort. It could, of course, choose to invite some bishops to the Conference and not others (such as those of small break-away factions), but even here there remains considerable ambiguity with some overlapping jurisdictions allowed. In terms of membership, beliefs and values the Anglican Communion, despite its patrician origins, is an overwhelmingly inclusive church.

CONFLICT AT THE LAMBETH CONFERENCE

So how does the Anglican Communion avoid moral relativism? This was a key question behind many of the debates at the 1998

Lambeth Conference. An inclusive church typically finds strong moral judgments difficult to sustain. Yet Lambeth 1998 was characterised by strong judgments on homosexuality, debt and human rights. Some important judgments on euthanasia and the environment were also made, albeit with more nuance than the other issues. Much vaguer judgments were also made about modern technology. The strength and force of the first set of judgments represent a significant departure from many previous Lambeth Conferences. How was this possible for an inclusive church?

Since the issue of homosexuality came to dominate the 1998 Conference it illustrates this question well. In the reports of the 1988 Conference homosexuality was also considered, but it was set there into an extended context of family, marriage, sexual abuse and the spread of AIDS. So there were just three paragraphs specifically on homosexuality, in contrast to fifteen on marriage, eleven on the family, five on sexual abuse and thirty-five on AIDS. These three paragraphs said little beyond the fact that 'we recognise that this issue is unresolved, and we welcome the fact that study is continuing'. They called for scientific, sociological and biblical study of the issue and 'continue to encourage dialogue with, and pastoral concern for, persons of homosexual orientation within the Family of Christ'.[30] The 1988 resolution reaffirmed the 1978 resolution calling for 'dispassionate study of the question of homosexuality, which would take seriously both the teaching of Scripture and the results of scientific and medical research' and then called 'each Province to reassess, in the light of such study and because of our concern for human rights, its care for and attitude towards persons of homosexual orientation'.[31]

From this it might have been expected that the agenda for the 1998 Conference would continue this study of homosexuality, albeit set into a broad context of family relationships, would dialogue with homosexual Christians, and would also encour-

30 ACC, *The Truth Shall Make You Free: The Lambeth Conference 1988: The Reports, Resolutions and Pastoral Letters from the Bishops*, The Anglican Consultative Council, London, 1988, p. 187.

31 *Ibid.* p. 237.

age provinces to share together the ways in which they were caring for homosexual people. The initial, preparation report on human sexuality, circulated with other section reports to all of the bishops some months ahead of the Conference, worked closely to this agenda. It was drafted and redrafted five times at the preparatory conference, the St Augustine's Seminar, which was held fifteen months before the Conference. Already there was considerable nervousness in the steering committee that the divisive issue of homosexuality might easily dominate the Conference. Ironically few of the initial reports from the nine provincial regions of the Anglican Communion (and none from the West) mentioned sexuality or homosexuality as a topic for the Conference. In contrast, all had specifically mentioned the topic of international debt. The latter was also a topic of central concern to the Archbishop of Cape Town, Njongonkulu Ndungane, the chair of the whole ethics section at the 1998 Conference. So it was decided that, although homosexuality would need to be discussed, the issue of international debt would receive the fullest treatment. It was felt that the Conference might be able to exert real moral authority and help to change the international culture to accept the need for debt remission for the world's most impoverished countries.

The initial report on human sexuality outlined the current situation in the Communion in which 'there are deep divisions between our cultures on a number of issues – divorce, cohabitation, marriage, polygamy, and homosexuality'. Some of the harmful effects of globalisation were noted, as well as some of the physical changes such as greater longevity and more effective control of human fertility. As at the 1988 Conference, the distressing spread of HIV/AIDS was also noted, as well as the increasing break-down of families in many countries. The report then asked: 'Faced with such difficult issues how can bishops provide effective and sensitive leadership?' In response it outlined 'three different ways of sexual living', which I derived initially from the Southern African report *The Church and Human Sexuality*[32] and then developed further elsewhere.[33]

32 *The Church and Human Sexuality*, Church of the Province of Southern Africa, 1995.

33 See my *Moral Leadership in a Postmodern Age*, T. & T. Clark, Edinburgh, 1997, pp. 81f.

The first of these ways is 'faithful and righteous family life, based on love and mutuality' which, together with 'singleness, dedicated celibacy and monastic community life', is an 'abiding way for Christians'. The second consists of 'expressions of sexuality, which are sadly present in all societies, are inherently opposed to the Christian way and are sinful', including 'promiscuity (both heterosexual and homosexual), adultery, prostitution, child pornography, active paedophilia, bestiality and sadomasochism'. It also mentioned that families too can be 'distorted by unfaithfulness or unrighteousness'. A third way is also suggested which 'allows for considerable differences among those who believe that they are faithful Christians' and allows Christians 'to be pastorally sensitive to those with whom they disagree'. This way suggests that there are 'forms of behaviour which some Christians claim should not be regarded as inherently sinful but which may be less than complete expressions of the Christian way'. Three examples are then given; the practice in parts of Africa of couples having children before marriage, faithful homosexual relationships in other parts of the Anglican Communion, and the remarriage of divorced people in church in increasing areas of the Communion. The full text of the example of faithful homosexuality is as follows:

> This sensitive issue continues to divide Christians. In many places, homosexual behaviour is identified simply with paedophilia and promiscuity, whereas in other places there are now many examples of faithful homosexual relations in society at large and within the Church. At present, there is a clear division of belief among Anglicans on homosexual behaviour and, indeed, medical knowledge is still developing in this area. While almost all would agree that promiscuous homosexuality (like promiscuous heterosexuality) is sinful and belongs to *Way 2*, Anglican opinion on faithful homosexuality is divided. Some believe it is sinful and belongs to *Way 2*; others believe it is acceptable to God and belongs to *Way 3*. Different cultures and different understanding of biblical texts are important elements in how one decides on these issues.

A section of theological reflection follows this depiction of the situation. Using the theological analysis originally written by John Suggit for the Southern African report, it argues that the biblical virtues of loving-kindness/faithfulness on the one hand

and righteousness/justice on the other are particularly important for the issue of human sexuality: 'a doctrine of atonement allows us to set these two ways of seeing God's relationship to the world into a context of our relationship to each other as human beings . . . as God has related faithfully and righteously to us, so we should try to relate to each other'. It then argues that '*Way 1* enshrines both faithfulness and righteousness and *Way 2* damages it':

> Many would argue that *Way 3* does contain some of the features of both faithfulness and righteousness. It has long been recognised in the Anglican Communion that polygamy in parts of Africa, and traditional marriage, do genuinely have features of both faithfulness and righteousness. In addition, there seem to have been many examples of faithfulness and righteousness among those who have remarried after divorce. An increasing number of Anglicans also maintain that faithful homosexuality contains features of both faithfulness and righteousness . . . An abiding pattern is faithful and loving monogamy, which is seen as the Christian way for sexual relationships and for the responsible bringing up of children. Nevertheless, faithful cohabitation and polygamy are seen as less than ideal but not as inherently opposed to this ideal.

Finally this preparatory report calls bishops to

> identify the theological virtues which are important in the Christian way of living; compare ways across the Communion in which we are seeking to strengthen faithful and righteous Christian marriage in the face of global pressures working against it; find ways of living together despite differences on issues such as divorce, homosexuality and polygamy; explore in what ways the Anglican Communion as a whole may find consensus on these issues, perhaps setting up an Inter-Anglican Commission on Human Sexuality.

Again, following the agenda suggested by the 1988 Conference, the chair of the human sexuality sub-section at the 1998 Conference, the Bishop of Johannesburg, Duncan Buchanan, proposed to invite a small group of homosexual Anglicans to meet the sub-section. However, after a series of widely reported and fractious meetings, the sub-section rejected this proposal and prepared a more normative statement specifically upon homosexuality.

The new statement notes at the outset that 'sexuality is the gift of a loving God'. Like the earlier report, it recognises marriage, singleness and dedicated celibacy 'as Christ-like ways of living', but omits any reference to mutual relations within marriage. It urges churches 'to find effective ways of encouraging Christlike living, as well as providing opportunities for the flourishing of friendship, and the building of supportive community life'. It, too, recognises that 'some expressions of sexuality are inherently contrary to the Christian way and are sinful' and includes some new examples of this – predatory sexual behaviour, violence against women and in families, rape and female circumcision. It adds a particular concern 'about the pressures on young people to engage in sexual activity at an early age' and urges churches 'to teach the virtue of abstinence'.

However, all mention of AIDS, which featured so prominently in 1988, or of such issues as remarriage after divorce, cohabitation or polygamy, has been removed, along with the specifically theological section on faithfulness and righteousness of the preparatory report. The main part of this short statement now focuses upon homosexuality. It assures people of homosexual orientation 'that they are loved by God and that all baptised, believing and faithful persons; regardless of sexual orientation; are full members of the Body of Christ'. It also calls on the church 'to work to end any discrimination on the basis of sexual orientation, and to oppose homophobia'. It then states:

We must confess that we are not of one mind about homosexuality. Our variety of understanding encompasses:

(1) those who believe that homosexual orientation is a disorder, but that through the grace of Christ people can be changed, although not without pain and struggle.
(2) those who believe that relationships between people of the same gender should not include genital expression, that this is the clear teaching of the Bible and of the Church universal, and that such activity (if unrepented of) is a barrier to the Kingdom of God.
(3) those who believe that committed homosexual relationships fall short of the biblical norm, but are to be preferred to relationships that are anonymous and transient.
(4) those who believe that the Church should accept and support or bless monogamous covenant relationships between homosexual people and that they may be ordained.

It appears that a majority of bishops is not prepared to bless same sex unions or to ordain active homosexuals. Furthermore many believe there should be a moratorium on such practices.

Although the style here still appears to be descriptive, the depiction of the second understanding (with a very wide gap between it and the third understanding) and the final two sentences are clearly much stronger than any wording adopted on this issue in the 1988 Conference Report. This 1998 Report then asks 'the Primates and the Anglican Consultative Council to establish a means of monitoring work done in the Communion on these issues and to share statements and resources' (but not, it should be noted, to set up an Inter-Anglican Commission on Human Sexuality since many bishops believed that this would give credence to the third and fourth understandings). It concludes with a quotation from the evangelical *St Andrew's Day Statement* about the call to redeemed humanity, male and female, in Christ.

The framing of a joint resolution from this sub-section proved even more difficult. The chair's suggested resolution – upholding 'faithfulness in marriage between one man and one woman in lifelong union' and celibacy, calling for a pastoral and sensitive ministry to people 'irrespective of their sexual orientation', condemning 'homophobia, violence within marriage and any trivialisation and commercialisation of sex', and asking for a central means of 'monitoring the work done on the subject of human sexuality in the Communion' – was soon judged by many in the sub-section to be inadequate. At the final plenary the word 'abstinence' was substituted for celibacy or chastity and the word 'homophobia' was replaced with 'irrational fear of homosexuals'. A majority of the sub-section also insisted upon adding a new resolution stating that the Conference 'cannot advise the legitimising or blessing or ordaining of those involved in same gender unions'. It was at this point in the sub-section that some of the North American bishops stated that they could no longer support the resolution as a whole. Undeterred one traditionalist Australian bishop attempted to strengthen this part of the resolution still further at the final plenary. He moved, unsuccessfully this time, that the word 'advise' should be changed to 'approve'. With more success, the Archbishop of Tanzania, Donald Mtemela, moved, again at the final plenary session, that a crucial new clause be added. In a carefully planned amendment he proposed that the words 'while rejecting homosexual practice as incompatible with Scripture . . .' should now preface the resolution calling for pastoral and sensitive ministry. Supported by 389 bishops (including most of those from Africa and Asia) and rejected by 190, these words give a new and firm normative tone to Lambeth Conference expressions on homosexuality. This vote proved to be the decisive moment in the 1998 Conference.

Set out in this way a process is clear. The broad setting and nonprescriptive character of the 1988 Conference report and resolutions have been replaced in the 1998 statement and resolutions with a specific focus upon homosexuality and with a clear normative rejection of homosexual practice as incompatible with Scripture. As a result, the mood of the 1998 Conference and the media attention given to it were inevitably dominated by the issue of homosexuality. Despite the emphasis upon international debt given by the Conference steering committee, by the chair of the ethics section and contained in all nine of the original provincial region reports, this will finally be remembered as the Conference which sought to reverse years of gradual acceptance of faithful homosexual relationships within parts of the Communion. An inclusive church which already contains many practising homosexual members, as well as homosexual priests and bishops, has adopted a firm moral stance rejecting homosexual practice.

How is this possible in a context of such obvious pluralism?

An important feature is still missing from this analysis, namely the inter-church movement (ICM) or, more accurately here, the intra-communion movement. The ICM is an obvious way of maintaining moral consistency and purity in a pluralistic world. It allows members of inclusive and morally pluralistic churches to join together in a common moral cause even while remaining members of these churches. The ICM also allows moral dissidents within exclusive churches to find additional Christian fellowship which matches their moral views more closely than their own churches. At its most effective the ICM is a single-issue movement, campaigning vigorously on that issue and avoiding division on other issues. ICMs can be strongly conservative, seeking to restore some older moral order or to retain some fast disappearing moral order. ICMs can also be radical, promoting moral change and innovation. The ICM is not itself a church. It exists solely to promote and protect a particular cause, not to replace the other functions of churches. Once an ICM with a specific and limited task has achieved this task – for example to make possible the ordination of women – it may well disband.

Elsewhere I have used the nineteenth-century movement around Josephine Butler as a vivid illustration of an ICM.[34] This single-minded and courageous evangelical campaigned for some thirty years against the Contagious Diseases Acts and, in the process, befriended many prostitutes. These Acts compelled women suspected of prostitution in certain ports to have compulsory inspections for venereal diseases. Josephine Butler argued that although the Acts were designed to reduce infection amongst British troops they were ineffective in controlling disease and actually encouraged the abuse and even virtual enslavement of women in publicly licensed brothels. To the embarrassment of members of her own church at the time, she campaigned vigorously in this area of such Victorian delicacy, despite the fact that her husband was headmaster of Liverpool College and then a canon residentiary of Winchester. Nonetheless she insisted that this was her Christian vocation and joined common cause with others who felt the same. The movement did finally succeed in having the Acts repealed in Britain (although not elsewhere in Europe) and, a century later, her work was finally recognised in the Church of England's *Alternative Service Book*. Throughout her campaigning she otherwise remained a respectable and pious member of the Church of England. The movement around her, although extremely demanding and socially risky, did not become a church. It had a clear and strictly limited task. And it allowed people across

[34] See my *Beyond Decline*, SCM Press, London, 1988, pp. 44f. and my *Moral Communities*, Exeter University Press, Exeter, 1992, pp. 73f.

denominational and social class divisions to work successfully together and to protect each other from the disapproval and ridicule of their peers.

Of course not all ICMs are successful. Sometimes their objectives are unattainable. Or sometimes ICMs try to combine divisive issues. For example, at a certain point key members of the *Prayer Book Society* assumed that all other members would be opposed to the ordination of women. Doubtless many were, but certainly not all. By combining the two issues the society risked alienating some of its own supporters. Similarly, groups opposed to abortion have sometimes assumed that all members will also oppose the withdrawal of nutrition and hydration from patients in a permanent vegetative state. Doubtless some will, but again this is an issue that has proved more divisive than they expected. It is after all logical to hold that new life should be supported while permanently damaged old life should not, or even to hold that both abortion and the nutrition and hydration of PVS patients constitute wrongful medical intervention.

An unprecedented, well financed and strategically organised ICM effectively took control of the agenda at the 1998 Lambeth Conference. A small group of conservative Western bishops, who were out of sympathy with the implicit and sometimes explicit tolerance of homosexual practice within their own parts of the Anglican Communion, shrewdly judged that with careful planning they could enlist the support of many fellow bishops in Africa (outside South Africa) and Asia. They were aware that many African and Asian bishops tended to conflate homosexuality with bestiality and paedophilia and, as a result, were astonished that anyone in the West could support it. They were also aware that they themselves needed to avoid any comparisons with remarriage after divorce in order to avoid offending their own supporters or with traditional marriage or polygamy in order to avoid offending some African supporters. However they wisely judged that an ICM directed solely at condemning homosexual practice could secure a firm resolution at the Conference. Some years ahead of the 1998 Conference they decided that *this* was indeed to be the dominating topic. In this way they believed that the Communion might be rescued from 'the liberal agenda' which had progressively weakened it from one Conference to the next.

There were two closely related organisations with a central role in this effective ICM. One was the American Anglican Council, whose president was James Stanton, Bishop of Dallas. He raised conservative American money to hire the premises of the Roman Catholic Franciscan Study Centre on the edge of the university campus. This served a number of interrelated groups, providing, for example, a venue for worship for those opposed to the ordination of women. The other organisation was the Oxford Centre for Mission Studies, represented at the Conference by Chris Sugden, its Director of Academic Affairs, and Vinay Samuel, its Executive Director. The latter, with their extensive knowledge of African and Asian bishops, were particularly active in circulating members of the Conference on the issue of homosexuality and in organising a well attended protest meeting. Conservative money also paid for mobile phones issued to supporters in the conference in order to allow greater strategic coordination. Unwittingly, the sexuality sub-group in the Conference accepted the invitation of the Bishop of Dallas to meet in the Franciscan Study Centre. His only direct intervention in the final plenary was significantly to propose changing 'one' to 'a' in the resolution upholding 'faithfulness in marriage between one man and one woman' – his opposition was to homosexuality rather than divorce. Together these two organisations had earlier arranged a series of international conferences to issue 'authoritative' statements on homosexuality which could then be referred to and used at the Conference. So, the Archbishop of South East Asia, Moses Tay, attempted to move two resolutions outside the ethics section approving of the *Kuala Lumpur Statement*. Similarly, the *St Andrew's Day Statement*, used in the sexuality statement, was published as an authoritative Anglican document in a reader specifically designed for the Conference again by the Oxford Centre for Mission Studies.[35]

All of this was achieved more through guile than coercion. Such an ICM represents an effective way in which members of

[35] Chris Sugden and Vinay Samuel, *Anglican Life and Witness: A Reader for the Lambeth Conference of Anglican Bishops 1998*, SPCK, London, 1997.

non-coercive, inclusive churches can still champion firm moral decisions. Despite the moral pluralism of their fellow churchgoers, in an ICM they can make common cause with like-minded churchgoers to defend, retain or even restore specific moral stances. These Lambeth Conference bishops were adopting a strategy which has proved effective on a variety of moral issues amongst churchgoers, lay and ordained, over the years. Unusually they did this so decisively at a Lambeth Conference and, in the process, they may well have secured a more united Anglican Communion. Before the 1998 Conference there were threats of schism, especially from some of the churches in South East Asia, if a liberal agenda triumphed. Well aware of this threat, many bishops from Western churches were anxious that homosexuality should not become a dominating issue at the Conference. Ironically, the effect of this ICM was to ensure that it did become so. In the circumstances, a conservative resolution allowed many Asian and African bishops to feel that their stance had prevailed and thus to abandon any idea of schism.

A number of Western bishops, while personally opposed to the Tanzanian resolution, regarded it as a price to pay for unity. Aware of the purely advisory status of the Conference, they agreed to disagree and reserved the right to act according to the conscience of their own part of the Communion. As the Conference drew to a close about a quarter of the bishops present signed an open letter of sympathy with gay and lesbian Anglicans:

> Within the limitations of this Conference it has not been possible to hear adequately your voices, and we apologise for any sense of rejection that has occurred because of this reality. This letter is a sign of our commitment to listen to you and reflect with you theologically and spiritually on your lives and ministries. It is our deep concern that you do not feel abandoned by your Church, and that you know of our continued respect and support . . . We must not stop where this Conference has left off. You, our sisters and brothers in Christ, deserve a more thorough hearing than you received over the past three weeks. We will work to make that so.[36]

Doubtless different ICMs opposing and supporting active

[36] Quoted in *Church Times*, 12 August 1998, p. 1.

(faithful) homosexuality will continue within the Anglican Communion for many years to come. As was discussed in chapter six, this is an issue which is unlikely to be resolved easily within inclusive churches. A majority of churchgoers and older members of the public in Britain still regard homosexual practice as wrong. Yet, across Western countries, there is a sharp age divide on this issue, which already appears to have influenced teenage churchgoers in Britain. However, given the fact that older people predominate in many Anglican congregations, the 1998 Conference resolution probably does accurately represent their moral view. Again, as was noted in the earlier chapter, the issue of homosexual practice is by definition a minority issue. Unlike cohabitation and divorce, homosexual orientation will not be part of the direct experience of most people, whether they are churchgoers or not. Finally, despite the Tanzanian resolution, biblical scholars are by no means agreed about the meaning of the condemnations of 'homosexuality' in Genesis 19, Leviticus 18.22 and 20.13, Romans 1.27, 1 Corinthians 6.9 and 1 Timothy 1.10.[37] For all of these reasons strong disagreements on the propriety of homosexual practices are likely to continue amongst Anglican churchgoers.

THE THEOLOGICAL SIGNIFICANCE OF DISAGREEMENT

This analysis has come full circle. The ICM does make moral consistency possible amongst like-minded churchgoers within inclusive, pluralistic churches. Yet, on an issue such as homosexuality, it does not eliminate sharp moral disagreements across all churchgoers. Over time there may eventually be convergence, as happened for example over the issue of slavery in the eighteenth and nineteenth centuries. On issues such as remarriage after divorce and heterosexual intercourse before marriage Anglican churchgoers have, as was seen earlier, changed very considerably since the 1950s. Yet even

[37] For contrasting scholarly views see L. William Countryman, *Dirt, Sex and Greed: Sexual Ethics in the New Testament and Their Implications for Today*, Fortress Press, Philadelphia, 1988 and SCM Press, London, 1989, and R. B. Hayes, *The Moral Vision of the New Testament*, Harper Collins, San Francisco and T. & T. Clark, Edinburgh, 1996.

here disagreements remain. On the issue of homosexuality change amongst churchgoers is at most embryonic. Conflict predominates.

Stephen Sykes would surely regard this as evidence of a dynamic church, 'the restlessness of a dialectic, impelled by criticism'.[38] Even Oliver O'Donovan, a signatory of the *St Andrew's Day Statement*, might give a similar account. In a commentary on the Statement, which is not accepted by all other signatories, he writes:

> It is worth pausing here to measure the width of the space between the lines; that is to say, how much the authors of the Statement have felt it safe to leave open as the subject for constructive disagreement. On the one hand, what they have said is compatible with the view that the serious gay Christian is simply mistaken; his or her position rests on a misunderstanding; the gay consciousness is a blind alley, with which the church simply has to be patient. Provided there is no attempt to stir up conflict, the church can respect the good faith of those who are mistaken, discuss the issues in a relaxed way as they arise, and wait for light to dawn. On the other hand, it is also compatible with the view that the serious gay Christian is a kind of prophet, acting in the loneliness of faith by stepping self-consciously and deliberately outside the church's tradition to point in a new direction that God is opening up and which the church will come to recognise in time. Precisely the seriousness of such an act rules out the hope for cheap or easily won concessions . . . These two outlooks, the authors imply, can exist together and argue their differences fruitfully.[39]

In the context of strong emotions at the Lambeth Conference in 1998, the style of disagreement that O'Donovan depicts appears too gentle. Yet, over time, inclusive churches may be able to express their differences here more constructively.

Troeltsch, and before him F. D. Maurice, might have suggested an even deeper theological analysis of such moral differences amongst churchgoers. First Maurice and then, quite independently as far as I have been able to establish, Troeltsch argued that apparently incompatible Christian movements are

38 Sykes, *The Identity of Christianity*, p. 17.

39 Oliver O'Donovan, 'Reading the St Andrew's Day Statement', in Sugden and Samuel, *Anglican Life and Witness*, pp. 48–9.

able together to express the fullness of the Christian Gospel. In his remarkable early work, *The Kingdom of Christ*, Maurice argued that the competing church parties of the early nineteenth century each had crucial weaknesses which were compensated by the other parties. Troeltsch, too, in his seminal study, *The Social Teaching of the Christian Churches*, argued that the three religious types – church, sect and mysticism – even though apparently contradicting each other, were each implicit within the Christian Gospel and could only express that Gospel adequately if their several contributions were each taken into account.

In words that could have been written for the 1998 Lambeth Conference, but in fact were written in the wake of the radical Reform Bill of 1832, F. D. Maurice analysed the Church of England of his day in terms of three parties or systems; the liberal system, the evangelical system, and the high church or catholic system. The first of these exclaims that 'opinions on everything are undergoing revolution' and asks 'Why not throw overboard your prejudices, and enter at once and heartily into the spirit of the age?' The second insists that others have 'lost sight of all spiritual influences and realities' and that 'the power of the Gospel . . . is not felt or regarded'. The third insists, in contrast to the others, that the church 'has divine sacraments, an apostolic order, a power of binding and loosing; the practices and rule of the age of the Fathers are her model'.[40]

Maurice was well aware that each of these parties tended to regard the others as profoundly mistaken. So liberals were then, and still are today, typically regarded as faithless, compromised by secular society, and relativised. Liberals, in turn, typically regard the others as simplistic, fundamentalist and anachronistic. Yet if conservatives – themselves divided on whether or not Scripture alone is their source of authority – succeeded in eliminating liberals, they would soon become repressive and, if liberals succeeded in eliminating conservatives, they would become indistinguishable from society at large. Each feeds

[40] F. D. Maurice, *The Kingdom of Christ: or Hints on the Principles, Ordinances and Constitution of the Catholic Church. In Letters to a Member of the Society of Friends*, Everyman edition, J. M. Dent, London and New York, (1837), vol.II, p. 308.

upon the other whilst remaining mutually suspicious and it is possible that churches that survive over time need alternating phases of liberalism and conservatism.

So, although the theologian 'is told by the supporter of each that he must embrace one or other of them', Maurice was not so convinced. Rather he argued:

> If we had more humility, we should probably have much fewer difficulties to encounter than we have . . . And that we may not be otherwise, do not let us hastily set ourselves up to condemn any of these systems, or those who propound them. Our consciences, I believe, have told us from time to time that there is something in each of them which we ought not to reject. Let us not reject it. But we may find, that there is a divine harmony, of which the living principle in each of these systems forms one note, of which the systems themselves are a disturbance and violation.[41]

I believe that this fine overview of theological conflict is still highly relevant to moral disagreements amongst churchgoers today. Held together by the distinctive Christian virtues of faith, hope and love, churchgoers nonetheless on occasion reach sharply different decisions on particular moral issues. So some churchgoers argue that Scripture condemns all homosexual practices and that colluding with an increasingly voracious gay, secular culture distorts and relativises the Christian faith. Others argue that Scripture and church tradition and experience condemn predatory sexual acts and promiscuity (heterosexual as well as homosexual) not faithful gay or lesbian relationships: as Christians we should openly support and encourage the latter. Perhaps there will eventually be scope for sustained theological and pastoral harmony between these two conflicting tones. Yet for the moment an inclusive church may need to hear both separately, suspecting that Christian moral truth may be larger than either.

[41] *Ibid.*

Postscript

Unusually for a work in ethics, this book has been preoccupied with data and with competing sociological theories. What I have attempted to show is that once moral communities take centre stage in ethics – as they do in virtue ethics – then there should be a greater interest in such data and theories. Virtue ethics makes assumptions about moral socialisation which do need to be tested empirically. Depictions of idealised communities are simply inadequate for this task.

Of course actual, as distinct from idealised, communities are likely to be ambiguous and messy moral carriers. People argue and fight, they disagree and conflict, and even in the most conformist communities there are always idiosyncratic nonconformists. Church communities are no exceptions. Nevertheless, what has been discovered in the course of this book is that there is a great deal of evidence showing that churchgoers are relatively, yet significantly, different from nonchurchgoers. On average they have higher levels of Christian belief (which is hardly surprising), but, in addition, they usually have a stronger sense of moral and civic order and tend to be significantly more altruistic than nonchurchgoers. I have argued that churchgoing is a distinctive culture and, as such, it is directly relevant to virtue ethics. Within this culture individuals are nourished in distinctively Christian values and virtues.

Now, of course, there is much research still to be done. If I have the energy there is a major work to be written about *The Future of Churchgoing*. Accurate information about churchgoing is gradually becoming available in many different countries.

There is a real need to correlate this information, to test it against different theories of churchgoing, and then to make cautious predictions about the future of churchgoing within these different countries. There are already some hints in the present book about the effects that urbanisation, immigration and other social factors which disturb a sense of identity may have in increasing rates of churchgoing. These need to be studied more systematically, distinguishing carefully between external social factors which churches themselves cannot control, but to which they can respond more or less vigorously, and internal factors which they might be able to change. If my thesis here is correct then churchgoing itself is an important factor in shaping moral beliefs and behaviour. And, if that is true, then future patterns of churchgoing will have direct implications for the future of these beliefs and patterns of behaviour in society at large. Precisely because my thesis puts so much emphasis upon the moral significance of regular churchgoing, the future of this churchgoing itself needs more scholarly attention.

There is also more qualitative research to be done on local congregations and parishes.[1] How do individuals articulate the various connections between their religious and moral beliefs and actions? In what ways might local congregations act as carriers of distinctive values and virtues? It would also be interesting to study voluntary work in a single locality to find out all the different interconnections between churchgoers and nonchurchgoers. The study of religious and moral socialisation is wide open for further research.

When I first started the research for this book I had no idea it would take so long. As I mention in the Preface, this is now the fifteenth book in the series *New Studies in Christian Ethics* and the series itself was first planned almost a decade ago. I thought at the time that my own contribution would come much earlier. In the event I am pleased that it has taken so long, since I have benefited enormously from the books that have already been

[1] An excellent example for such research is provided by Penny Edgell Becker, *Congregations in Conflict: Cultural Models of Local Religious Life*, Cambridge University Press, Cambridge and New York, 1999.

published in the series and have tried to build upon many of their conclusions in my own book. For me this is very much a shared venture in theological scholarship. I hope it continues for many years to come.

Works cited

ABC Television, *Television and Religion*, London University Press, London, 1965.

Abrams, Mark, Gerard, David and Timms, Noel (eds.), *Values and Social Change in Britain: Studies in the Contemporary Values of Modern Society*, Macmillan, London, 1985.

ACC, *The Truth Shall Make You Free: The Lambeth Conference 1988: The Reports, Resolutions and Pastoral Letters from the Bishops*, The Anglican Consultative Council, London, 1988.

Acquaviva, S. S., *The Decline of the Sacred in Industrial Society*, 1966, trans. P. Lipscomb, Harper & Row, New York, 1979.

Albrecht, Gloria, review of Stanley Hauerwas' *In Good Company* in *Scottish Journal of Theology*, 50, 1997.

Ashford, Sheena, and Timms, Noel, *What Europe Thinks: A Study of European Values*, Dartmouth, Aldershot, 1992.

Avery, William O. and Globbel, A. Roger, 'The Word of God and the Word of the Preacher', *Review of Religious Research*, 22:1, 1980.

Barnett, Steven and Thomson, Katarina, 'How We View Violence', in Roger Jowell, John Curtice, Alison Park, Lindsay Brook, Katarina Thomson and Caroline Bryson (eds.), *British Social Attitudes the 14th Report*, Social and Community Planning Research, Ashgate, Aldershot, 1997.

Baum, Gregory, *Essays in Critical Theology*, Sheed and Ward, Kansas City, 1994.

Becker, Penny Edgell, *Congregations in Conflict: Cultural Models of Local Religious Life*, Cambridge University Press, Cambridge and New York, 1999.

Beckford, James A. and Gilliat, Sophie, *Religion in Prison: Equal Rites in a Multi-Faith Society*, Cambridge University Press, Cambridge, 1998.

Benson, Peter L. 'Religion and Substance Use', in John F. Shumaker (ed.), *Religion and Mental Health*, Oxford University Press, New York, 1992.

Bentley, Peter and Hughes, Philip J., *Australian Life and the Christian Faith: Facts and Figures*, Christian Research Association, Kew, Victoria, Australia, 1998.

Berger, Peter L., *The Sacred Canopy*, Doubleday, New York, 1967; British title, *The Social Reality of Religion*, Faber & Faber, London, 1969.

A Far Glory: The Quest for Faith in an Age of Credulity, Anchor Books, New York, 1992.

Bibby, Reginald, *Fragmented Gods*, Irwin Publishing, Toronto, 1987.

Black, Alan W., 'Religion and Environmentally Protective Behaviour in Australia', *Social Compass*, 44:3, 1997.

Bocock, Robert, *Ritual in Industrial Society: A Sociological Analysis of Ritualism in Modern England*, George Allen and Unwin, London, 1974.

Bouma, Gary D. and Dixon, Beverly R., *The Religious Factor in Australian Life*, MARC Australia, World Vision and the Zadok Centre, 1986.

Bradney, Anthony, *Religions, Rights and Laws*, Leicester University Press, Leicester, 1993.

Brewer, Priscilla J., *Shaker Communities, Shaker Lives*, University Press of New England, New Hampshire, 1986.

Brierley, Peter, *Prospects for the Nineties: Trends and Tables from the English Church Census*, MARC Europe, London, 1991.

'Christian' England: What the English Church Census Reveals, MARC Europe, London, 1991.

British Broadcasting Corporation, *Religious Broadcasts and the Public*, Audience Research Department, BBC, 1955.

Bruce, Steve, *Religion in the Modern World*, Oxford University Press, Oxford, 1996.

Cahill, Lisa Sowle, *Sex, Gender and Christian Ethics*, Cambridge University Press, Cambridge and New York, 1996.

Cairns, D. S. (ed.), *The Army and Religion: An Enquiry and its Bearing upon the Religious Life of the Nation*, Macmillan, London, 1919.

Casanova, José, *Public Religions in the Modern World*, University of Chicago Press, Chicago, 1994.

Church of England, *Church Statistics: Parochial Membership and Finance Statistics for January to December 1995*, The Central Board of Finance of the Church of England, Church House, Westminster, 1997.

Church of the Province of Southern Africa, *The Church and Human Sexuality*, Church of the Province of Southern Africa, 1995.

Church of Scotland, *Lifestyle Survey*, Church of Scotland Board of Social Responsibility, 121 George Street, Edinburgh, 1987.

Countryman, L. William, *Dirt, Sex and Greed: Sexual Ethics in the New*

Testament and Their Implications for Today, Fortress Press, Philadelphia, 1988 and SCM Press, London, 1989.

Cox, Jeffrey, *The English Churches in a Secular Society: Lambeth, 1870–1930*, Oxford University Press, Oxford, 1982.

Cronin, Kieran, *Rights and Christian Ethics*, Cambridge University Press, Cambridge and New York, 1992.

Davie, Grace, *Religion in Britain Since 1945: Believing Without Belonging*, Blackwell, Oxford, 1994.

Dekker, Paul, Ester, Peter, and Nas, Masja, 'Religion, Culture and Environmental Concern: An Empirical Cross-national Analysis', *Social Compass*, 44:3, 1997.

Demerath, N. J., *A Tottering Transcendence*, Bobbs-Merrill, New York, 1974.

Donnison, David and Bryson, Caroline, 'Matters of Life and Death: Attitudes to Euthanasia', in Roger Jowell, John Curtice, Alison Park, Lindsay Brook and Katarina Thomson (eds.), *British Social Attitudes the 13th Report*, Social and Community Planning Research, Dartmouth, Hants, 1996.

Eckberg, Douglas Lee and Blocker, T. Jean, 'Christianity, Environmentalism, and the Theoretical Problem of Fundamentalism', *Journal for the Scientific Study of Religion*, 35:4, 1996.

Fergusson, David A. S., *Community, Liberalism and Christian Ethics*, Cambridge University Press, Cambridge and New York, 1998.

Field, Clive D., 'Non-Recurrent Christian Data', *Reviews of United Kingdom Statistical Sources*, vol. xx, *Religion*, Royal Statistical Society and Economic and Social Research Council, Pergamon Press, London, 1987.

Finney, John, *Finding Faith Today*, British and Foreign Bible Society, Swindon, 1992.

Ford, David and Hardy, Daniel, *Jubilate: Theology in Praise*, Darton, Longman & Todd, London, 1984; American title *Praising and Knowing God*, Westminster Press, Philadelphia, 1985.

Forrester, Duncan, *Christian Justice and Public Policy*, Cambridge University Press, Cambridge, 1997.

Forster, Peter G., *Church and People on Longhill Estate*, University of Hull, 1989.

Francis, Leslie J. and Kay, William K., *Teenage Religion and Values*, Gracewing, Fowler Wright Books, Herefordshire, 1995.

Gallup, George H. (ed.), *The Gallup International Public Opinion Polls: Great Britain 1937–1975*, Random House, New York, 1976; see also: *The International Gallup Polls* (1978); and *Gallup Political and Economic Index* (annual).

Gardner, E. Clinton, *Justice and Christian Ethics*, Cambridge University Press, Cambridge and New York, 1995.

Giddens, Anthony, *Modernity and Self-Identity*, Stanford University Press, Stanford, 1991.

Gill, Robin, *Theology and Social Structure*, Mowbrays, Oxford, 1977.

Beyond Decline, SCM Press, London, 1988.

Christian Ethics in Secular Worlds, T. & T. Clark, Edinburgh, 1991.

Moral Communities, Exeter University Press, Exeter, 1992.

The Myth of the Empty Church, SPCK, London, 1993.

A Textbook of Christian Ethics, T. & T. Clark, Edinburgh, 2nd edn, 1995.

Moral Leadership in a Postmodern Age, T. & T. Clark, Edinburgh, 1997.

Gill, Robin, Hadaway, C. Kirk and Marler, Penny Long, 'Is Religious Belief Declining in Britain?', *Journal for the Scientific Study of Religion*, 37:3, 1998.

Gorer, Geoffrey, *Exploring English Character*, Cresset Press, London, 1955.

Death, Grief and Mourning in Contemporary Britain, Cresset Press, London, 1965.

Greeley, Andrew M., *Unsecular Man: The Persistence of Religion*, Schocken Books, New York, 1972, and SCM Press, London, 1973.

'Religion in Britain, Ireland and the USA', in Roger Jowell, Lindsay Brook, Gillian Prior and Bridget Taylor (eds.), *British Social Attitudes the 9th Report*, Social and Community Planning Research, Dartmouth, Hants, 1992.

'Religion and Attitudes Toward the Environment', *Journal for the Scientific Study of Religion*, 32:1, 1993.

Gunter, Barry and Viney, Rachel (eds.), *Seeing is Believing: Religion and Television in the 1990s*, John Libbey/ITC, London, 1994.

Gustafson, James, 'The Sectarian Temptation', *Proceedings of the Catholic Theological Society of America*, 40, 1985.

Halman, Loek and Pettersson, Thorleif, 'Morality and Religion: A Weakened Relationship', *Journal of Empirical Theology*, 9:2, 1996.

Hallett, Garth L., *Priorities and Christian Ethics*, Cambridge University Press, New York and Cambridge, 1998.

Harding, Stephen, Phillips, David and Fogarty, Michael, *Contrasting Values in Western Europe: Unity, Diversity and Change*, Macmillan, Basingstoke, 1986.

Harrison, Ted, *Members Only?*, Triangle, SPCK, London, 1994.

Hauerwas, Stanley, *Vision and Virtue*, Fides, Notre Dame, Indiana, 1974.

Character and the Christian Life, Trinity University Press, San Antonio, 1975.

A Community of Character: Toward a Constructive Christian Social Ethic, University of Notre Dame, Indiana, 1981.

The Peaceable Kingdom: A Primer of Christian Ethics, University of Notre Dame, Indiana, 1983, and SCM Press, London, 1984.

Suffering Presence, University of Notre Dame, Indiana, 1986, and T. & T. Clark, Edinburgh, 1988.

Naming the Silences, William Eerdmans, Grand Rapids, Michigan, 1990.

Against the Nations, University of Notre Dame, Indiana, 1992.

Dispatches from the Front, Duke University Press, Durham, N.C., 1995.

Hauerwas, Stanley and Willimon, William H., *Resident Aliens: Life in the Christian Colony*, Abingdon, Nashville, 1989.

Where Resident Aliens Live, Abingdon, Nashville, 1996.

Hayes, R. B., *The Moral Vision of the New Testament*, Harper Collins, San Francisco and T. & T. Clark, Edinburgh, 1996.

Heald, Gordon and Wybrow, Robert J. (eds.), *The Gallup Survey of Britain*, Croom Helm, London, 1986.

Herberg, Will, 'Religion in a Secularized Society', *Review of Religious Research*, 3:4, 1962.

Hoge, Dean R., Zech, Charles, McNamara, Patrick and Donahue, Michael J., *Money Matters: Personal Giving in American Churches*, Westminster John Knox Press, Louisville, Kentucky, 1996.

Hornsby-Smith, Michael P. and Procter, Michael, 'Catholic Identity, Religious Context and Environmental Values in Western Europe: Evidence from the European Values Surveys', *Social Compass*, 42:1, 1995.

Horton, John and Mendus, Susan (eds.), *After MacIntyre: Critical Perspectives on the Work of Alasdair MacIntyre*, Polity Press, Oxford, and University of Notre Dame, Indiana, 1994.

Hughes, Philip J., *Religion in Australia: Facts and Figures*, Christian Research Association, Kew, Victoria, Australia, 1997.

Hughes, Philip J., Thompson, Craig , Pryor, Rohan and Bouma, Gary D., *Believe It or Not: Australian Spirituality and the Churches in the 90s*, Christian Research Association, Kew, Victoria, Australia, 1995.

Independent Television Authority, *Religion in Britain and Northern Ireland: A Survey of Popular Attitudes*, ITA, London, 1970.

Inglehart, Ronald, *Culture Shift in Advanced Industrial Society*, Princeton University Press, New Jersey, 1990.

Jacobs, Eric and Worcester, Robert, *We British: Britain Under the MORIscope*, Weidenfeld & Nicolson, London, 1990.

Joad, C. E. M., *The Present and Future of Religion*, Ernest Benn, London, 1930.

Johnston, Michael, 'The Price of Honesty', in Roger Jowell, Sharon Witherspoon and Lindsay Brook (eds.), *British Social Attitudes the 5th Report*, Social and Community Planning Research, Gower, Aldershot, 1988.

Johnston, Michael and Wood, Douglas, 'Right and Wrong in Public and Private Life', in Roger Jowell and Sharon Witherspoon (eds.), *British Social Attitudes the 2nd Report*, Social and Community Planning Research, Gower, Aldershot, 1985.

Kaldor, Peter, *Who Goes Where? Who Doesn't Care?*, Lancer, Homebush, NSW, Australia, 1987.

Kaldor, Peter and Powell, Ruth, *Views from the Pews: Australian Church Attenders Speak Out*, Openbook Publishers, Sydney, 1995.

Kaldor, Peter, Bellamy, John and Powell, Ruth, *Shaping a Future: Characteristics of Vital Congregations*, Openbook Publishers, Sydney, 1996.

Kay, William K. and Francis, Leslie J., *Drift from the Churches: Attitude Toward Christianity During Childhood and Adolescence*, University of Wales Press, Cardiff, 1996.

Kerkhofs, Jan, 'Between "Christendom" and "Christianity" ', *Journal of Empirical Theology*, 1:2, 1988.

Küng, Hans, *A Global Ethic for Global Politics and Economics*, SCM Press, London, 1997.

Lechner, Frank J., 'Secularization in the Netherlands?', *Journal for the Scientific Study of Religion*, 35:3, 1996.

Lindbeck, George A., *The Nature of Doctrine: Religion and Theology in a Postliberal Age*, Westminster Press, Philadelphia, and SPCK, London, 1984.

Loughlin, Gerard, *Telling God's Story: Bible, Church and Narrative Theology*, Cambridge University Press, Cambridge, 1996.

Luckmann, Thomas, *The Invisible Religion*, Macmillan, London, 1967.

'Shrinking Transcendence, Expanding Religion?', *Sociological Analysis*, 50, 1990.

MacIntyre, Alasdair, *After Virtue: A Study of Moral Theory*, Duckworth, London, 1985.

Response in John Horton and Susan Mendus (eds.), *After MacIntyre: Critical Perspectives on the Work of Alasdair MacIntyre*, Polity Press, Oxford, and University of Notre Dame, Indiana, 1994.

Mackey, James P., *Power and Christian Ethics*, Cambridge University Press, Cambridge, 1994.

McDonald, J. I. H., *Biblical Interpretation and Christian Ethics*, Cambridge University Press, Cambridge, 1993.

Mahoney, John, *The Making of Moral Theology: A Study of the Roman Catholic Tradition*, Clarendon Press, Oxford, 1987.

Mannheim, Karl, *Ideology and Utopia*, Routledge and Kegan Paul, London, 1936.

Markham, Ian S., *Plurality and Christian Ethics*, Cambridge University Press, Cambridge and New York, 1994.

Martin, David, *A Sociology of English Religion*, Heinemann, London, 1967.

The Religious and the Secular, Routledge and Kegan Paul, London, 1969.

'The Secularisation Question', *Theology*, vol. 76, no. 630, Feb. 1973.

Reflections on Sociology and Theology, Clarendon Press, Oxford, 1996.

Does Religion Cause War?, Oxford University Press, Oxford, 1997.

Mass-Observation, *Puzzled People: A Study of Popular Attitudes to Religion, Ethics, Progress and Politics in a London Borough*, Victor Gollancz, London, 1947.

'Why Do People Come to Church?', *British Weekly*, 13 January 1949.

Maurice, F. D., *The Kingdom of Christ: or Hints on the Principles, Ordinances and Constitution of the Catholic Church. In Letters to a Member of the Society of Friends*, Everyman edition, J. M. Dent, London and New York, 1837.

Meeks, Wayne A., *The Origins of Christian Morality: The First Two Centuries*, Yale University Press, New Haven and London, 1993.

Milbank, John, *Theology and Social Theory: Beyond Secular Reason*, Blackwell, Oxford, 1990.

'Enclaves, or Where is the Church?', *New Blackfriars*, vol. 73, no. 861, June 1992.

Miller, William R., 'Researching the Spiritual Dimensions of Alcohol and Other Drug Problems', *Addiction*, 93:7, 1998.

MORI, *Christian Beliefs*, Research Study Conducted for BBC Songs of Praise, Nov. 1993: see also *British Public Opinion* (monthly).

Nichols, Aidan, 'Non Tali Auxilio: John Milbank's Suasion to Orthodoxy', *New Blackfriars*, vol. 73, no. 861, June 1992.

Northcott, Michael S., *The Environment and Christian Ethics*, Cambridge University Press, Cambridge, 1996.

O'Donovan, Oliver, *The Desire of Nations: Rediscovering the Roots of Political Theology*, Cambridge University Press, Cambridge, 1996.

'Reading the St Andrew's Day Statement', in Chris Sugden and Vinay Samuel, *Anglican Life and Witness: A Reader for the Lambeth Conference of Anglican Bishops 1998*, SPCK, London, 1997.

Osborn, Lawrence and Walker, Andrew (eds.), *Harmful Religion: An Exploration of Religious Abuse*, SPCK, London, 1997.

Osmond, Rosalie, *Changing Perspectives: Christian Culture and Morals in England Today*, Darton, Longman & Todd, London, 1993.

Parsons, Susan Frank, *Feminism and Christian Ethics*, Cambridge University Press, Cambridge, 1996.

Pilkington, G. W., Poppleton, P. K., Gould, J. B. and McCourt, M. M. 'Changes in Religious Beliefs, Practices and Attitudes Among University Students over an Eleven-year Period in Relation to Sex Differences, Denominational Differences and Differences Between Faculties and Years of Study', *British Journal of Social and Clinical Psychology*, 15, 1976.

Porter, Jean, *Moral Action and Christian Ethics*, Cambridge University Press, Cambridge and New York, 1995.

Reimer, Samuel H., 'A Look at Cultural Effects on Religiosity: A Comparison Between the United States and Canada', *Journal for the Scientific Study of Religion*, 34:4, 1996.

Richter, Philip and Francis, Leslie J., *Gone But Not Forgotten: Church Leaving and Returning*, Darton, Longman & Todd, London, 1998.

Roof, Wade Clark, *A Generation of Seekers: The Spiritual Journeys of the Baby Boom Generation*, Harper, San Francisco, 1993.

Roof, Wade Clark, Carroll, Jackson W. and Roozen, David A., *The Post-War Generation and Establishment Religion*, Westview, Oxford, 1995.

Rudman, Stanley, *Concepts of Persons and Christian Ethics*, Cambridge University Press, Cambridge, 1997.

Sacks, Jonathan, *The Persistence of Faith*, Weidenfeld & Nicolson, London, 1992.

Faith in the Future, Darton, Longman & Todd, London, 1995.

Schweiker, William, *Responsibility and Christian Ethics*, Cambridge University Press, Cambridge and New York, 1995.

Sedgwick, Peter H., *The Market Economy and Christian Ethics*, Cambridge University Press, Cambridge and New York, 1999.

Selznick, Philip, *The Moral Commonwealth: Social Theory and the Promise of Community*, University of California Press, Berkeley, 1992.

Shand, Jack D., 'The Decline of Traditional Christian Beliefs in Germany', *Sociology of Religion*, 59:2, 1998.

Smith, Harmon L., *Where Two or Three are Gathered Together: Liturgy and the Moral Life*, Pilgrim Press, Cleveland, 1995.

Song, Robert, *Christianity and Liberal Society*, Clarendon Press, Oxford, 1997.

Stark, Rodney and Iannaccone, Laurence R., 'A Supply-Side Re-interpretation of the "Secularization" of Europe', *Journal for the Scientific Study of Religion*, 33, 1994.

Stark, Rodney and Bainbridge, William Sims, *Religion, Deviance and Social Control*, Routledge, New York and London, 1996.

Startup, Richard and Harris, Christopher C. 'Elements of Religious

Belief and Social Values Among the Laity of the Church of Wales', *Journal of Contemporary Religion*, 12:2, 1997.

Sugden, Chris and Samuel, Vinay, *Anglican Life and Witness: A Reader for the Lambeth Conference of Anglican Bishops 1998*, SPCK, London, 1997.

Svennevig, Michael, Haldane, Ian, Spiers, Sharon and Gunter, Barrie (eds.), *Godwatching: Viewers, Religion and Television*, John Libbey/ IBA, London, 1988.

Sykes, Stephen, *The Identity of Christianity: Theologians and the Essence of Christianity from Schleiermacher to Barth*, SPCK, London, 1984.

Timms, Noel, *Family and Citizenship: Values in Contemporary Britain*, Dartmouth, Aldershot, 1992.

Troeltsch, Ernst, *The Social Teaching of the Christian Churches*, Harper, New York, 1960 (1919).

United Reformed Church, *Rejoice and Sing*, Oxford University Press, Oxford, 1991.

Wainwright, Geoffrey, *Doxology: The Praise of God in Worship, Doctrine and Life: A Systematic Theology*, Clarendon Press, Oxford and New York, 1980.

Wallace, Anthony F. C., *Religion: An Anthropological View*, Random House, New York, 1966.

Wallis, Roy, *The Road to Total Freedom: A Sociological Analysis of Scientology*, Heinemann, London, 1976.

Warner, R. Stephen,'Religion, Boundaries and Bridges', *Sociology of Religion*, 58:3, 1997.

'Religion and Migration in the United States', *Social Compass*, 45:1, 1998.

Weber, Max, *The Protestant Ethic and the Spirit of Capitalism*, Unwin, London, 1930 (1904–5).

White, Lynn, 'The Historical Roots of our Ecologic Crisis', *Science*, vol. 155, no. 3767, 10 March 1967.

Williams, Rowan, 'Saving Time: Thoughts on Practice, Patience and Vision', *New Blackfriars*, vol. 73, no. 861, June 1992.

Wilson, Bryan, *Religion in Secular Society*, C. A. Watt, London, 1966.

Contemporary Transformations of Religion, Clarendon Press, Oxford, 1974.

Religion in Sociological Perspective, Clarendon Press, Oxford, 1987.

The Social Dimension of Sectarianism, Clarendon Press, Oxford, 1990.

Wilson, John and Janoski, Thomas, 'The Contribution of Religion to Volunteer Work', *Sociology of Religion*, 56:2, 1995.

Witten, Marsha G., *All is Forgiven: The Secular Message in American Protestantism*, Princeton University Press, New Jersey, 1993.

Wuthnow, Robert, *Rediscovering the Sacred: Perspectives on Religion in Contemporary Society*, William Eerdmans, Grand Rapids, 1992.

Sharing the Journey: Support Groups and America's New Quest for Community, The Free Press, New York, 1994.

Yeo, Stephen, *Religious and Voluntary Organizations in Crisis*, Croom Helm, London, 1976.

Index